I Have Someone To Tell You
A Jesuit Heralds the Gospel

Fr. Robert McTeigue, SJ

Edited by Roxanne Perko

Introduction by
Bishop Michael Olson

Copyright © 2017 Fr. Robert McTeigue, SJ

All rights reserved.

ISBN: 1514255960
ISBN-13: 978-1514255964

DEDICATION

To the Most Reverend Howard George Tripp, Auxiliary Bishop Emeritus of Southwark, England, who ordained me to the diaconate, and said to me the life-changing words: "Receive the gospels of Christ, Whose herald you now are…"

CONTENTS

	Introduction by Most Rev. Michael Olson	1
	Editor's Note	5
	Author's Note	6
	A Special Message for Clergy	8

ADVENT

1	**What Time Is It?** First Sunday of Advent	25
2	**Is the Gospel Good News or Great News?** First Wednesday of Advent	31
3	**Obedience *and* Freedom?** First Thursday of Advent	33
4	**Do You Want to Be Healed?** First Friday of Advent	36
5	**How Will You Prepare the Way of the Lord?** Second Sunday of Advent	39
6	**Fear Not?** Third Sunday of Advent	44
7	**What Do You Want for Advent?** Third Friday of Advent	48

LENT

8	**The Dangers of "Business-As-Usual"** Ash Wednesday	54
9	**Some Choices Are Hard; Some Choices Are Easy** Thursday After Ash Wednesday	60
10	**It's Time to Come Home** First Sunday of Lent	63
11	**Is Anger a Sin or a Gift?** First Friday of Lent	66

12	**Do You Have a Good Memory?**	68
	Second Sunday of Lent	
13	**Can You Follow Directions? Can You Ask?**	74
	Third Wednesday of Lent	
14	**"Let's Play Hide-And-Seek!"**	76
	Fourth Sunday of Lent	
15	**Would You Like Some Help?**	82
	Fourth Monday of Lent	
16	**"Is There No One to Condemn You?"**	85
	Fifth Sunday of Lent	
17	**Do You Have Enemies?**	88
	Fifth Friday of Lent	
18	**Stay Awake!**	91
	Palm Sunday	
19	**How Strong Are You?**	97
	Palm Sunday	
20	**What Are You Waiting For?**	102
	Monday of Holy Week	
21	**What Do You See?**	104
	Good Friday	

EASTER

22	**Do You Need a Savior?**	110
	Thursday of the Octave of Easter	
23	**Can You Endure?**	114
	Second Sunday of Easter	
24	**Never Mind!**	118
	Second Monday of Easter	
25	**Have You Ever Been Amazed?**	121
	Third Sunday of Easter	
26	**Do You Believe? How Do You Know?**	126
	Third Monday of Easter	
27	**What Happens to Useless Branches?**	129
	Fifth Sunday of Easter	

28	**Christ's Cross and Resurrection Are Inseparable**	134
	Fifth Sunday of Easter	
29	**Do You Have a Motto?**	139
	Fifth Tuesday of Easter	
30	**Only Real Love Leads to True Joy**	142
	Fifth Thursday of Easter	
31	**Where Is Your Weakness?**	146
	Fifth Friday of Easter	
32	**Will You Run Away?**	149
	Seventh Monday of Easter	
33	**A Useless Gift?**	152
	Pentecost Sunday	

ORDINARY TIME

34	**Follow Me**	158
	First Monday of Ordinary Time	
35	**"They Have No Wine"**	161
	Second Sunday of Ordinary Time	
36	**How Good Is Your Hearing?**	167
	Third Sunday of Ordinary Time	
37	**The Sin Against the Holy Spirit**	171
	Third Monday of Ordinary Time	
38	**Why Are Christians Persecuted?**	174
	Fourth Sunday of Ordinary Time	
39	**Marriage and Celibacy**	178
	Fourth Sunday of Ordinary Time	
40	**Salt and Light**	183
	Fifth Sunday of Ordinary Time	
41	**Let Go**	190
	Sixth Friday of Ordinary Time	
42	**Why Should We Proclaim the Christ?**	192
	Twelfth Sunday of Ordinary Time	
43	**No Excuses**	197
	Thirteenth Sunday of Ordinary Time	

44	**Why Doesn't God Do Something About Evil?**	200
	Fifteenth Saturday of Ordinary Time	
45	**Goals and Feelings**	203
	Twenty-Second Thursday of Ordinary Time	
46	**Do We Have Enemies?**	206
	Twenty-Third Wednesday of Ordinary Time	
47	**"Oh Well, I Guess You Had to Be There…"**	209
	Twenty-Fourth Tuesday of Ordinary Time	
48	**A Vow of Silence?**	212
	Twenty-Fifth Wednesday of Ordinary Time	
49	**"It Is Not Good for the Man to Be Alone"**	214
	Twenty-Seventh Sunday of Ordinary Time	
50	**How Much Does Heaven Cost?**	219
	Twenty-Seventh Sunday of Ordinary Time	
51	**Are You Hiding Anything?**	224
	Twenty-Eighth Friday of Ordinary Time	
52	**Disintegration or Consummation?**	228
	Twenty-Eighth Saturday of Ordinary Time	
53	**Are You Ready?**	231
	Twenty-Ninth Tuesday of Ordinary Time	
54	**Why Call God "Father"?**	234
	Twenty-Ninth Thursday of Ordinary Time	
55	**"It Can't Happen Here"**	236
	Thirtieth Monday of Ordinary Time	
56	**The Problem of Pain**	239
	Thirtieth Tuesday of Ordinary Time	
57	**"Lord, Will Only a Few Be Saved?"**	241
	Thirtieth Wednesday of Ordinary Time	
58	**Unrequited Love**	244
	Thirtieth Thursday of Ordinary Time	
59	**Promises**	247
	Thirty-First Sunday of Ordinary Time	
60	**Time**	251
	Thirty-First Tuesday of Ordinary Time	
61	**Innocent Blood**	253
	Thirty-First Friday of Ordinary Time	

62	**Generosity**	256
	Thirty-Second Sunday of Ordinary Time	
63	**Millstones and Blindness**	261
	Thirty-Second Monday of Ordinary Time	
64	**"Her Value Is Far Beyond Pearls"**	264
	Thirty-Third Sunday of Ordinary Time	
65	**The Day and the Hour**	270
	Thirty-Third Sunday of Ordinary Time	
66	**Honesty, Clarity, and Courage**	274
	Thirty-Third Sunday of Ordinary Time	
67	**How to Write a Letter**	277
	Thirty-Fourth Wednesday of Ordinary Time	

SAINTS AND SOLEMNITIES

68	**Now It's Our Turn**	281
	Memorial of Ss. Campion, Southwell, & Companions	
69	**Are You Exhausted?**	285
	Solemnity of the Immaculate Conception	
70	**How Are Martyrs Made?**	288
	Memorial of European Martyrs of the Society of Jesus	
71	**Are You Crazy?**	291
	Memorial of Saint Agnes	
72	**Lambs and Wolves**	293
	Memorial of Saints Timothy and Titus	
73	**Is Jesus a Gift or a Burden?**	296
	Feast of the Presentation of the Lord	
74	**Excuses**	300
	Solemnity of the Ascension of the Lord	
75	**What Difference Does It Make?**	308
	Solemnity of the Most Holy Trinity	
76	**How Do You Know When You Are in Love?**	312
	Memorial of the Immaculate Heart	
77	**How Much Does Love Cost?**	315
	Memorial of Our Lady of Sorrows	

78	**Treasures and Riches**	317
	Memorial of Saint Ignatius of Antioch	
79	**Scholars and Knowledge**	320
	Memorial of Saint Ignatius of Antioch	
80	**What Holds You Back?**	323
	Memorial of the North American Martyrs	
81	**Can You Be a Saint?**	326
	Solemnity of All Saints	
82	**"I Miss You"**	332
	The Commemoration of All Souls	
83	**Courage**	336
	Memorial of Blessed Rupert Mayer, SJ	
84	**Who Needs a King?**	340
	Solemnity of Christ the King	

MEDLEY

85	**First Homily: Jesuit Companions**	348
	Feast of all the Saints & Blesseds of the Society of Jesus	
86	**Called, Equipped, and Missioned**	353
	Mass of the Holy Spirit, Baccalaureate Mass	
87	**Why Would Anyone Do Something Like That?**	357
	Wedding Homily	

INTRODUCTION

Since my ordination and installation as a diocesan bishop in January 2014, I have become more conscious about my responsibility to preach the Word of God and to preach well. Along with this awareness has come a new responsibility to see to the appropriate formation of my priests and deacons in the ministry of preaching—most especially the preaching of the Sunday homily. Some of this awareness has been offered to me from the generous praise and challenges offered by the lay and religious faithful who participate weekly at the Sunday Eucharist. Their comments manifest the distinction between their needs and wants as the People of God for being nourished by authentic preaching as it occurs in the context of the Eucharistic Liturgy as a profoundly ecclesial act. It is evident when the homilist hits the mark—it is equally evident when he does not.

Homilists frequently miss the mark when they confuse the Sunday homily with such endeavors as entertainment, autobiography, political rhetoric, popular psychology directed at self-help, dialogue, apologetics, or academics. The result of these mistakes is an obscuring of the Church's mission and ministry for the gathered assembly, offering them mere words but not the Word that nourishes them. Homilists hit the mark when their preaching is the fruit of their own prayer—their ecclesial prayer—centered upon Jesus Christ, the Word of God, the Word made flesh. As Pope Benedict XVI wrote in his post-synodal apostolic exhortation, *Verbum Domini*, "The sacramentality of the word can thus be understood by analogy with the real presence of Christ under the appearances of the consecrated bread and wine. By approaching the altar and partaking in the Eucharistic banquet we truly share in the body and blood of Christ. The proclamation of God's word at the celebration entails an acknowledgment that Christ himself is present, that he speaks to us, and that he wishes to be heard" (*Verbum Domini* 56). A well-preached homily opens up the Scriptures for the Eucharistic assembly and makes known anew what the Father has done for us in Christ, what Christ in turn asks of us in return, and sends us forth in the Spirit to complete the mission entrusted to us as His Church. To accomplish this, a homilist must foster the appropriate attitude of generosity and be formed in the aptitude for the ministerial task at hand.

It has been my privilege to know Father Robert McTeigue, S.J. for many years since our days as students of philosophy at the Catholic University of America. Much of our shared experiences as students involved the understanding and clear reading of texts authored by great philosophers. Father McTeigue has consistently displayed this appropriate attitude of generosity in his preaching because he has always first been a grateful recipient of the Grace that the Word of God has offered him as a redeemed and loved sinner, on the road to sanctity. This attitude has been coupled with Father McTeigue's consistent response to the Word by the cultivation of the aptitude for preaching, particularly at the celebration of the Sunday Eucharist through prayer, study, and reflection upon the needs of the faithful as encountered by him in his ministry as a religious and a priest. As Pope Francis wrote in *Evangelii Gaudium*, "The preacher needs to keep his ear to the people and to discover what it is that the faithful need to hear. A preacher has to contemplate the Word but he also needs to contemplate his people" (*Evangelii Gaudium* 154). Father McTeigue first knows the Word and in its service knows the text that makes known the Word to the People of God.

In his book *I Have Someone to Tell You: A Jesuit Heralds*

the Gospel, Father McTeigue generously shares with the reader the Good News of what the Word of God continues to accomplish in the life of the Church as well as in his own life and ministry as a Jesuit priest. He provides examples of sound preaching that befit the dignity of the Eucharistic setting as well as provide for the complete nourishment of the faithful in need of substance required to fulfill their baptismal vocation. He also offers concrete assistance for the formation of homilists to cultivate the aptitude for preparing a Sunday homily and in executing its effective delivery to the faithful. On the basis of these aspects I highly recommend the use of this book in the formation of seminarians and in the ongoing formation of deacons and priests in their ministry of preaching. I would further recommend this book to the lay faithful for the formation of their understanding of what their authentic needs are for their faith formation. Father McTeigue's offering will help them to understand how the homily is to be a vehicle and means to provide for that sound formation so that none of us might settle for mediocrity in the proclamation of the Word by permitting the substitutions of sources other than Sacred Scripture, or uses of means unworthy and ill-suited for proclamation from the pulpit.

In the second chapter of *Lumen Gentium*, the Second Vatican Council taught us that "the Eucharistic sacrifice is the source and summit of the Christian life." The source and summit are most clearly achieved when this Sacrifice is offered, received, and celebrated with due and fitting dignity by the joyful hearts and prepared minds of both clergy and laity. Father McTeigue's book offers clergy and laity assistance in this prayerful preparation and reverent execution of their respective liturgical ministries, especially in preaching and hearing the homily. I hope your appreciation of the homily in the celebration of the Eucharist will be heightened by the reading of this book as much as mine has been. I hope your reading of this text will clarify for you what precisely is so good about the Good News of the Word made flesh.

+Michael F. Olson
Bishop of Fort Worth, Texas

EDITOR'S NOTE

"A journey of a thousand documents begins with a single flash drive…"

As a student at Ave Maria University, I had the blessing of hearing Father McTeigue preach and speak on many occasions. Like many of my fellow students, I found his homilies to be both educational and inspirational. I always looked forward to hearing him preach—he took to heart his mission as a shepherd of souls and prepared himself accordingly. When Father McTeigue asked me if I would consider helping him with a project to compile a book of his homilies, I jumped at the opportunity.

At the beginning of this adventure, Father McTeigue handed me a flash drive containing hundreds of homilies and other documents, spanning eighteen years of preaching. Through my university years, I organized and sorted through the files, and with the much appreciated assistance of Susan Waldstein and Kathy Dittus, we selected the 87 homilies contained here.

This book is the compilation of many labors. I am grateful to Father McTeigue for the opportunity to work on it, and for the support we have received from so many people in the process. It was an honor and a privilege to serve as editor of this book, and I am glad to see it reach completion. May Father McTeigue's words be a source of blessing to all who read them. *Ad maiorem Dei gloriam*!

Roxanne Perko
Solemnity of Christ the King
November 20, 2016

AUTHOR'S NOTE

"You have called me, Lord, to minister to your people. I do not know why you have done so, for you alone know that. Lord, lighten the heavy burden of the sins through which I have seriously transgressed. Purify my mind and heart. Like a shining lamp, lead me along the straight path. When I open my mouth, tell me what I should say. By the fiery tongue of your Spirit make my own tongue ready. Whatever I do, let it be in accordance with your will, now until the end."
—Saint John Damascene

Would a long list of names, names almost certainly of people you don't know and won't meet, interest you? Probably not. That's one reason why I hesitate to begin this introduction with a typical, "I'd like to thank..." As a reader, I usually skip that part of a book's introduction; as a writer with an imperfect memory, I am likely to forget the names of people whom, in justice, I should thank in public and in print. Nonetheless, I will speak here of gratitude—and of amazement.

I must not fail to say that I am grateful to God, Who chose to create, save, and sanctify me. With wonder I thank my Heavenly Father for calling me to be a companion of His Son and a priest of His Christ. I am grateful to my brothers in the Society of Jesus for helping me to find and keep my vocation. I am grateful to my family and friends for loving me faithfully across the miles and the years. And I am grateful to those many people who have confirmed my mission as a homilist, especially my students. Their hunger for the Word of God inspires me daily. And I must not fail to express my gratitude to my editor, Roxanne Perko. When I handed her stacks of wrinkled papers, assorted scribbles on envelopes and napkins, and a flash drive with hundreds of files named "HOMILY" or "NOTES", she did not run away. Without her persistence, this book would not have been possible.

I must speak also of amazement. I am amazed that over the years people have asked me to take my notes and scribbles and turn them into a book on preaching. Now that I have done so, I urge the readers of this book to let these words here lead you to the Word of God, and to cling to Him.

I can tell both clergy and laity that good preaching is like mortal sin—both require grave matter, sufficient reflection, and full consent of the will; neither happens by accident. For bishops, priests, and deacons, who have been ordained to preach the Gospel with authority, especially at Sunday Mass, I urge you all to love your mission to feed the Word to hungry souls. To the laity I make a request. Prepare to receive at Mass the Word of God when He is proclaimed and preached at Mass. You are more likely to receive blessings from the pulpit if you have studied and prayed over the Scriptures before coming to Mass.

My hope for all who read this book is that they will raise their expectations for what a homily can do for them, whether one is standing in the pulpit or sitting in the pew.

Father Robert McTeigue, S.J.
Solemnity of the Assumption of the Blessed Virgin Mary
August 15, 2016

A SPECIAL MESSAGE FOR CLERGY

This is a talk I gave at a priests conference in 2013 at Ave Maria University, in Ave Maria, Florida, as we celebrated the Year of Faith in 2013-2014.

Heralds of the Gospel: Our Ministry of Preaching

How good is your memory? Let's put it to the test by asking you this question—when did you hear the following words? "Receive the gospels of Christ Whose herald you now are. Believe what you read; teach what you believe; practice what you teach."

Every priest here heard those words at least once. We all heard them at our ordination as deacons, when we received the commission to preach. Do you remember the moment? Each one of us knelt before the bishop, who put the Book of the Gospels into our hands. Do you remember how you felt at the moment? Do you recall that moment often?

I was ordained a deacon in London, England—Wimbledon to be precise—by Bishop Howard Tripp. When I knelt before the bishop to receive the commission to preach, I expected that he would simply stick the Book of the Gospels horizontally into my hands, as I had seen that gesture done many times before. But Bishop Tripp did something different. He held the Book of the Gospels, upright, with his hands at the top corners. I stuck out my hands and he let the book fall into my hands, so that I could feel the weight of the gospels falling upon me. I gasped; he smiled.

Ten years later, I was in mission work in Southeast Asia, meeting with a newly-ordained auxiliary bishop from London. I asked him if Bishop Tripp was still alive. He said, "Yes, he's still alive. He just retired, but none of us can tell because he hasn't slowed down one bit." I told him the story of my ordination as a deacon. I asked him, as a personal favor to me, to relate to Bishop Tripp the story of my ordination, and how the experience of receiving the Book of the Gospels from his hands changed my life. It was that experience that inflamed my passion for preaching, and it was that experience that led me to choose the topic of my talk today, which is, "Heralds of the Gospel: Our Ministry of Preaching."

As our nation and our Church move towards times of trial, and as we make our way through the Year of Faith declared by Pope Benedict XVI for 2013-2014, I believe that our ministry of preaching is a great privilege and perhaps an even greater urgent necessity. The people entrusted to our care need the life-giving, liberating, and healing truth, Who is the Person of Christ, Whom we are ordained to herald from our pulpits. My goal this afternoon is to offer you encouragement, some advice, and, above all, the wisdom of the Church for all of us who have been given the ministry of liturgical preaching.

Now, let me ask you another question: "Do you look forward to preaching?" I think if we priests are really honest, we probably should say, "Sometimes. But sometimes not." It is a difficult challenge, sometimes even a burden, to break open the Word of God in public, before congregants who—let's be frank—probably came to church three minutes after Mass started, are tired and distracted, and could not, even if their lives depended on it, tell you what the readings of the day are.

And we see, at least sometimes, that lack of preparation and engagement on the part of the congregation in other parts of the Mass as well. I won't ask for a show of hands, but I think all of us here have had the following experience:

PRIEST: **THE LORD BE WITH YOU!**

CONGREGATION: *(Mumbled, quiet, passive response)* "And with your spirit."

PRIEST: **LIFT UP YOUR HEARTS!**

CONGREGATION: *(Mumbled, quiet, passive response)* "We lift them up to the Lord."

PRIEST: **LET US GIVE THANKS TO THE LORD, OUR GOD!**

CONGREGATION: *(Mumbled, quiet, passive response)* "It is right and just."

How can such an experience not be dispiriting? I once had such an experience at a parish on Pentecost Sunday!

Ok, that's one side of the issue. Now let's take a look at another side. Once again, I will ask a question, and I believe that this question may be an uncomfortable one, one that may be difficult to answer honestly: "What do our people think and feel at the prospect of hearing us preach?" Do people vie for seats in the front of the church so that they can see and hear us more clearly? Do our people arrive with pen and paper to take notes? Do they come ready with tissues to dry their tears? Again, I won't ask for a show of hands, but if we're honest, I think we would likely have to answer, "Probably not."

Let me describe to you an experience in a parish that I think is likely quite typical. I was travelling, and went to a parish in civilian clothes, attending Mass "incognito," as it were. At the start of the homily, I looked at the congregation and it appeared to me that most of the people had tuned out before the priest spoke the first word of his homily. People opened up bulletins, started thumbing through hymnals, or assumed the vacant stare of good people who are bored, longsuffering, and polite. The priest spoke for just under ten minutes about propitiation, atonement, and sacrifice. Everything he said was true and sound —and utterly forgettable. There was no invitation to the congregation, he used no "hook" to get their attention or appeal to their interest; there was no apparent beginning, middle, or end. He started, he continued, and then he just stopped. Along the way, there were no gestures or vocal variety. He spoke as if he were in an empty room. His whole presentation would make it difficult to infer that what he was saying mattered to him or to anyone else.

Now, I could be wrong, but it seemed to me that at that parish, the priest and the congregation had an understanding—one that was unspoken but quite real and binding: He would not preach too long, and they would not expect too much. Then everyone could go on with the *real* business of Mass, which appears to be the orderly distribution of Holy Communion followed by an orderly evacuation of the parking lot. (You can tell that I am not a pastor, because I did not say that the real business of the Mass is to take up the collection!)

In other words, the pastor and the congregation, by their respective behaviors and preparation—or *lack* of preparation—indicated that there is not much difference between the Mass and a Communion service. In other words, what matters is not participating in the Sacrifice of Christ at the altar (of which Holy Communion is the fruition, and the Liturgy of the Word is a preparation). Of course, such a view represents a colossal failure of catechesis and formation, and if expressed in those terms, many people would deny it. But, having spent my whole life either in the sanctuary or in the pew, I believe the following.

I believe that one reason that priests in general are not renowned for their preaching, and one reason that congregations demand so little from homilists and expect even less, is that all too many do not see preaching as an important element of the Mass. People just want to get their bit of sacramental Jesus and go home. Many congregations do not look for much from homilies; and my observation is that many homilists do not often exceed the expectations of their congregations. The root of the problem, I believe, is that Word and Sacrifice have been shorn from the Sacrament of the Eucharist.

Because so little is expected of liturgical preaching, bishops, priests, and deacons generally do not have to do much to rise to the occasion. We all have concelebrated at enough Masses to have heard many homilies that clearly result from a process that I call "P.F.A.", which stands for "Pious Free-Association." Homilies arising from P.F.A. sound something like this: "Isn't God nice? Mary wore blue. Footprints in the sand. Kids are cute. Jesus had a beard. Amen." Such a homily, which has clearly not passed through the mind and heart of the homilist, will not remain in the mind and heart of the congregation.

The issues of how we got that way and what we can do about it reach far, far beyond the scope of my presentation today. Instead, I wish us to focus specifically on the ministry of liturgical preaching, and the opportunities we have to revive, refresh, and restore that ministry during the Year of Faith.

That brings me to another question, a hypothetical question. And the question is this: "What if we were convinced that liturgical preaching is at once the most important and least effective ministry we exercise in these times of darkness and distress?" Of course, that question presents several others: "If we really believed in the urgency of liturgical preaching, what would we do with our time, energy, and talents? What would our priorities be? What would our weekdays and weekends look like if we really believed that liturgical preaching could bring the greatest blessing to the greatest needs our people have?"

I suggest that if we really believed that liturgical preaching, blessed by God's grace and crafted to the best of our ability, was a primary duty and premier privilege of our priesthood in our present difficult and worsening days, then our lives would likely look and feel differently from our present routines. Now, I hasten to add that I am not at all presenting myself as one who has perfectly mastered the stewardship of his time and energy, his duties and priorities. I stand before you as a quite flawed sinner and a struggling learner in the face of the questions I am putting before you today. Nonetheless, I can state with confidence that our ministry of liturgical preaching demands our maximum effort. With that in mind, I offer you now what I have found in my experience, prayer, and research to be fruitful. I ask of you only that you give it a fair hearing, take it to prayer, and make a good discernment of what may be useful in your life and ministry.

Let's take on another question. How about this? "What are the best compliments that can be said of a homilist?" I want to offer two suggestions that for decades have guided my views on preaching. First, a great compliment to a homilist would be: "Wow! What got into him? Can I get some of that too?" In other words, truly inspiring liturgical preaching must be truly inspired. The message and the messenger together must point to a more-than-human source. That brings me to the next great compliment that a homilist can receive, namely: "You can't fake that—you only get that by praying."

Those two compliments point to a principle, and the principle is this: Truly inspired and inspiring liturgical preaching must be rooted in a meeting of grace and nature; it must be the work of the Holy Spirit upon the preacher, and then again upon the congregation. Consider these words by Charles Spurgeon, the great 19th-century British preacher:

"The gospel is preached in the ears of all men; it only comes with power to some. The power that is in the gospel does not lie in the eloquence of the preacher; otherwise men would be converters of souls. Nor does it lie in the preacher's learning; otherwise it could consist of the wisdom of men. We might preach till our tongues rotted, till we should exhaust our lungs and die, but never a soul would be converted unless there were mysterious power going with it – the Holy Ghost changing the will of man. O Sirs! We might as well preach to stone walls as preach to humanity unless the Holy Ghost be with the word, to give it power to convert the soul."

So says Charles Spurgeon, to which I answer, "Amen." Apart from prayer, our preaching will be indifferent, or, worse, a "clever" attempt at marketing. C.S. Lewis warns us against seeking to be popular by appealing to what may be preferred by the populace. Lewis wrote these words of warning: "A man who first tried to guess 'what the public wants,' and then preached that as Christianity because the public wants it, would be a pretty mixture of fool and knave."

The ministry of preaching is always also a call to prayer, for both the preacher and the congregation. Especially in times such as these, when our nation and our Church seem to be on a collision course, we dare not preach without prior prayer. A priest aflame with the Holy Spirit can be a desperately needed beacon of light as shadows fall around us. I was surprised to find that the 19th-century British art critic John Ruskin had made an observation about preaching that is especially appropriate to our times. Ruskin said: "No lying knight or lying priest ever prospered in any age, but especially not in the dark ones. Men prospered then only in following an openly declared purpose, and preaching candidly beloved and trusted creeds."

If we are to preach well in these our dark times, if we are to preach "candidly beloved and trusted creeds," we must be men formed by meeting Christ the Word of God in Scripture and in prayer. Now, I know, I know, we hear incessant exhortations to pray. And we may very often say to ourselves, "Look—if there were 36 hours in a day, and I didn't need to sleep, then, sure, I would certainly have time to pray as much as I ought and still get everything else done." I understand the reasons for those words, having spoken them very often myself, so please understand me. I am not suggesting that we insist upon *more prayer*; instead, I am suggesting that we *insist more* upon prayer, and that we insist more upon prayer of a certain kind. In other words, I am suggesting not expanding our prayer *time*, but rather expanding our prayer *life*. Remember that Jesus Himself did not direct His disciples to pray more; He instructed them to pray always.

A very busy priest, working in a parish, university, or hospital—and I've done all three—can't be expected to spend 12 hours a day in a chapel, sighing and enjoying ecstatic inspirations. Yes, there must be time set aside for formal prayer and for silent prayer. And, yes, very often it is nearly impossible to expand the length of that time. But the size of our prayer life can be expanded even if the size of our prayer time cannot. To understand what I mean, I ask you to consider making homily preparation the cornerstone of your prayer. In other words, bring the lion's share of your time and the focus of your life to the habit of always preparing for preaching.

Here's what I mean. Regarding your prayer time, let your time with Scripture and intercession and dialogue with God revolve around your preaching, as you prepare to preach to the specific needs of your specific congregation. Regarding your prayer life, let every waking moment be spent alert to the possibility of gathering matter and inspiration for preaching. Every event, every conversation, when taken as a possibility for illustrating or enlivening preaching, can take on new and unexpected richness and vitality. Anything that brings laughter or tears, joy or sorrow, indeed, any person or event can be a gift from God that can be incorporated into our preaching. Going through the day alert, expecting the unexpected, attuned to the possibility of a "God-sighting," establishing such a habit, that is the prayer life of a preacher. And that constant openness, that constant practice of the presence of God, can, over time, become the life of prayer that transforms the homilist from a mere speaker to a true herald of the gospel. In my own life, what keeps me praying every day is that constant prayer of alertness in preparing for homilies.

Let me use a computer metaphor to illustrate my point. Maintaining a prayer life (in contrast to a prayer time) in order to cultivate a habit of near-constant homiletic preparation, is akin to a computer program that "runs in the background." An anti-virus program or spyware program that runs in the background runs constantly, is vigilant, and is unobtrusive; ideally it is unnoticed until it "catches" something that should be called to your attention. That habit of a prayer life for the sake of homiletic preparation is analogous to that vigilant program running in the background on your computer. That practice of a homiletically-motivated prayer life has been very fruitful in my life as a preacher, and I commend that practice to you.

Now let's get more specific. Is there a way of keeping ourselves motivated to cultivate that habit of a prayer life for the sake of preaching? I believe that we can make use of a phrase as a kind of motto for the priest who identifies himself centrally as a preacher. The phrase is this: "I have someone to tell you." The meaning of that phrase points in two directions, with both a more obvious sense and a less obvious sense. In the more obvious sense, the words, "I have someone to tell you," are spoken by Christ, and He speaks it of each of us who are His preachers, His heralds. In His mysterious Providence, He has chosen each of us to proclaim the gospel, above all in the liturgy.

In the less obvious sense, the words, "I have someone to tell you," are spoken by each of us who have received the ministry of liturgical preaching. The emphasis is on the word "someone." As priests, we preach, primarily, not an idea or cause or hypothesis or opinion; we preach the

Person of Christ, Who is the Word of the Father. Our mission, our privilege, and our burden is to make Christ known and loved through our preaching. And we cannot preach credibly and fruitfully if we do not know the One we preach. To make Christ known and loved from the pulpit, we must first know and love Him in our own lives.

But it is not enough to know and love Christ. We must also know and love our congregation. We must know and love the people to whom we preach. We must know their needs, longings, fears, hopes, doubts, and joys. And for the love of God we must love them in all of their goodness and all of their weakness. Building our lives around the ministry of preaching is an act of charity and compassion for our congregations, the people entrusted to our care by Christ and His Church. During the Year of Faith, and during these times of growing darkness, our people have an even greater need for a ministry of anointed and authoritative liturgical preaching.

Yes, we need to know our congregation in their concrete circumstances, and we must also know that our congregation is made up of human beings. Now, that's an obvious statement, of course, but it is a statement that has some not-so-obvious implications. Let me unpack that statement. When I say that human beings comprise our congregation, I am also noting that our congregation is not made up of angels or of machines. Not angels, our congregants have bodies and emotions; not machines, our congregants have free will. Those facts present a homilist with great opportunities and great challenges. To understand and manage those opportunities and challenges well, I urge you to turn to Aristotle's treatise on rhetoric. Aristotle understood, imperfectly of course, but nonetheless better than most, what it means to speak to a human audience.

Aristotle noted that the three elements of rhetoric are ethos, pathos, and logos. Ethos is the speaker's reputation for moral rectitude. My university students would call it "street cred." Pathos refers to emotion as a means of engaging the will, so as to move one's audience to action. Logos, of course, is the truth. Without a commitment to the truth, a speaker is a mere sophist; if a sophist can find a big enough audience to whip into a frenzy, we would call him a demagogue.

As priests, of course, we are drawn to the Logos, Who is Christ Himself. And each of us, I'm sure, would do all in our power to avoid sophistry and demagoguery. That is good, but that is also not enough. Simply stating the truth is not enough because a human being is more than just an intellect. Human beings are not angels. We know that of course, but I wonder how often we act accordingly, especially when we are in the pulpit.

Here's what I mean: I warn my students against what I call the "Rationalist Fallacy," which I have committed in my life countless times. The Rationalist Fallacy may be stated as follows: "If only I explain myself clearly enough, then people will understand and agree with me, and they will act accordingly." We all know, brothers, that the Rationalist Fallacy is a trail of tears. Clear and reasonable explanations are almost never sufficient, because even when people are reasonable, they are never purely rational. We as preachers must also be concerned with the emotions and the free will of our people.

Our people have bodies and emotions. That is why pure reason is insufficient. People need to be rationally convinced of the truth; they must also be emotionally moved to the truth, and to the right action that the truth demands. Our task as preachers is to move them without manipulating them. In other words, we must engage their emotions while respecting their freedom and their intelligence. That's a fine line for us to walk, but we must learn to walk it.

Our appeal to emotion must be authentic, not merely sentimental and certainly not fake. I'm not suggesting that we hire televangelist Jimmy Swaggart to give us crying lessons. I think that the most honest way to engage the emotions of our non-angelic congregations is to allow them a glimpse of our own emotions. We don't have to emotionally disrobe in the pulpit—of course not! But our voices and our bodies must give some indication that the Word we are proclaiming shakes us, shatters us, comforts us, and heals us. It is not enough for us to believe what we preach; our congregation must believe that we believe it.

Perhaps an illustration from the life of Mark Twain might help. Mark Twain was known, perhaps even notorious, for his use of salty language in every day conversation. His longsuffering wife was scandalized and disturbed by his behavior. One day, in exasperation, she herself cursed a blue streak and asked how he liked hearing those words himself. His reply was, "My dear, I hear the lyrics, but not the melody." In other words, he did not believe that she believed what she was saying, even though she was using all the right words. We must not make the same mistake.

I noted before that our congregation is not made up of angels. We are speaking to human beings with bodies and emotions. That is why Aristotle's reference to the role of pathos in rhetoric is essential. Aristotle also knew that human beings are naturally social, naturally relational. That is why ethos, the reputation, the credibility of the speaker, is so important. A congregation is more likely to accept the "truthiness" of the truth spoken by the speaker if they find the speaker to be credible. Let me give you an example.

I might write a speech proclaiming the full humanity of the unborn child. Every word of it would be true. But if I asked that the speech be delivered by Bill Clinton, would the speech be credible? Of course not! He does not have the proper pro-life reputation for the words of a true pro-life speech to be credible when spoken by him.

The issue of ethos presents us with a challenge. How

do we establish our credibility with our congregation? By our valid and licit ordination to preach the gospel with authority? Yes, partly. By evidence of our erudition and education? Yes, partly. By our daily compassionate and charitable service and companionship? Yes, primarily. Our preaching, especially when our message is difficult, is more likely to be received by our congregations when they are convinced that we preachers are speaking with love to people who are loved—loved by God and loved by us. Just as our ministry of preaching is fed by our daily prayer life, our ministry of preaching is fed by our daily care for our congregation, as we establish a relationship of spiritual father, shepherd, and friend with our people.

I mentioned before that our people are not machines. They have free will. We must move them to action. We want them to be not only "hearers of the Word" but "doers of the Word." Here's what I have in mind. Someone was trying to explain the difference between a speech given by Senator Adlai Stevenson and a speech by Senator Bobby Kennedy. The difference, one observer noted, is that after a speech by Stevenson, people would say, "What a nice speech." In contrast, after a speech by Kennedy, people would jump up and say, "Oh my God! We've got to DO something!"

I hope that all of us have in mind as one of the goals of our preaching that our people should stand up and say, "Oh my God! We've got to DO something!" We can lead them to that point by presenting the truth with love and passion, in a way that rouses tears, anger, faith, hope, charity, joy, and gratitude. But if we want them to go from *saying*, "We've got to DO something!" to actually *doing* something, we have to help them with some concrete directives. These directives must be specific enough so that they are measurable rather than vague. In other words, our homiletic rallying cry must be more specific than shouting, "Let's be nice!" How do you measure "nice"? And yet the directives must be flexible enough that individuals can apply them to the unique circumstances of their lives. An excerpt from one of my own homilies may be helpful here. And please be sure that I am offering this excerpt only as an illustration and not as an archetype.

I was preaching here last year, on the Third Sunday of Ordinary Time. The gospel passage was Mark's account of the call of the first disciples. In that homily I focused on hearing and acting on Christ speaking to us both by way of Scripture and by way of our neighbor. I concluded the homily with some concrete steps for the congregants to take. I also included a Scripture verse to serve as both a mnemonic and as a measure for their action. Here's how I wrapped up the homily:

"Christ Who is the Word of the Father is always speaking to us. Can we hear Him? If we hear Him, do we understand Him? If we understand Him, will we act on what He says? Today, and for each day this week, I ask that you will pray for three graces, for three special blessings. First, pray for alertness, that you might hear Christ when He speaks to you. Second, pray for wisdom, that you might understand Christ when speaks to you. Third, pray for obedience, that you might act when Christ speaks to you. If we do that, if we pray and live to hear, understand, and act, then we will be telling the truth when we join the psalmist and pray: 'Teach me your ways, O Lord.'"

There are, of course, many means of calling a congregation to action in a way that they can remember and measure. This way seems to work for me and the congregation I preach to most often. You, of course, will have to find ways that are suitable for you and your congregation.

My brothers, during this Year of Faith, during this present darkness, our people are in great need of the best liturgical preaching that grace and nature can offer them. Pope Benedict, in calling the Year of Faith, wrote that:

"We cannot accept that salt should become tasteless or the light be kept hidden (cf. *Mt* 5:13-16). The people of today can still experience the need to go to the well, like the Samaritan woman, in order to hear Jesus, who invites us to believe in him and to draw upon the source of living water welling up within him (cf. *Jn* 4:14). We must rediscover a taste for feeding ourselves on the word of God, faithfully handed down by the Church, and on the bread of life, offered as sustenance for his disciples (cf. *Jn* 6:51)."

So said Pope Benedict. That is why, brothers, I believe that we must make a maximum effort to be men of prayer, men of passion, and men of preparation, for the sake of the Word we preach and for the sake of the people we preach to. If we do that, then we will become the heralds of the Gospel of Christ, we will believe what we read, and we will practice what we preach.

I thank you for your time and attention. *Oremus pro invicem*! ("Let us pray for one another!")

ADVENT

What Time Is It?

First Sunday of Advent, Lectionary 3
Ave Maria, FL, 2012

Jeremiah 33:14-16
Psalm 25:4-5, 8-9, 10, 1
1 Thessalonians 3:12-4:2
Luke 21:25-28, 34-36

What time is it? Well, I suppose your answer might depend on how you count such things. You might look at your watch and see that it is a little bit past ten o'clock. You might look at a calendar and see that it is December 2. That's just two days after the end of Islamophobia Awareness Month—I don't know how I missed that—I wish someone here would have told me; December 2— that's two days into the month of December, which means that the year 2012 is drawing to a close, for better or for worse; December 2— that's just a few days before the last day of classes—thank you Jesus!

If we check our calendar carefully, we can see that December 2 is just two days past the end of hurricane season for 2012—which means we are more or less safe until the start of the next hurricane season on June 1, 2013.

We can look at the calendar again and see that December 2 is just nineteen days short of the start of winter, assuming that a northerner like me can honestly speak of winter in southwest Florida.

And, if we look into the current issue of Magnificat magazine, we can see that December 2 is the First Sunday of Advent. But what does that mean? For me, the First Sunday of Advent means the start of the season that I call, "The Onset of Father McTeigue's Pre-Christmas Spiritual Dyspepsia," or, said more simply, "Advent is when Father McTeigue's spiritual ulcer kicks into high gear." Why do I say that?

Well, among other things, the Season of Advent is a time of preparation for the Season of Christmas, which itself is the liturgical season that our culture gets most wrong. Do I exaggerate? You can find out by going online and searching these words: "YouTube Walmart Black Friday Mob." If you do so, you will get, by my latest count, 42 million hits. You can watch countless hours of human beings, made in the image and likeness of God, Americans who are not hungry, beating the stuffing out of each other for foreign-made junk that no one really needs and few can afford. If we as a nation mark our preparation for Christmas by Black Friday, then I think I might want to start looking for a hermitage somewhere very far away...

But that is only part of the story. My spirit sinks low on the First Sunday of Advent not only because it is a reminder that Christmas Madness is coming, but also because of the foolish things that people thoughtlessly say about Advent. Every year, for as long as I can remember, some well-intentioned soul spouts pieties about Advent being a "Season of Patience," with words like these: "Behold the serene, patient stillness of the pregnant woman waiting in joyful composure for the arrival of her child." Whoever says that has never spent much time with a pregnant woman.

Worse, well-intentioned souls spout glibly about

Advent as a "season of hope," with hope understood as a whimsical wishful thinking, along the lines of, "Hopefully it won't rain on our picnic today." Whenever one of these Pollyannas presents hope with the cheerful sounding "Don't worry—I just know everything is going to be okay!", in that moment, my inarticulate suffering releases all souls from Purgatory.

Worst of all—if we are not careful, we can note that today is the First Sunday of Advent, and then read, somewhat thoughtlessly, today's Scripture lessons. For example, I tend to think of Jeremiah as an admirably sober and sullen prophet, but in today's reading, God speaks these words through him: "The days are coming, says the LORD, when I will fulfill the promise I made to the house of Israel and Judah…In those days Judah shall be safe and Jerusalem shall dwell secure…" Doesn't that sound like wishful thinking? Either God hasn't been keeping up with the news lately or someone needs to send the Prophet Jeremiah to Iran…

And now let's turn again to the Gospel of Luke. Listen to these words from "gentle Jesus, meek and mild": "There will be signs in the sun, the moon, and the stars, and on earth nations will be in dismay, perplexed by the roaring of the sea and the waves. People will die of fright in anticipation of what is coming upon the world, for the powers of the heavens will be shaken." When you hear that, are you inclined to jump up to sing a few rousing choruses of the hymn "He's Got the Whole World in His Hands"? Me neither.

And then, just when you think you might finally be able to sleep at night for just a little while, if for no other reason than sheer exhaustion, Jesus warns us with these words: "Be vigilant at all times and pray that you have the strength to escape the tribulations that are imminent and to stand before the Son of Man." Who can live like that?

So, now, I will ask you again: "What time is it?" It is

December 2, 2012, the First Sunday of Advent, which *is* a season of patience and a season of hope. I say this to you because I was ordained to preach what our Lord has entrusted to His Church, and I am glad to say this to you because it is true and because it is good news.

A season of patience: Patience is not a resigned dithering, a form of pacing back and forth waiting for the future to hurry up and arrive. Patience is a resolution to endure the storm; the Medievals said that "patience is the pillar that cannot be shaken." During Advent, we choose to remain patiently faithful during this present darkness, waiting for Christ the Sun to rise upon our world, as He promised.

A season of hope: True hope is not wishful thinking! Hope is a choice to make oneself available to a good future offered by God. During Advent, we make a choice to hope by showing up, ready to greet Christ who comes to us in history, in mystery, and in glory. The only worthy response to the Season of Advent is life lived in hope. Hope is not merely a comforting fantasy. It is an obligation we must embrace fiercely and firmly. It is an obligation to choose to show up, with our heart and hands, with our time, talent, and treasure, to cooperate with whatever good thing God wishes to work through us over time.

A life of hope is a life that is both utterly realistic and marked by a readiness to be amazed by God and what He can do with human instruments living through time and living for eternity. Consider these words of Cardinal Francis George of Chicago. He said, "I expect to die in bed, my successor will die in prison and his successor will die a martyr in the public square. His successor will pick up the shards of a ruined society and slowly help rebuild civilization, as the Church has done so often in human history."

Cardinal George is speaking words of hope, because he is speaking words that are both sober about the human condition and confident in God's sovereignty. He knows that true hope is not casually spoken of nor easily lived. He knows that the triumph of hope rests upon human beings who are carried by the Providence of God. And he knows that a living Christian hope is not lived alone but is always lived within the mission of the Church. Cardinal George, as a man of hope, knows that part of the work of the Church on Earth is to prepare people for eternity by helping them to live well in time, building and rebuilding civilization, handing on the good fruits of both faith and reason, from one generation to the next. In God's providence, we must continue to do so until He comes again in glory, to judge the living and the dead, and the world by fire.

Let's get specific. Let's take the demands and opportunities of Advent, let's take the resolution of patience and the choice for hope and see how we might live that vocation, in our time, right here in Ave Maria. I think it would help us all greatly if we stop from time to time and marvel that we are all here together, by God's providence, in a community that shares the same faith and the same values. What a privilege to be in such a community that is at once a town, a parish, and a university. What good things God can do through us here when we let Him!

The opportunities we have here as Advent begins also put great responsibilities in our hands. We need to reach out to each other in mercy, humility, compassion, and generosity. We need to admit our faults and our incompleteness. We need to declare that our cooperation with God requires that we cooperate with each other.

How shall we do that? Let's start with something simple. Find a friend. Pray with your friend. Join your friend in doing something kind for your neighbor. That simple formula, you will quickly find, will require patience and hope, just in time for Advent. Finding and welcoming Christ Who is in need within your neighbor will help prepare you to welcome Jesus of Nazareth, Son of God and Son of

Mary, Who is the Word-made-flesh, Whose birth we celebrate at Christmas.

Prayer, patience, hope, friendship, service—these are the ingredients of the vigilance Jesus calls for in today's gospel. They are proof that the Spirit of God is still at work in the world. They are the hand of our Heavenly Father leading us to our true home, where already a banquet is prepared for us. Prayer, patience, hope, friendship, service—these are the signs we must look for within ourselves and among God's faithful people. Whenever and wherever we see them, let us then recall these words of Jesus: "...when these signs begin to happen, stand erect and raise your heads because your redemption is at hand."

May God's Holy Name be praised now and forever.

IS THE GOSPEL GOOD NEWS OR GREAT NEWS?

First Wednesday of Advent, Lectionary 177
Ave Maria, FL, 2013

Isaiah 25:6-10a
Psalm 23:1-3a, 3b-4, 5, 6
Matthew 15:29-37

For whom is today's gospel passage good news? Well, if we don't think of ourselves, as Matthew records, as lame, blind, deformed, or mute, maybe we won't receive today's passage as good news. But a medieval commentator had this to say about today's gospel passage. He wrote: "The dumb are they that do not praise God; the blind, they that do not understand the paths of life; the deaf, they that obey not; the lame, they that walk not firmly through the difficult ways of good works; the maimed, they that are crippled in their good works."

I won't ask for a show of hands, but I know those words surely describe me, at least some of the time, if not most of the time. That Jesus would gladly heal such as these brings joy to my heart, and draws me closer to Him.

For whom else is this gospel passage good news? For the hungry and the tired. Matthew records that the heart of Jesus is moved with pity for the hungry and tired who follow Him. Again, I won't ask for a show of hands, but I know that I am hungry, and hungry for more than just food; I am hungry, as I suspect you are as well, for peace of mind, for mercy, and for a place to rest my wounded heart.

But for whom is this gospel passage *great* news? It is great news for those who know they have little to give but are willing to give it all to the Lord. The disciples ask, "Where could we ever get enough...?" The needs before us always seem overwhelming. Jesus asks them, "How much do you have?" He asks the same question of us. I will not ask for a show of hands to see how many of us are ready to hear, much less answer, that question. The disciples answer that question, and give all—*all*—of the little they have. And Jesus makes what they give to be enough and more than enough.

That fact presents us with a difficult but intriguing question: What great thing could the Lord do with my little life if only I would give it to Him? If you would like to find the answer to that question, you could begin by placing your life on this altar, and offer it to the Father in union with the sacrifice of Christ. If you do that, your life would become fruitful beyond what you can now imagine.

Let's pray with and for each other today, that we each will have the courage, generosity, and, really—the good sense, to place our lives on the altar today.

May God's Holy Name be praised now and forever.

OBEDIENCE *AND* FREEDOM?

First Thursday of Advent, Lectionary 178
Ave Maria, FL, 2013

Isaiah 26:1-6
Psalm 118:1, 8-9
Matthew 7:21, 24-27

There are some phrases that make a faithful Christian writhe with pain and indignation. For example, when someone says, "I'm not really religious, but I am spiritual," or "I like Jesus, but not the Church," or "I think it would be great to be a Christian, if it weren't for all the rules," a faithful Christian can feel his eye twitch and can start to feel his stomach acid churn. Those statements are wrong for too many obvious reasons to list here and now. However, whenever people articulate such foolishness, we should thank them. We should thank them because—alas—they are holding up a mirror and asking us to notice the resemblance between them and us.

The people I just described upset us because they are talking about accepting the Lord only on their terms rather than on His. But—really—are we so very different? Can we honestly claim that we have never been tempted to praise Christ while pushing away His Cross? Can we honestly claim that there is no area of our lives that we withhold from the Lordship of Jesus? Can we honestly claim that we never say to the Lord, "Yes, but…"?

I think of these things because of what we heard in today's gospel passage. Jesus said to his disciples: "Not everyone who says to me, 'Lord, Lord,' will enter the kingdom of heaven, but only the one who does the will of my Father in heaven." Jesus is referring to a word which we dare not mention in polite company, one which seemingly has no place in civilized society. Jesus is referring to the dreaded "O-word." Jesus is speaking about obedience.

The roots of the word obedience come from the Latin word for hearing. Obedience requires that we hear a command, and then that we act upon it. But that does not tell us enough, and it does not guide us to the obedience that Jesus is pointing to. However, Saint Ignatius Loyola can be our guide to proper Christian obedience.

Saint Ignatius said that the lowest level of obedience is that of execution—in other words, mere compliance. Those of you who are parents have seen this kind of obedience countless times. When one of your children performs an onerous household chore while sulking, whining, and slamming doors, that is mere compliance—the lowest level of obedience.

The next level of obedience is that of the intellect. One does what one is commanded, if begrudgingly, but one can imagine a possible world wherein that command might be reasonable, and perhaps even wise. We see this kind of obedience when a patient reluctantly complies with a doctor's order to quit smoking and start exercising. The patient mutters, "The doctor may be right, and I will do what he says, but I don't have to like it."

Saint Ignatius says that the highest form of obedience,

truly Christ-like obedience, is the obedience of the will. At this level, the person embraces with full consent and desire what has been commanded. This person says, "I give myself, wholeheartedly, without reserve, to what has been commanded."

This is how Jesus obeyed our Heavenly Father. The Son loves and trusts our Heavenly Father and thus Jesus always says to our Heavenly Father, "Thy will be done."

Obedience, the readiness to hear and do what we ought—that is true freedom, as Pope John Paul II taught us. That is the freedom that Christ calls us to daily. That true freedom can take root in us and bear good fruit, if we bring ourselves to place our lives on the altar, and in union with Christ offer our lives to the Father Who loves us.

The moral of the story is this: Those who are ready to give are those who are ready to obey.

May God's Holy Name be praised now and forever.

Do You Want to Be Healed?

First Friday of Advent, Lectionary 179
Ave Maria, FL, 2013

Isaiah 29:17-24
Psalm 27:1, 4, 13-14
Matthew 9:27-31

The other day I happened upon a curious statistic. Right now, in the United States, the number of people receiving government disability payments exceeds the total population of the nation of Greece. Now, it is undeniable that some folks have suffered terrible injuries, such as, losing an eye or suffering a spinal injury, and as a result are unable to work.

But it is very likely true that a non-trivial number of people are probably gaming the system; they may have suffered some injury, but not one truly severe enough to render them unable to work. Yet, somehow, they have gotten a medical certificate that qualifies them to collect disability payments. Now, what if we went up to those people and said, "Good news! Jesus of Nazareth, the great healer, Jesus the wonder-worker is coming to town! Let's go out and meet Him and call on His name, and He will heal you, and then you can go back to work! Won't that be great?"

It isn't hard to imagine that some of those folks would politely decline the offer of meeting up with Jesus-the-healer. While being "disabled" might be an inconvenience, the free money is more appealing than having to work for a living. I think of this as we consider today's gospel passage. The two blind men were almost certainly beggars. It was a marginal existence of course, but it was also quite free of responsibility. They would have no businesses to run, no families to feed. Yet they wanted sight so much that they called out for the healing of Jesus, even though that healing would bring upon them the requirement to support themselves, and perhaps others, through hard work, for the rest of their lives.

Why do I speak of these things? I do so because I think they can help us to understand sin and conversion. Picture this. Let's imagine ourselves walking to confession. We say to ourselves, "Every time I go to confession, I confess the same sin. 15 minutes after I've completed my penance, I've committed that same sin again. I wonder why that is?" Well, I think we can see how our reflection on fraudulent disability claims and the account of the healing of the blind men can help us to answer that question.

The disability frauds love their disability, as they find it useful, and it keeps them from taking on the ordinary responsibilities of life. The blind men hated their disability, and sought healing, knowing full well that once they were healed they would have to take on the responsibility of hard work. You see, the disability frauds represent insincere penitents, and the blind men calling for healing represent sincere penitents.

In other words, if we are confessing the same sins time after time, then we likely desire the benefit of forgiveness, but don't really desire to take on the hard work of conversion. We want to have our cake and eat it too. We want the benefit of forgiveness for our sin, while we still love our sin. That's why we confess but we don't really repent. Receiving absolution and performing our penance are necessary steps, but they are not the whole process. After going to confession, whether we like it or not, we have the solemn responsibility to reform our lives so that the sin we just confessed does not reappear. We have to uproot the patterns of thought, feeling, and action that feed our sin. We must walk away from the people, places, and things that are the near occasions of sin for us. If we do not do that, then we are like the disability frauds who want the benefit of the disability payment while hiding from the One who could heal us of our supposedly regretted disability.

During this season of Advent, we have a choice to make. We can, as we hear again and again this season, "prepare the way of the Lord," by removing every obstacle to the exercise of His sovereign Lordship over our lives. We can be like the blind men who cry out, "Have pity on us!" and who, like them, are ready to take full responsibility for the gift of mercy that the Lord offers. Or we can be like the frauds who tell themselves that their dishonesty will not catch up with them.

Let's spend some time in prayer today, asking the Lord to reveal to us just one sin that He would like to see gone from our lives. And let's ask Him to show us how, by Midnight Mass on Christmas Eve, we can be relieved of that sin which we have clung to for so long. If we do that, then, as we celebrate the birth of the Christ of God, we can hear the echo of the Lord's voice from today's gospel passage: "Let it be done for you according to your faith."

May God's Holy Name be praised now and forever.

How Will You Prepare the Way of the Lord?

Second Sunday of Advent, Lectionary 4
Ave Maria, FL, 2013
Isaiah 11:1-10
Psalm 72: 1-2, 7-8, 12-13, 17
Romans 15:4-9
Matthew 3:1-12

I have always had a special regard for Saint John the Baptist. That may be because I was born on one of his feast days. I was born on the Feast of the Beheading of John the Baptist. I like to tell myself that it was just a mere coincidence that I was born on that particular feast day and not a foreshadowing of things to come, but that remains to be seen. So far, I've been right.

On this Second Sunday of Advent, in this particular time and place for our Church, our nation, and our own little community here at Ave Maria, what must we remember, pray over, and act upon from today's gospel passage? Let's remember four words today, which are taken directly from today's reading: travel, trees, fire, and fan.

Travel—John recalls these words from the prophet

Isaiah: "Prepare the way of the Lord, make straight his paths." In the Middle East in ancient times, roads were few and hazardous. Consequently, the people of John's time had a proverb which said: "There are three states of misery—sickness, fasting, and travel." That will help us to appreciate that Saint Matthew records that the people were "going out" to John, and "were being baptized by him in the Jordan River as they acknowledged their sins." To leave your town or village to go out to the Jordan was not a mere stroll—it was a hardship. The merely curious would not undertake such a perilous trip. Going out to the Jordan River for John's baptism indicated a readiness to begin the difficult process of leaving your sins behind. That "going out" and "leaving behind" reminds me of an entry recorded in the diary of John Bunyan, the author of the famous work, "The Pilgrim's Progress." Bunyan wrote that one day, while standing on the village green, he heard a voice ask him this question: "Wilt thou leave thy sins and go to heaven, or wilt thou have thy sins and go to hell?" John the Baptist asks us the same question today. Will we make the hard journey to repentance, or sit at home comfortably with our sins?

But as we reflect on travel in light of today's gospel, we must remember that we live on a two-way street. We have a journey to make, but so does the Lord. Jesus, Who is Son of God and Son of Mary, He Who is the Word made flesh, became man and entered our world so that He could enter our souls, and reclaim His rightful place upon the throne of our hearts. If we wish to "prepare the way of the Lord" and "make straight his paths," then we have to remove any obstacles that keep our hearts from Him. We must clear our lives of the people, places, and things that are near occasions of sin for us. And we must throw down the idols that now sit on the throne of our crooked hearts.

So far, we've spoken of travel. The second word we need to remember today is "trees." The Baptist said: "Even now the ax lies at the root of the trees. Therefore every tree that does not bear good fruit will be cut down and thrown into the fire." A medieval abbot named Rabanus wrote this about today's gospel and trees: "There are four sorts of trees: the first totally withered, to which the Pagans may be likened; the second, green but unfruitful, as the hypocrites; the third, green and fruitful, but poisonous, such are heretics; the fourth, green and bringing forth good fruit, to which are like the good Catholics." Are we fruitful trees in the Lord's vineyard? We may judge that not by the number of our pious words or thoughts, but by our works of charity and by the cultivation of virtues that follow from true conversion. God is patient, but John makes clear that time is running out for all of us. The Season of Advent is given to us as a reminder to get busy.

Travel and trees. The third word we need to remember from today's gospel is "fire." John said of the coming Messiah, "He will baptize you with the Holy Spirit and fire." Fire brings light. Jesus is the beacon of light to guide us home to our Heavenly Father. Fire brings warmth. Jesus sparks in us the warmth of love of God and neighbor. The biblical scholar William Barclay wrote that, "Christianity is always the religion of the kindled heart." And fire brings purification. Fire burns away dross; it strengthens and tempers metal. The fire of Jesus will burn away the dross of evil from us, and leave us with a heart that may become a strong instrument in His hands.

Travel, trees, fire. Finally, we must talk about today's gospel and the word "fan." The Baptist said of the coming Messiah that, "His winnowing fan is in his hand. He will clear his threshing floor and gather his wheat into his barn, but the chaff he will burn with unquenchable fire." Now, if you are a city boy like me, and you've never ground your own wheat in a granary, the meaning of that image is not immediately obvious. In the time of John and Jesus, a large mill stone would grind the grain, and leave on the floor the wheat and the chaff, which is the junky leftovers of the plant. The winnowing fan was a great wooden shovel. The grain was lifted from the threshing floor with that shovel and tossed into the air. The heavy grain fell back to the ground, while the light chaff was carried away on the wind. The good grain was brought into the barn, and the leftover chaff was used as fuel for the fire.

What John is pointing to is an unavoidable sifting of all humanity. Those heavy with fruitfulness for Christ will be gathered into the Kingdom, and it will not end well for the rest. One medieval commentator said that the Church will be subject to four winnowings, that is, four times of persecution and sifting. The first sifting or persecution will be by the Jews, the next by the Romans, the third by heretics, and the fourth by the anti-Christ. I will leave it to you to check your calendar and see where we are today in that four-step process. But it is certainly true that in every age of the Church, the Body of Christ has its persecutors, and we are kidding ourselves if we think that this age is an exception.

Travel, trees, fire, and fan. These are the words that I said we ought to remember from today's gospel passage. What shall we *do* with them? Let's be practical, and let's be simple. First, I ask you today, to take time in prayer, and ask God to reveal to you one obstacle, that is, one habit of sin that keeps you from Christ. Then resolve today that, with God's grace, that obstacle will be removed by Midnight Mass on this Christmas Eve. Second, take time in prayer today, and ask God to reveal to you one fruitfulness, that is, one habit of charity, that He would like to see take root in your heart. Then resolve today that, with God's grace, that good seed will be well planted by Midnight Mass on this Christmas Eve. Between this moment and Christmas Eve night, let us intercede for each other with these words of Saint Paul: "May the God of endurance and encouragement grant you to think in harmony with one another, in keeping with Christ Jesus, that with one accord you may with one

voice glorify the God and Father of our Lord Jesus Christ."
May God's Holy Name be praised now and forever.

Fear Not?

Third Sunday of Advent, Lectionary 9
Moody Air Force Base, Valdosta, GA, 2012

Zephaniah 3:14-18a
Isaiah 12:2-3, 4, 5-6
Philippians 4:4-7
Luke 3:10-18

Do you want to hear a story? Well, I will tell you two. The first one might be a bit familiar to you.

There is a deacon in my parish back home, named John, a very fine man, who is about fifteen years older than me. He is a quiet, soft spoken, gentle man. I can't imagine him raising his voice. So I was very surprised to learn that he had served our country as a Marine. He was a rescue swimmer for the Marines during the Vietnam war, jumping out of helicopters into the ocean to rescue downed pilots. I cannot imagine having that kind of courage and I told him so. John smiled, and shrugged off my implicit compliment. He said, "Well, when you're 20 you assume that you are immortal, so it is easy to be convinced to do very dangerous things."

Of course, convincing young people to do very

dangerous things is an important part of military training. The key requirement, as I understand it, is to convince young people to do very dangerous things under very controlled conditions, for very good reasons, and under the guidance of legitimate authority. Part of the recklessness that characterizes youth, alas, is when young people, apparently incapable of the thoughtful reflection that leads to healthy fear, take it upon themselves to do very dangerous things under uncontrolled conditions, for little or no good reason, and without any guidance or authority at all. That sort of thing frequently keeps commanders, chaplains, and parents from getting the good night's sleep that they deserve.

So, let's keep that image in mind, that of fearlessness leading to recklessness, and let's turn to another image. In my office at the university, I have a painting called "Watchers in the Night." It depicts a guardian angel watching over a sleeping child. This angel is not a cute little cherub that we see on some Christmas cards. No, no. This angel is 7 feet tall, holding an even taller spear in one hand, and a ball of flame in the other. His wings are spread out as a protective mantle about the child and his bed. This angel is clearly full of the Holy Spirit and of testosterone.

I once showed that painting to a student in distress and said to her, "Don't you find that image reassuring?" She said, "No, not all." I asked her why not. She replied, "Father—if I need that kind of protection, what the heck is after me?!?" Hers was a fear that could not be calmed or relieved.

I tell you these two stories because they represent two extremes. On the one hand is a fearlessness that could lead to recklessness; on the other hand is a fearfulness that could lead to paralysis. Neither approach serves us well; neither approach is suitable for a Christian; neither approach glorifies God. What Christians are called to is an honest recognition that sometimes our world is dangerous, that often we have to do hard and risky things, and, above all, that we live in a world governed by a provident and loving Father.

So, with that in mind, let's turn to today's Scripture passages. The prophet Zephaniah writes these words: "Fear not, O Zion, be not discouraged! The LORD, your God, is in your midst, a mighty savior…" Why does Zephaniah tell us not to be afraid? Because there is nothing or no one to be afraid of? Well, no, we know that isn't true. He tells us to fear not, because God is with us, our savior is among us. Our savior, who defeated sin and death, lives with us, among us, within us, and He wishes to share His victory with us.

Now let's listen again to Saint Paul. Saint Paul writes these words: "Have no anxiety at all, but in everything, by prayer and petition, with thanksgiving, make your requests known to God." We are sons and daughters of our Heavenly Father. Orphans live in fear; orphans are anxious for they have nothing and no one. We are not orphans! And we dishonor our Heavenly Father when we live as if we were orphans. We deny our adoption when we live as if we have to fend for ourselves because there is no one to love us or protect us. Someone who is confident in his father's love never hesitates to ask for what he needs; someone who is confident in his father's love is glad for another opportunity to receive his father's love. Jesus taught us that—He lived His whole life that way. We must do the same.

We human beings are weak, prone to worry and anxiety, and we live in a world that can be indifferent or dangerous. What the world does to our heart and mind and body can cause us to believe that we are unloved orphans, abandoned by life. We have to stand against that lie, and insist that we are sons and daughters of the living God Who will never abandon us and Who shares with us His victory. Let's show the world the truth about fear and the truth about being Christians, by confidently calling upon the

Heavenly Father Who made us, Who saved us, and Who guides us to Heaven our true home, where already a banquet is prepared for us. If we believe and pray with a confidence that is stronger than fear, then, as Saint Paul tells us, "…the peace of God that surpasses all understanding will guard your hearts and minds in Christ Jesus." And what could be better than that?

May God's Holy Name be praised now and forever.

What Do You Want for Advent?

Third Friday of Advent, Lectionary 197
Ave Maria, FL, 2012

Isaiah 56: 1-3a, 6-8
Psalm 67:2-3, 5, 7-8
John 5:33-36

What do you want for Christmas? No doubt you've been asked that question many times in recent weeks, and you have surely asked that question of your family and other loved ones. When I was a boy, I would ask my parents, "What do you want for Christmas?", and they would say, "Nothing…just peace of mind…SIGH…" At the time, I would be so frustrated with them, but, now that I am about their age when I asked that question, I am starting to appreciate their honest answer.

Today I want to put before us another question: "What do you want for Advent?" That question, I am sure, is much more rare, and to most people, scarcely intelligible. I do not doubt that as Advent approached, we asked ourselves what graces we would like to receive during Advent, and what special efforts we might make to observe the season of Advent. But don't worry—I will neither ask for nor offer statements of how zealously or fruitfully any of us have lived the first three and a half weeks of Advent.

Now we are coming down to the wire. Sunday is the Fourth Sunday of Advent, and Tuesday is Christmas Day. So, I ask the question more urgently: "What do you want for Advent?" In other words, in the brief time of Advent that still remains, what would you like to receive from the Lord, and what would you like to offer Him?

To answer those questions, let's take some guidance from Dietrich Bonhoeffer, the pastor who heroically resisted the Nazis. Regarding Advent, Bonheoffer wrote these words: "A prison cell, in which one waits, hopes—and is completely dependent on the fact that the door of freedom has to be opened from the outside—is not a bad picture of Advent."

Waiting for the door of freedom to be opened, waiting to be liberated from our captivity, from our limitations—those are very fine images of Advent. We are like Lazarus in the tomb, waiting to be called forth. But once the prison door is opened, once we have been called from death to life, when we find ourselves at the threshold, half in the dark and half in the light, what shall we do with our freedom? What shall we do with our undeserved second chance? How shall we who have been unexpectedly born again live our vocation as liberated and free?

I want to relate those questions, inspired by Bonheoffer's image of Advent, to my earlier question, namely, "What do you want for Advent?" For me to answer that question publicly, in this forum, for a moment I beg your indulgence and ask that you allow me to address primarily the men present here today. I will gladly talk about women, my sisters in Christ, at any time, but today, at this time, I need to speak especially to the men.

My brothers, what I want for Advent is to be freed to unite with a strong company of Godly men, men who know that they are called to be husbands, fathers, priests, and heroes. I want to walk out of the tomb into the light, with other Godly men, who are ready and eager to use their God-given manly freedom and strength to stand up for the honor of faith, family, and community. Our nation, our Church, our culture, our communities suffer—*suffer*—from the lack of such Godly men. You know that is true; I know that you do not doubt it. But why do we lack such men?

To answer that question, consider these words from Louis Cardinal Pie and his Christmas homily of 1871. Cardinal Pie, by the way, was a favorite of St. Pius X. Cardinal Pie preached these words:

> "Is not ours an age of mis-lived lives, of un-manned men?
> Why?
> Because Jesus Christ has disappeared. Wherever the people are true Christians, there are men to be found in large numbers, but everywhere and always, if Christianity wilts, the men wilt. Look closely, they are no longer men but shadows of men. Thus what do you hear on all sides today? The world is dwindling away, for lack of men; the nations are perishing for scarcity of men, for the rareness of men. I do believe: there are no men where there is no character; there is no character where there are no principles, doctrines, stands taken; there are no stands taken, no doctrines, no principles, where there is no religious faith and consequently no religion of society.
> Do what you will: only from God you will get men."

We need men—we need real, Godly men. What we see around us is a generation of not men but merely "boys-who-shave," that is, males who are unwilling to shoulder the cross of being a true man, a man who sacrifices and leads and provides. We suffer from a lack of men willing to take responsibility for the children they beget, or for the women who love them, or for the civil liberties they enjoy. Today we are surrounded by countless Peter Pans, boys who refuse to become men. They are not all of the problem, but these Peter Pans who live in their parents' basement, spending their days smoking dope, using pornography, and demanding a free ride are surely not now ready to be part of the solution. And we have been reminded, again and again, that these shallow and selfish Peter Pans have a very dark side that can explode in selfish and murderous rage.

So, as Advent draws to a close, we may ask, "What is the solution?" First, we must turn to the Lord and cry out, we must clamor for our liberation, we must ask for the cells and tombs of our lives to be opened. Second, we must obey the call to emerge from the darkness and live as free men, men made in the image and likeness of God—men redeemed at a terrible cost and consecrated for a greater glory. Finally, we—all of us, men and women, young and old—we must prepare our boys to be Godly men. We can begin to do so by honoring the heroic fathers of our past and present; we can do so by proclaiming Jesus Who is true God and true man; we can do so by insisting again and again that God is above all a great and loving Father.

Is all that wishful thinking? The scriptures tell us otherwise. Remember these words from the prophet Zephaniah we heard today. The prophet wrote: "Fear not...be not discouraged! The LORD, your God, is in your midst, a mighty savior..."

You see, God does not call us to an impossible task. God, our Lord and mighty savior, is with us, offering us all we need to live and die as we ought. Let us turn to Him and say "yes" to all that He offers us.

What should we want for Advent? I believe that we should want to turn to the Lord and ask Him to liberate males and call them to be Godly men who can provide for, protect, and serve all who are entrusted to their care. And when we see the blessings that flow from Godly men who have become true husbands, fathers, priests, and heroes, then we can echo the words of the psalm we heard today: "...the plan of the LORD stands forever; the design of his heart, through all generations."

May God's Holy Name be praised now and forever.

Lent

The Dangers of "Business-As-Usual"

Ash Wednesday, Lectionary 219
Elizabethtown College, Elizabethtown, PA, 2006

Joel 2:12-18
Psalm 51
2 Corinthians 5:20–6:2
Matthew 6:1-6, 16-18

Do you make a lot of noise when you pray? I ask this question with some urgency because of what happened to me a few years before I became a priest. I was asleep in my apartment in Northern Virginia when I was awakened by a tremendous shout from the apartment downstairs: **"THANK YOU JESUS!!"** I sat up in bed without opening my eyes and said, "Oh no! I've died! And heaven is a Baptist church—I feel so foolish…"

I opened my eyes and saw by my digital clock that it was four in the morning. The woman downstairs continued to shout, and then cranked up her stereo, playing the hymn "Go Tell It On A Mountain!" I thought I was losing my mind. "This has to stop!" I said to myself. "It's a Saturday and I sleep in late on Saturdays. Someone has to stop this woman." I picked up my shoe and started banging on the floor yelling, "Jesus said to go to your Heavenly Father *in secret!* **In secret!**"

Now the gospel reading for today makes clear that we're not to put our religious practices on display for the approval of others. So, then, why are we all here to get ashes smeared on our foreheads? Have we forgotten already what Jesus said?

We don't get ashes on our forehead for anybody else's benefit or approval. We get the ashes on our forehead to remind us that "Business-As-Usual" is dead. What do I mean by "Business-As-Usual"? It refers to all the ordinary things we do, and how we do them and why we do them, without really thinking about them. It's all the stuff that we take for granted, without question or doubt. Business-As-Usual means that we act and choose and live without thought, without feeling, without purpose. And Business-As-Usual is dangerous because of the effects that it causes. What effects? I invite you to use your imagination for a bit and bear with me.

Hold up your right hand. Now with your other hand, check it for calluses. Calluses are developed over time by repeated action, hardening the skin. A callus is simply a pile of dead skin. You're students, and spend a whole lot of your time with books, so you're not likely to have many calluses on your hands. But if you were a bricklayer, or a carpenter, and worked with your hands all day, your hands would be covered with them. I bring this to your attention to alert you to the fact that Business-As-Usual builds calluses on your heart. What do I mean by that?

During the Second World War, there were special training programs designed for guards in the Nazi death camps. Soldiers were each given a puppy to raise for six weeks. Then the men lined up with their puppies, and were ordered to pick up the puppy and break its neck. Anyone who hesitated was kicked out. Why? Because anyone who hesitated could still feel, could still be compassionate. Anyone who hesitated still had a heart. The ones who followed orders without thinking, the ones with the calloused hearts, they became the monsters who ran the death camps. Now do you understand when I say that Business-As-Usual builds calluses on your heart? Calluses on your heart harden your heart against the grace of God. It puts you on the highway to hell.

Now, here you may sigh with relief. You may say, "Well! I'll never be a Nazi puppy killer! I'll never go to hell!" Oh...not so fast! One doesn't have to be a Nazi prison guard to be on the road away from God. Each one of us here can get calluses on our hearts, and so become numb to the touch of God. Bit by bit, slowly, without warning, without alarming us or even alerting us, Business-As-Usual can lead us quietly away from God, away from grace and love, and into the arms of darkness, into the nothing. That's why we wear ashes today. To remind us that we have to kill Business-As-Usual before it kills us.

Let me identify for you three ways that Business-As-Usual, those thoughtless, heartless patterns of valuing and behaving, can lead to calluses on the heart. And I'll identify some ways that this Lent, you can prevent and remove calluses of the heart.

There are at least three areas of life where hardheartedness, the calluses of Business-As-Usual, can creep in: 1) Praying as if God doesn't speak; 2) eating as if no one else is hungry; 3) spending as if we have not been blessed.

A few words about prayer: Many people tell me, "I don't really pray much because when I do I fall asleep." Well here's a suggestion—don't pray in bed! Pray where you might hurt yourself if you fall asleep, like while you're flossing your teeth. And many people tell me, "Well, I say some prayers every day—so I'm okay, right?" Well, it's good to talk to God, but we also have to learn how to let God speak to us.

Here's the bottom line: If you don't have a daily habit of prayer, a habit of speaking to and listening to God, you will certainly get deadly calluses on your heart. This Lent, make a commitment to learn how to pray. Go online tonight and order a book called "Too Deep For Words." That can get you started in learning how to pray. Then promise God that you will block out 15 minutes every day just for you and Him—it's your date with God. Do it. Every week, add a few more minutes, so that by the time Easter comes around, you're up to 30 minutes a day with God. People spend more time on the treadmill than that.

"Eating as if no one else is hungry." This country has more food than it knows what to do with. There is so much food in this country that we have an epidemic of overweight dogs; Purina sells us "diet" dog food. When we eat, do we remember at all that every night millions of people go to bed hungry? When we eat, do we remember that we consume more calories in a day than many people do in a week? Fasting is abstaining from food for religious reasons. It's not dieting. When we fast, we let ourselves go hungry to remind us that we need to be hungry for God, that we need God even more than we need food. And when we fast, we let ourselves go hungry so that we can remember those who go hungry because there is no food for them. This Lent, choose to fast. Choose to skip a meal on Wednesdays and Fridays; then take the money that you save and send it to Bread For The World, an organization that feeds the hungry. Donate at www.bread.org.

A third way that Business-As-Usual calluses our hearts is through thoughtless spending, spending as if we have not been blessed. What do I mean by that? Two words: "**My** money." You may say, "Darned right—my money! I earned it. No one can take it away from me and no one can tell me what to do with it. I deserve whatever I can buy with it." But wait a minute—what about being blessed? Yes, you earned the money, you worked for it. But the ability to get up and go to work—did you give that to yourself? Did you give yourself hands and feet and eyes and a mind to work? Didn't God bless you with all that? If you are so blessed by God, can you rightly close your fist around your cash and say, "***Mine!!***"? Doesn't God deserve a cut? If you want to give God His share, give to the poor. Jesus said, "Whatever you do to the least among you, you do for me." Believe Him, and give to the poor. In older times, giving to the poor was known as "almsgiving." This Lent, make a commitment to give alms. Go to www.catholiccharitiesusa.org and make a donation to help someone in need.

Prayer, fasting, and almsgiving are the three traditional Catholic practices for Lent. They are good ways to keep calluses from growing on your heart. They're a good way to move you towards God. But what about the calluses that are already there? How do they get removed? Confession. Lent is the perfect time to go to confession. Confession is an essential part of practicing good spiritual hygiene. This Lent, find a priest and say, "Hey! I need to get right with God! Please hear my confession." And then, promise yourself and God (you can do it during your daily prayer) that from now on you will go to confession at least once per month. It's the only way to keep yourself clean.

I challenge you this evening not to leave this room until you make a commitment to prayer, fasting, almsgiving, and confession. Then be marked with ashes to remind yourself that Business-As-Usual is dead. We make these changes because we want all the life and love that God can offer; we make these changes because we reject the death and hate that sin can offer. We make these changes to prove to our Heavenly Father that Jesus did not die for us in vain. We make these changes because the bitterness of the Cross and the glory of the Resurrection have touched our lives. We say "yes" to prayer and fasting and almsgiving and confession so that we can say "yes" forever to the God who invites us to the happiness of Heaven. What we do for God, let us do for love and gratitude and joy. Yes, we know that we are sinners, but we are loved sinners. Therefore even in Lent we can rejoice because we loved sinners have been given a second chance, we have been caught safely by the mercy of God. So with gladness, we can echo the words of Saint Paul: "Behold, now is the acceptable time; now is the day of salvation."

May God's Holy Name be praised now and forever.

SOME CHOICES ARE HARD; SOME CHOICES ARE EASY

Thursday after Ash Wednesday, Lectionary 220
Ave Maria, FL, 2012
Deuteronomy 30:15-20
Psalm 1:1-2, 3, 4, 6
Luke 9:22-25

Some choices are easy to make. For example, what if someone approached you and said, "Which do you prefer? The key to the executive washroom, or this moist towelette?" The answer would be obvious, wouldn't it?

Saint Polycarp, a holy martyr whose memory we honor today, was given what some thought to be an easy choice to make. He was asked, "Which do you choose? Will you renounce Christ and embrace Caesar, or will you choose a martyr's death?" For Polycarp, the choice was easy—he chose Christ, and a brief death and eternal life.

Moses, too, presented the people with an apparently easy choice. He said to the people: "I call heaven and earth today to witness against you: I have set before you life and death, the blessing and the curse." How hard of a choice can that be? Let's see: "In the sight of heaven, I can choose life or death, blessing or curse. Hmmm." Seems like a no-brainer, doesn't it?

But what if the choice were just as far-reaching, but presented subtly, even seductively? What if you were told: "Behold! I will provide for you from cradle to grave. I will take care of all your needs from life—as I define life—till death—as I define death. I will tell you all you need to know and I will tell you of all that you should hold dear. All you need to do is nothing, simply nothing, and enjoy." Would you accept that offer? Do you think it would be easy or hard to resist? I think that we in America are now being offered such a choice by those who believe that the center of all wisdom, authority, and goodness is and ought to be in the hands of the federal government.

Faithful Catholics, however, know better. They know that only the living God is the true sovereign Lord over life and death. They know that in this fallen world man must earn his living by the sweat of his brow, and no government plan, however well financed, can make that hard fact go away. Faithful Catholics know that true wisdom resides not in Washington but in Jesus of Nazareth, Who is Son of God and Son of Mary, Who alone is the way, the truth, and the life.

We must be clear that we Catholics in America are now being faced with a very hard, which is to say costly, choice. If we do not agree to be seduced towards the idolatry of the next Caesar, then we will be coerced to accept such idolatry. In the brief time that remains before the coercion begins in earnest, we must use every good and legal means to insist and ensure that we will live what we know to be true—namely, that only God is God; that only God is sovereign over life and death; that we must bend our knee only before Christ and never before Caesar.

To fight and win this good fight we will need the help of each other to take up and carry our cross with our Lord, to Calvary and beyond. And we will need the strength that can only be found at this altar, in the gift of the Holy Eucharist. Let's begin this battle with great hope, for as the psalm says, "For the LORD watches over the way of the just, but the way of the wicked vanishes."

May God's Holy Name be praised now and forever.

It's Time to Come Home

First Sunday of Lent, Lectionary 24
Yangon, Myanmar, 2007

Genesis 2:7-9; 3:1-7
Psalm 51: 3-4, 5-6, 12-13, 17
Romans 5:12-19
Matthew 4:1-11

What is the farthest you have ever been from home? For me, being here in Yangon is the farthest I've ever been from home—a distance of about nine thousand miles. Everything here is so different: the languages, the food (I like *mohinga*), the *longyi*, the pagodas. In the time I've been here, I've felt like I was not quite on the same planet.

Next week, I will make the long journey back home to America. Although I have enjoyed my stay in Myanmar, I am happy to return to the love of family and of old friends, the favorite foods of hamburgers and hot dogs, and the comfortable ease of being surrounded by my native language, English. It's time to come home. It's time to come home.

Today's gospel makes me think of going home. The younger son left his home and family and went off to a distant land. After some adventures, he came upon hard times. He lowered himself by caring for pigs, the lowest job a good Jew could have. He was so desperate, so hungry that he wanted to eat the pigs' food. To a Jew, that would be worse than eating garbage. But he remembers that he once had a home. There was a place where he could find what he needed and be with his loving father. He is ready to admit that he has sinned terribly, that he has made a horrible mess of his life, and he decides to return home. The difference is that he will not ask to be welcomed back as a son; he will simply ask to be a servant of his good father.

His father surprises him. He runs to him, welcomes him back as a son and heir, and has a great feast in his honor. The son who was dead has come back to life! The lost son is back with his father. His father couldn't be happier.

Now, what has all that got to do with us? Well, let me begin by sharing a little secret with you. You see, we're all sinners. We're all like the younger son. When we sin, we slap our Heavenly Father in the face and leave home. The more we live with sin in our lives, the farther we go from home, to live with the pigs and eat their food. We can get so used to living with sin that we even forget that we once had a home, a place of love where we belonged, and that we have a Heavenly Father who loves us deeply, who longs for us to return.

Now, it's not enough for me to just wag my finger at you and say, "Ok, you sinners! Go home to the Father! He's waiting!" That would not be enough. I must tell you that I am a sinner. I, like the younger son in today's gospel, have slapped my Father in the face and left home. Like the younger son, I have awakened in the middle of pigs and filth and cried out, "What have I done?" Like the younger son, I have made the journey back home, hoping just to be a servant.

And like the younger son, I have known the joy and

amazement of receiving a hero's welcome from the Father. My Heavenly Father has welcomed me back as His son and heir. He told me of how He missed me and longed for my return. My Father ran to me as I took the first step back to Him. He took me into His home and gave me a place at His table. I know that I am a sinner, and I know that I am a loved sinner. And I know that what God has done for me, He wants to do for you.

Is there a habit of sin in your life? Is there something keeping you from enjoying life with your Heavenly Father? Do you hope only to be a servant and not a son and heir in the heavenly kingdom? Do you think that you have done something unforgivable? If so, I can only tell you this—come home. Let me echo the words of Saint Paul which we heard this morning when he wrote: "So we are ambassadors of Christ, as if God were appealing through us. We implore you on behalf of Christ, be reconciled to God." Come home to the Father Who is waiting for you, Who will run to you if you take the first step. Come home to the Father Who wants you to be part of His family and His kingdom.

In Lent, we are given a season of homecoming. During Lent we can say, "If I want to know the joy of the risen Jesus, I must first come home to the Father. I must repent, I must be reconciled to God." My brothers and sisters in Christ, during this holy season, God Himself is calling you to His home and to His heart. Leave the foreign land of sin behind and come home to the place of grace and mercy. This Lent, offer yourself to God in prayer. This Lent, make a good confession and get free from what keeps you away from God. This Lent, unite yourself to Christ in the Eucharist as a perfect gift to the Father. My friends, now, now, it is time to come home.

May God's Holy Name be praised now and forever.

Is Anger a Sin or a Gift?

First Friday of Lent, Lectionary 228
Ave Maria, FL, 2012

Ezekiel 18: 21-28
Psalm 130:1-2, 3-4, 5-7a, 7bc-8
Matthew 5:20-26

When I was a boy, my buddies and I would read comic books and argue about which superhero was the best. We would ask questions like, "If Batman and Superman had a fight, who would win?" I don't read comic books very much anymore, but I still find myself asking speculative questions. For example, "If there was a debate between Saint Augustine and Jesus, who would win?"

I ask that question because it appears that Saint Augustine and Jesus are at odds with each other. Consider this quote from Augustine. He writes, "Hope has two beautiful daughters: their names are anger and courage. Anger that things are the way they are. Courage to make them the way they ought to be." If Augustine is right, and I think he is, lack of anger can be a terrible thing. Without a capacity for righteous anger, we will not have the energy or passion to defend the weak and the vulnerable.

But in today's gospel passage, Jesus says, "…whoever is angry with his brother will be liable to judgment." So, which is it? Is anger good or is anger bad? Neither.

In biblical Greek, there are two words commonly used for anger. One is *thumos*. *Thumos* is like the flame that comes from dry straw. It blazes quickly and it just as quickly dies down. The other common word for anger is *orge*. That anger is a long-lived, slow-burning fire. It is like a fire in a coal mine underground that can burn for decades. This is the anger of wrath, of brooding, bitter, toxic resentment. It is that anger which never forgives and never forgets; it is the anger that is savored and caressed and is not appeased even by revenge. That is the anger Jesus warns us against.

Very often, people tell me that they plan to give up anger for Lent. Nowadays I am inclined to say, "Please don't do that. In fact, God will be glorified if you find something to be angry about every day." Ask God to cultivate in your heart hope's beautiful daughter, anger—the passionate energy that will move you to resist evil and protect the vulnerable. And ask God to cultivate in your heart hope's other beautiful daughter, courage—the readiness to work for the good that ought to be. And above all, ask God to heal those wounds of yours that may stir you to wrath and resentment.

If we ask for and gratefully receive the gift of righteous anger and the gift of relief from wrathful resentment, we will be God's powerful instruments and joyful witnesses, and we will be able to echo the psalm we heard today: "I trust in the LORD; my soul trusts in his word. My soul waits for the LORD more than sentinels wait for the dawn."

May God's Holy Name be praised now and forever.

Do You Have a Good Memory?

Second Sunday of Lent, Lectionary 25
Ave Maria, FL, 2011

Genesis 12:1-4a
Psalm 33:4-5, 18-19, 20, 22
Timothy 1:8b-10
Matthew 17:1-9

Who is the most annoying person at a wedding? Is it your niece, who announces her arrival at puberty with a shockingly immodest dress? The dress that moves you to say, "My, what an informative outfit you're wearing, Murlene!" Or is it your cousin, who uses too much cologne and not enough mouthwash, who tries to sell you insurance during the reception?

I think that the most annoying person at a wedding is the photographer. It is the photographer who intrudes clicks and flashes at solemn moments, and forces everyone into unnatural poses and smiles for what seems to be an eternity. And it is the photographer who records for posterity our most furtive attempts at blowing our nose or our most awkward attempts at dancing.

Yet, we put up with the photographer. Why? Because

the photographer is essential for securing memories. More important than looking at dated hairstyles or ridiculous tuxedos, we turn to what the photographer provides us with in order to see again the innocence and hopefulness of a newly married couple. We want to show to our children the faces of grandparents who died before their grandchildren were born. We want to marvel at the passage of time as we look at the pictures of the young ring bearer and little flower girl who have grown up and started families of their own. We accept the photographer with grudging gratitude, for he is essential for securing our memories, memories that delight us in the good times and sustain us during the bad times.

Securing memory. That is why Jesus led Peter, James, and John to the mountaintop to witness His transfiguration. Jesus knew that His agony and death were not far away. He knew that His followers would be shattered and scattered by those events. Jesus hoped that if His three closest friends could catch a glimpse of His glory, if they could see clearly that He is the fulfillment of the law and the prophets, if He could impress upon their memories the full truth of Who He is, then, in His darkest hour, Peter, James, and John would not lose heart but would remain faithful. It was not to be. When the soldiers came to arrest Jesus in the garden, all His followers, including His dearest friends who had seen His glory, abandoned Him.

We should not be quick to judge Peter, James, and John. Yes, they had seen a glimpse of the truth of Jesus that the others had not seen, but they had not yet meet Christ Risen, they had not yet received the Holy Spirit Who would be given at Pentecost, they had not the witness of the New Testament, nor the aid of two thousand years of theological reflection and saintly testimony offered by the Church. But we have had all those benefits and more. So, it is right, as we have heard this gospel account of the Transfiguration of Jesus, to ask about the quality of our own memory and memories.

When has the goodness of God been most brightly clear to you? Was it on your wedding day? Or the birth of your child? Or the healing of your sick friend? Was the sovereignty of God most evident to you at the conversion or reversion of a loved one? When did you most powerfully feel the hand of God rest upon your heart? Was it after making an overdue confession? Was it during Adoration and Benediction? When did you most clearly hear God call you by name? Was it at your First Communion? At your Confirmation? When were you most convinced of the triumph of love? Was it when you put a ring on her finger? Was it when you welcomed home a wayward child? When did you feel in your bones that creation is good? Were you atop a mountain or afloat on the ocean? Watching a sunrise or a sunset? How often do you recall such revelations of God's glory? How much time do you take to savor those revelations?

Our ability to recognize, remember, and receive God's gracious presence to us is essential, if we are to survive and remain faithful while in dark times and in desert places. And we are all subject to the darkness and the desert and the alien voices that dwell therein, for we live in a finite and fallen world. Are we prepared to recognize, receive, and remember God's fidelity during the times and places and seasons of desolation? We must be able to answer that question well, as individuals, as a community, as a Church, and as a nation.

As individuals: When your doctor says "cancer"; when your spouse says "divorce"; when your teenager says "pregnant"; when your boss says "fired"; when your bank says "foreclosed"; when your professor says "failure"—in that moment, will we as individuals then be able to recognize, receive, and remember that Christ is victorious, that the Holy Spirit anoints us, that our Heavenly Father is sovereign?

As a community: When we hear "revenue shortfall"; when we hear "budget cuts"; when we hear "rightsizing"; when we hear "doing more with less"—in that moment, will we as a community then be able to recognize, receive, and remember that Christ is victorious, that the Holy Spirit anoints us, that our Heavenly Father is sovereign?

As a Church: When the press says "scandal"; when a diocese says "bankrupt"; when a pastor says "goodbye"—in that moment, will we as a Church then be able to recognize, receive, and remember that Christ is victorious, that the Holy Spirit anoints us, that our Heavenly Father is sovereign?

As a nation: When unemployment is up and housing starts are down; when inflation erodes the value of the dollar and bloats the price of food; when tempers are short and lines are long at the gas pump; when the Chinese will no longer lend us money and the world rejects the dollar—in that moment, will we as a nation then be able to recognize, receive, and remember that Christ is victorious, that the Holy Spirit anoints us, that our Heavenly Father is sovereign?

Even in the best of times, we live in a finite and fallen world, so we must prepare for when people and events will shake our faith. Who can deny that we live in a fallen world? And who is willing to say that we are now living in or heading towards the best of times?

Jesus, in His transfiguration, teaches us that to be prepared to face the trials of life we must be able to recall and savor what we have seen of His glory. Such memories, relished with a grateful heart and a clear mind, are essential if we are to remain faithful until the end. But even memories are not enough.

To be faithful to the end, through good times and bad, also requires a firm and consistent choice to be alert to God's revelations and invitations throughout each moment of our daily and seemingly ordinary lives. We must be alert to God in nature, and see His wisdom and artistry in the sunsets over the canal, in the owl that perches atop the Oratory at night, and in the animals that are at home around us.

We must make a firm and consistent choice to be alert to God's revelations and invitations in our daily walk of faith, as we pray grace before meals, as we celebrate the sacraments, and as we clutch ever more tightly our Rosary beads in our hands.

We must make a firm and consistent choice to be alert to God's revelations and invitations even from that apparently most unlikely source, our neighbor. In the weak and the proud, in the needy and the smug, in the beautiful and the ugly, there we can find icons of God and temples of the Holy Spirit. We would do well then to recall the words of the Jesuit poet, Gerard Manley Hopkins, who wrote: "...for Christ plays in ten thousand places, Lovely in limbs, and lovely in eyes not his, To the Father through the features of men's faces."

Be sure of this: Only firm habits of alertness, remembering, and savoring will secure for us the saving truths that Christ is victorious, that the Holy Spirit anoints us, and that our Heavenly Father is sovereign. Only those truths will sustain us in the hard times that are coming, hard times which are as predictable as the sunrise, as startling as lightning, and as undeniable as an earthquake.

However else we may prepare for hard times, whether practically, financially, socially, or emotionally, our preparations are for naught if we are not first spiritually prepared. Let our preparation be founded upon the faithful recalling of God's faithfulness, and constant mindfulness of God's constant presence.

Only if we are alert, remembering and savoring the revelations of God, will we be able to obey these words of Saint Paul which we heard this morning: "Beloved—bear your share of hardship for the gospel with the strength that comes from God."

Only if we are alert, remembering and savoring the revelations of God, will we be able to obey these words of the Gospel which we heard this morning: "This is my beloved Son, with whom I am well pleased; listen to him."

Only if we are alert, remembering and savoring the revelations of God, will we be able to pray these words of the Psalmist which we heard this morning: "LORD, let your mercy be on us, as we place our trust in you."

May God's Holy Name be praised now and forever.

Can You Follow Directions?
Can You Ask for Directions?

Third Wednesday of Lent, Lectionary 239
Donahue Academy, Ave Maria, FL, 2012

Deuteronomy 4:1, 5-9
Psalm 147:12-13, 15-16, 19-20
Matthew 5:17-19

Are you good at following directions and rules?

I used to think so. Then I visited my little nieces last week.

My two-year old niece, Brigid, taught me how to eat an Oreo cookie. "No, no, Uncle Bob! You're doing it wrong. Eat it like this!"

My four-year old niece, Teigan, taught me how to set up a chess board. She was very precise. She said, "Well, Uncle Bob, this is how it's going to be. You sit still and I will tell you what to do." Sound familiar? Doesn't it seem sometimes that your whole life is like that?

My mother liked following rules and orders, as long as they were *her* rules and orders. When she set the table for dinner, she laid the utensils out with such precision you would think the fate of the world depended on it. I took this fact as an invitation to mischief. After Mom set the table, I would make a point of walking into the dining room and moving a fork three inches to the left. Mom would come running into the room and slam the fork back into place on the table. "You're not doing it right!" she'd yell at me. Doesn't it seem sometimes that your whole life is like that, somebody yelling at you for not doing it right?

That brings us to the readings we just heard this morning. We hear about laws and decrees and statutes and commandments and prophets and scribes and everyone is throwing stones at everyone else because someone is breaking some rule and everyone thinks that nobody else is doing it right and everyone is telling everybody else that everyone is going to hell because somebody somewhere is breaking some kind of rule. And it all gets so confusing and so annoying.

Just like today. Today there are people who are afraid to scratch their own nose unless first they check the Bible, the catechism, the code of canon law, the documents of Vatican II, the *Summa Theologica*, and the collected letters of nine different saints. In other words, even today people make a relationship with God a burden and a source of anxiety.

What shall we do about that? Well, let's turn to a Jesuit. Let's turn to Saint Jose Maria Rubio, who died in Madrid in 1929 and was canonized by Pope John Paul II in 2003. Saint Jose Maria Rubio's instructions were very clear. He said this: "Do what God wants and want what God does."

What does God want? He wants us to love Him and to love our neighbor. What does God do? He gives us the grace to love Him and to love our neighbor. Especially during this season of Lent, let's take up the vocation to love and the gift of grace, and let's leave anxiety aside. If we do that, God will be glorified, and we will all be a lot easier to live with.

May God's Holy Name be praised now and forever.

"Let's Play Hide-and-Seek!"

Fourth Sunday of Lent, Lectionary 31
Ave Maria, FL, 2012

1 Samuel 16:1b, 6-7, 10-13a
Psalm 23:1-3a, 3b-4, 5, 6
Ephesians 5:8-14
John 9:1-41

Do you like to pretend? When we were kids, we always played games of "Let's Pretend" or "Make-believe." For example, we would play "Let's pretend this giant cardboard box is a castle" or "Let's make-believe that our tricycles are race cars." As you can imagine, the best of my "Let's Pretend" days are long behind me. But not so long ago, I was asked to combine two classic children's games. I was asked to combine "Let's Pretend" with "Hide-and-seek."

A friend of mine had a little boy named Jacob, and he gave me instructions about how to play this game. He would tell me, "I'm going to hide here, behind the couch, where you can't see me, so that you won't know where I am. Then I want you to look for me under the table and under the rug and inside the laundry basket. Then I will jump out from behind the couch and you will be surprised." We even rehearsed so that he could be sure that I would look for him in the wrong places, overlook him in the right place, and then appear properly surprised when he jumped out at me. Combining "Let's Pretend" with "Hide-and-seek" is a very delicate and serious business, and Jacob wanted to make sure that I got it right. I had to be blind when he wanted me to be blind, and I had to see only what he wanted me to see.

But that sort of pretending is something that only children do, right? Adults don't play such games, do they? Maybe I used to think that way, but not anymore. The gospel passage we heard this morning focuses on blindness and seeing. People are pointing fingers and arguing about who is really blind and who isn't, arguing about who can truly see and who can't, arguing about who has the light and who doesn't. It seems that the people around Jesus were combining "Let's Pretend" and "Hide-and-seek" long before that little boy Jacob ever thought of it. And, sad to say, today, in our own time, we are asked to play that game of seeing only what people want us to see, and to play the game of being blind to what they don't want us to see. Let me give you a few examples to explain what I mean.

Today, we are being asked to cooperate with another game of pretend-blindness. We are asked to pretend that we are blind to the fact that the federal government, through its mandate requiring free contraceptives, abortifacients, and sterilizations for all employees, is assaulting human life and the free exercise of religion, which are guaranteed by our Constitution.

We are asked to pretend that we are blind to the fact that this federal mandate is an existential threat to faithful Catholic institutions in the United States.

We are asked to pretend that we are blind to the fact that self-identified Catholics in and out of government have betrayed the trust that they should be worthy of.

I know what *I* think of such things; I can easily guess what *you* might think about such things—but what does *God* think about such things? Well, let's listen again to what Saint Paul wrote to us this morning. Saint Paul writes: "Brothers and sisters: You were once darkness, but now you are light in the Lord. Live as children of light, for light produces every kind of goodness and righteousness and truth." Saint Paul makes it clear that we have only two choices—we can live as children of light or we can live as children of darkness. Light produces goodness; darkness produces wickedness.

Let's listen again to the words of Saint Paul. Saint Paul writes, "Take no part in the fruitless works of darkness; rather expose them..." By our baptism, we have become children of the light, and our vocation is to know and tell and do the truth. And we are to name the darkness for what it is, wherever we find it. It is in the light of Christ that all motives and actions must be examined.

A Jesuit friend who is also a biologist is fond of saying, "Sunlight is the best disinfectant." How much more so for the light of Christ! Satan likes to work with whispers in the shadows. The surest way to overcome evil is to drag it into the light and expose it for the fraud that it is. When evil is taken into the light, it dies a natural death. The surest way to purify our hearts and society is to expose them to the light of Christ.

Now we can understand the task at hand. Self-identified Catholics, both in and out of government, are spreading darkness. They ask us to pretend that dark is light and light is dark; they ask us to pretend that true is false and false is true; they ask us to pretend that good is evil and evil is good. They ask us to pretend that it is not the mission of the Church to hand on what she has received from Christ. Indeed, members of the White House staff recently told representatives of the American bishops that the bishops should consult with "more enlightened people" in the Church about the goodness of the contraceptive mandate. Who now can deny that some children of the light have become darkness? Who now can deny that some children of the light have become blind but claim to see? Who now can deny that some children of the light refuse to see what they have been shown by the light of Christ?

My friends, we here must never boast or claim that we are wise or holy. But we must admit that we have received from the Church Christ founded all of the saving truths that Christ entrusted to His Church. And we have an obligation to proclaim and insist upon those saving truths as long as the breath of life is within us. We have an obligation to shine the bright light of Christ into every dark corner, wherever lies and deceit and fraud may hide. If we do not take up that hard task right now, if we do not wield the light to turn back the tide of darkness now, then I do not know what hope we can have for the future.

In today's gospel, we heard Jesus speak these words: "I have to do the works of the one who sent me while it is day. Night is coming when no one can work."

For a while, yet, it is still daylight, and we have work to do. I fear that a darkness may be coming, and if we do not resist it now, then, sometime soon, we may be unable to do the work of God openly, as we may now do in daylight. If we do not resist this present darkness now, openly, then we may have to resist the darkness later, in the catacombs. I do not want to see your children fight such a battle later because we failed to fight our battle now.

Let's listen again to these words we heard this morning from the Gospel of John: "Then Jesus said, 'I came into this world for judgment, so that those who do not see might see.'"

We must bring the light of Christ to those who have been spiritually blinded by the beguiling and dazzling darkness of this fallen world. How shall we do that? We must proclaim the culture of life against the culture of death. As citizens we must ensure by every legal means that our rights guaranteed by the Constitution are respected. As

Catholics, we must with Christ gather those who have been scattered. We must gather into the heart of the Church those who have left it. We must call back to the splendor of truth those who have chosen to make sacrifice to ideologies and to idols. We must pray and fast and do penance and make reparation for those Catholics who have wandered and who now scatter rather than gather with Christ. Above all, we must invite them home by means of our charity, by our unity, and by our joy—the joy that comes from fidelity to Christ and His Church. If we cannot win them over by argument, perhaps we can speak to their hearts by letting them see the goodness that fidelity to Christ produces.

And just as our Lord was opposed for His fidelity to His Father, so too we may expect to be opposed for our fidelity to Christ. Those children of darkness who are armed with worldly wisdom and worldly power will oppose the Faith and the faithful.

To understand what I'm getting at, let's listen again to these words of John's gospel which we heard this morning: "Some of the Pharisees who were with him heard this and said to him, 'Surely we are not also blind, are we?' Jesus said to them, 'If you were blind, you would have no sin; but now you are saying, "We see," so your sin remains.'"

Jesus told us that boasting of your sight and denying your blindness leave you not only blind but incurably blind. The only antidote, the only cure for the blindness that comes from pride and darkness is humility, for only with humility can we enter into the light of Christ, and ask that our own darkness be revealed and removed. Only then can we hope to be credible witnesses to Christ; only then can we hope to see what is trying to hide before our very eyes. However we cling to sin, whatever we try to hide in the shadows, whatever deceits we wish to cloak—all these must be brought to the light of Christ.

If we are humble and repentant, if our own blindness and love of darkness are removed, then we can be bright shining mirrors reflecting the light of Christ into our culture and our country, shining the light of Christ into a world determined to hide in the shadows.

All right, we all have work to do. How shall we get started? Today, and for each day this week, I will ask you to pray for three graces, for three special blessings. I will ask us all to repent, repeat, and rejoice. Let us repent, because we loved sinners are still imperfectly reflecting the light of Christ. Let us repeat—let us repeat again and again that human dignity demands a culture of life and religious liberty. And let us rejoice, as Pope Pius XI once said, that we live in times such as these, for now it is permitted to no one to be mediocre.

If we do that, if we repent, repeat, and rejoice, then we can echo the words of Saint Paul, and proclaim to a world drowsing in darkness: "Awake, O sleeper, and arise from the dead, and Christ will give you light."

May God's Holy Name be praised now and forever.

Would You Like Some Help?

Fourth Monday of Lent, Lectionary 244
Ave Maria, FL, 2010

Isaiah 65:17-21
Psalm 30
John 4:43-54

I need you to exercise a little imagination.

There's a knock at door—who is it? A voice says, "I'm from the government and I'm here to help!" Think: the people who gave us the post office and public schools are outside and want to come in and "help" me? You'd nail the door shut, wouldn't you?

There's a knock at the door—who is it? "I'm from God and I'm here to help!" What would you do? I think it would depend on how you viewed God.

What if our view of God is so distorted, that even when we have read to us this glorious passage from Isaiah, we hear the following:

"Thus says the LORD: Lo, I am about to create a new wasteland in which to abandon you. There the things of the past shall haunt you forever, and there will always be shame, regret, and fear. I created this world to be a torment, and its people in constant dread, as they are relentlessly put to the test, so that they may be reminded again and again that there are infinite ways to sin, and no way to please me or appease me."

If our view of God is so twisted that we hear those words as we listen to today's reading from Isaiah, then we shall not find any rest in this life, unless we reject completely and forever such a monstrous view of God.

My heart breaks as I watch people tiptoe through life, fearing that they might step into hidden piles of "grave matter," fearing to breathe or move or think or feel or desire lest they inadvertently commit a mortal sin. My heart breaks because the suffering such poor souls endure is unnecessary, and it is not redemptive. My heart breaks because the idolatrous tyrant that some people call God looks nothing like the loving Father whom Jesus has revealed to us.

Let's listen again to what God has put on the lips of the prophet Isaiah:

"Thus says the LORD: Lo, I am about to create new heavens and a new earth; The things of the past shall not be remembered or come to mind. Instead, there shall always be rejoicing and happiness in what I create; For I create Jerusalem to be a joy and its people to be a delight; I will rejoice in Jerusalem and exult in my people."

Every year people ask me, "Father, what shall I give up for Lent?" I know that they are expecting me to urge them to give up something non-essential: desserts or soda or some silly pleasure. I am now convinced that what Jesus wants us all to give up for Lent is a distorted view of His Father.

It is God's nature to only give His best, which is Himself; He can only offer us Himself, for it would defeat His purposes to force Himself upon us; and He knows, as I fear we do not, that we can only receive the true God if we let go of every false god in our lives. And the image of God as an unhappy, exacting, maniacal tyrant is a false God.

Today, let's throw down all our idols, let's tear down all our false gods, let's rebuke and reject any image of God that does not look like the loving Father of Jesus.

If we do that, then we can make the words of today's psalm our own and declare to God and the world: "You changed my mourning into dancing; O LORD, my God, forever will I give you thanks."

May God's Holy Name be praised now and forever.

"Is There No One to Condemn You?"

Fifth Sunday of Lent, Lectionary 36

Isaiah 43:16-21
Psalm 126
Philippians 3:8-14
John 8:1-11

In today's gospel, Jesus asks the woman a most important question: "Is there no one to condemn you?" Why is that question so important? It's important because we are sinners, and we need to know what God thinks about sin and about sinners.

God is all good; He is perfect love. Therefore He must hate sin. All sin offends Him. But He loves sinners. When sinners rejected God and condemned themselves to eternal death, God chose to save them. God sent His only Son as savior for us all. Jesus, on the cross, took on all the consequences of sin and death. God raised Jesus up and gave Him the victory over sin and death, a victory that Jesus shares with us, His followers.

God hates sin; God loves sinners. I am a sinner. I am a loved sinner. You are sinners. You are loved sinners. What should we do when we sin? Well, we could imitate Adam and Eve and try to hide from God, but that never works. We could despair of ever being reconciled with God, and hang ourselves like Judas, but that gives us nothing. We could listen to the nagging voice that says that we are no good and will never be any good and resign ourselves to living under the burden of toxic shame, never daring to hope that we could ever be pleasing to God.

But wait! Jesus asks, "Is there no one to condemn you?" When we sin, and that nagging voice says that we are no good, that we are failures, that there is no hope for us, that voice is the voice of condemnation. The voice of condemnation, the voice of no hope, is the voice of the devil himself. We must not listen to it.

What then shall we do? Shall we ignore any suggestion that we have sinned against God? No! Saint Paul says that the Holy Spirit convicts us of sin. When we sin, it is the work of the Holy Spirit to convict us, to convince us that we have sinned and need to repent. The voice that tells us to get on our knees and beg God for mercy is the voice of the Holy Spirit. The Holy Spirit convicts and the Holy Spirit never condemns. Conviction says, "You have sinned—now repent!" Condemnation says, "You have sinned, you are no good—now give up!" Conviction turns us to the light of the Divine Mercy; condemnation turns us to the darkness of despair.

My friends, Lent is a time of conviction. It is a time to invite the Holy Spirit into our lives, to examine our hearts, and show us where there is sin in our lives. It's a time to ask the Holy Spirit to convict us of sin so that we might repent. Lent is not a season of condemnation. Lent is not a season to decide that we are worthless and should just give up.

The good news of the gospel today is that Jesus does not condemn us. He came to save sinners. He sends the Holy Spirit to convict us of sin so that we might repent. Do you want to have a joyful celebration of Easter? Do you want to have a share in Christ's victory over sin and death?

Saint Paul writes for us today when he says, "I wish to know Christ and the power flowing from his resurrection." If that is what you want, then reject the voice of condemnation, reject the voice that says you are no good. Ask the Holy Spirit to convict you of sin and send you into the mercy of the Father. Run into the arms of the merciful Father.

If the Holy Spirit convicts you of sin, resolve to make a good confession before Easter. Become free from the dead weight of sin. And may the words of Saint Paul be yours today as he writes, "My entire attention is on the finish line as I run toward the prize to which God calls me—life on high in Christ Jesus."

May God's Holy Name be praised now and forever.

Do You Have Enemies?

Fifth Friday of Lent, Lectionary 255
Ave Maria, FL, 2009

Jeremiah 20:10-13
Psalm 18
John 10:31-42

Did you ever wonder about how many ways there are to be crazy? I had never given it much thought until I encountered the MMPI, the Minnesota Multi-Phase Personality Inventory. The MMPI is a test that every candidate for priesthood or religious life for the past 20 years has taken as part of a psychological evaluation before entering a seminary or novitiate. It takes several hours to answer several hundred true/false questions on the test.

After taking the test, one cannot help but begin to identify forms of maladjustment in the people one meets. You find yourself thinking, "That guy over there—they definitely had him in mind when they wrote question 42 for the MMPI! And that woman—doesn't she just scream question 179?" Of all the different types of anxiety alluded to in that test, the most frequently asked questions had to do with what "they" were doing.

For example: "True or false—they are trying to put ground glass in my food." "True or false—they are trying to control my thoughts." "True or false—they are listening to my private conversations." "True or false—they are always watching me." It is something of a cliché to snicker about the man wearing the tin foil hat to block out the radio waves that "they" are using to read his thoughts.

In literature, the great evangelist of paranoia was Franz Kafka. He said that the paranoid are the only true realists. In popular culture, one still sees the t-shirts that read, "Just because I'm paranoid doesn't mean they're not after me!"

These things come to mind in light of our reading today from Jeremiah: "I hear the whisperings of many: 'Terror on every side! Denounce! Let us denounce him!' All those who were my friends are on the watch for any misstep of mine. 'Perhaps he will be trapped; then we can prevail, and take our vengeance on him.'"

Paranoid? Perhaps. But only with good reason! Jeremiah annoyed a lot of powerful, sinful people who did not want to hear the message that God gave him. Jeremiah was such a threat to business-as-usual that the powers-that-be tried to put a stop to him.

How about us? Are we worth the attention of evil? Does Satan find us to be a threat to his plans? Are we living our faith in such a way that evil men want to pass laws against us? Does our fidelity to God attract the scorn of powerful sinners?

Or do we live in such a way that we are obviously following the advice of prisoners who say, "Never do anything to attract the guard's attention"?

Here, in this parish, in this university, in this town, we have the opportunity and obligation to form young Catholic leaders who will be smart, wise, holy, prudent, courageous, humble, aggressive troublemakers who will not give a moment's peace to the world, the flesh, and the devil.

Here, in this parish, in this university, in this town, we

have the opportunity and obligation to form young Catholic leaders who will be such a threat to the lies and blasphemies that comprise the culture of death that the enemies of God will cry out, as they did against Jeremiah, "This must be stopped!" True disciples of Christ could form such young leaders. True disciples of Christ would have to.

Or....we can just coast along, keep our heads down, live quietly, and hope that when the enemies of God finally come for the People of God, that they will kill us gently, and that they will kill us last. And who knows? Maybe we'll be luckier than Terri Schiavo!

May God's Holy Name be praised now and forever.

Stay Awake!

Palm Sunday, Lectionary 38
Ave Maria, FL, 2010

Isaiah 50:4-7
Psalm 22:8-9, 17-18, 19-20, 23-24
Philippians 2:6-11
Luke 22:14–23:56

What would the perfect movie look like? A famous movie producer once said, "The perfect movie would start with an earthquake and lead up to something really exciting." I would like to start this homily with an earthquake. More specifically, in light of the horrific earthquakes recently in Haiti and Chile, I would like ask you to use your imagination, and picture what it would be like to wake up in the middle of an earthquake.

Imagine being thrown out of your bed without warning. You hear crashes and screams. You choke from dust; you panic as you smell smoke. You stagger across broken glass, trip over furniture, and as you collapse in pain, you wonder if you will ever see your family again.

When you regain consciousness, you pick yourself up, dust yourself off, and start looking for your family members.

Imagine finding all of them but one. "Where is Grandpa?" you ask your children. You start tearing through the rubble, trying not to show your children your panic and your dread. Finally, you find him under a pile of lumber. He is not moving. You fear the worst. He opens his eyes and asks, "Is it time for breakfast already?" You cannot believe your ears! How could Grandpa have slept through an earthquake?

Let's stretch your imagination a bit further. After the earthquake, you are told, "An aftershock is coming. The next earthquake may be even bigger than this one." What would you do then? Well of course, you would try to prepare as best you could. But what if Grandpa told you, "Hey! I'm going back to bed. I slept through one earthquake and I was fine, so I know that earthquakes can't hurt me." What would you say to him? "Grandpa, you slept through an earthquake once and you got lucky. But now you know the earthquake is coming! You have to get ready!" Sleeping through an unexpected earthquake seems almost miraculous; going to sleep when you know that an earthquake is coming seems insane.

I think of earthquakes, and sleeping through earthquakes, as we celebrate Palm Sunday, the beginning of Holy Week. Jesus entered Jerusalem, the holy city, to consummate His mission from the Father. He would go to His violent death, to His resurrection, and to His glory. He caused a stir in the city as He fulfilled all the prophecies spoken of Him throughout the ages. The arrival of Jesus was prophesied for centuries; John the Baptist prepared the way; and Jesus entered Jerusalem and went unacknowledged by most, rejected by many, and scorned by those who should have welcomed Him. The arrival of Jesus in Jerusalem came like a long-predicted earthquake, upsetting what man had built, pulling down man's monuments, and pointing to powerful realities that man cannot control. Tragically, rather than bringing about humility and repentance and faith, those who were most thoroughly warned to prepare for the earthquake that is Jesus responded with a convulsion of rage and violence. They rejected Jesus, and He was nailed to a cross.

Two thousand years ago, Jesus suffered violence at the hands of angry and hateful men. And I fear that we may be tempted to console ourselves by saying that whatever else might be true of us, it is surely true that had *we* seen Jesus in Jerusalem, He would not have suffered violence at *our* hands. Maybe. Maybe.

And I fear that in our own time, in the lives that we lead, Jesus again suffers unto death, a savage death brought about not by hatred and cruel violence, but a uniquely humiliating death brought about by neglect and a blistering indifference.

This is what I mean: I fear that we have let ourselves become so busy, so fast-paced, so distracted, so self-absorbed, so scattered, so inattentive, so noisy, so careless, so unrecollected that we will let Jesus go to His death without offering Him a tear, a tender gesture, or a word of kindness. And so we send Jesus to His death—this time a death brought about not by violence but a death brought about by neglect.

The horror of it all is that we can be like those who are forewarned of an earthquake and then promptly fall asleep. I fear that we know that Jesus is even now in our midst, yet we do not see Him, hear Him, touch Him, wait for Him, watch for Him, call out to Him, or listen to Him. As Holy Week begins, it may well be time to look into our lives, and see if we daily pass by Jesus, whom we send to a brutal death of neglect.

Do we neglect Jesus when we fail to pray and worship? Yes, we do. But cutting corners on prayer is not the only way that we can turn our back on Jesus. Today, today, in our midst, as we recall Jesus' long-prophesied and quickly-rejected entry into Jerusalem, today, here and now, Jesus cries out in anguished loneliness outside of every chapel and church. Jesus cries out in anguished loneliness from within a spouse who aches for the nearness of a beloved who has grown cold. Jesus cries out in anguished loneliness from our children, who need our time and our embrace as much as they need our correction and direction. Jesus cries out in anguished loneliness from our students, who need our hope and our wisdom as much as they need our information and our expertise. And can any of us deny that Jesus calls out in anguished loneliness from within ourselves, we who need compassion and kindness from our neighbor and from ourselves, as much as we need food and shelter?

Today, this Palm Sunday, the start of Holy Week, something more powerful, more unsettling, more life-changing than an earthquake has entered our lives. Jesus has come here, ready to carry His cross. Today He comes among us prepared to go to death and resurrection and glory. And that fact leaves us with three choices. We can look at Jesus and His cross and scorn them both, and so hand Him over to angry and violent men, in imitation of the leaders of governments and churches that remain silent as Christians are martyred everyday throughout the world.

Or we can look at Jesus and His cross and simply not see Him, letting Him melt into the crowd, to die of neglect. If we do that, we are like the fools who have decided to sleep through the earthquake.

Or we can have compassion for Jesus, and help Him carry His cross, whether we find Him in the chapel or on the street or in our classrooms or in our own homes or within the pain and grief of our own wounded hearts.

Jesus suffers unto death in all those whom we meet, including the person we meet when we look in the mirror. If we wish, we can acknowledge Him and offer Him words of comfort and gestures of tenderness. If nothing else, we can stay with Him, so that He does not suffer the cruelest violence of dying alone and neglected.

Holy Week has begun. No matter what we do, Jesus

will go to His death. He will die violently through hate or He will die quietly through savage neglect, or He will die in our arms, knowing that He had a faithful companion who stayed with Him to the end.

If we stay with Him in His need, in His loneliness and His anguish; if we stay with Him and let our own grief over His death break our hearts; if we choose to die with Him, then we shall rise with Him, lifted up by the Holy Spirit, raised up to the Father's glory, and share in Jesus' victory over sin and death. The Scriptures are clear: Only those who die with Jesus can rise with Him to eternal life.

But how can we be compassionate with the dying Jesus, how can we be faithful until the end, if we cannot find Him? And how can we find Him if we do not look for Him? And how can we look for Him if we are so busy, so distracted, so scattered, so self-centered, that we ignore Him, even as He enters our lives carrying His cross, calling out to us through the Scriptures and the sacraments, calling out to us from our spouse and our children, calling out to us from our neighbor and from our own aching heart?

The tragedy and horror of our time is that the calling and suffering Jesus is being neglected by people who knew all along that He was coming. None of us are surprised that Holy Week begins today; none of us are surprised to hear of a cross and an empty tomb; none of us are surprised to hear of Jesus' commandment to love God and to love our neighbor as ourselves.

I fear that if we do not open our eyes and our hearts, we will be like those who knew the earthquake was coming and fell asleep, sure that the earthquake would do nothing significant. We Christians have the greatest story to tell, and the story is this: Christ has died, Christ is risen, Christ will come again.

But we will have only the greatest tragedy to tell if our story goes like this: Christ has died, Christ is risen, Christ will come again—and I slept through it all. Please, God, may that tragic story never be true of us!

Today, Palm Sunday, the start of Holy Week 2010, Jesus has come among us, prepared to take up His cross. Who will go with Him? Shall He go alone? Or shall we go with Him, to die and rise with Him for the life of the world?

If we look around us, if we look at recent headlines, if we look within our families and within our own hearts, if we look at the history of nations, if we look at the history of God's own people, we see again and again the bitter fruit of neglecting, avoiding, or rejecting Jesus and His cross as He comes to us to fulfill all prophesies. Let us resolve that we will not be like those who would fall asleep knowing that the earthquake is coming. Let us resolve, at least for this Holy Week, that we will put aside whatever distracts us, whatever addicts us, whatever seduces us, whatever misleads us, and instead focus on Jesus. Let us resolve to be alert, so that when Jesus cries out to us in His loneliness, whether He calls to us in a chapel, or in the workplace, or within our schools, or within our homes or within our hearts, that we will run to Him, and embrace Him, and promise to stay with Him, so that He will not die alone. Let our prayer be that this year, the last words that the dying Jesus will hear will be these: "Jesus, remember me when you come into your kingdom." And Jesus, who, as Saint John tells us, loves His own to the end, will allow us to hear in our last moment the words our hearts have ached to hear from the first moment of life, and the words are these: "Amen, I say to you, today you will be with me in Paradise."

May God's Holy Name be praised now and forever.

How Strong Are You?

Palm Sunday, Lectionary 37-38
Ave Maria, FL, 2013

Luke 19:28-40
Isaiah 50:4-7
Psalm 22:8-9, 17-18, 19-20, 23-24
Philippians 2:6-11
Luke 22:14–23:56

The portion of Luke's Gospel we just heard this morning contains the heart of our faith, the truth of our worship, the meaning of our living and of our dying. Even if I could, I would not dare try to say all that could be said about what we just heard. And even if I could, I would not dare to say, "The most important thing we just heard is…" Instead, I will offer a modest suggestion. I will say this: "I know the Word of God and the People of God here well enough to say that there are certain words from today's gospel reading that we must attend to and remember."

Let's listen again to these words of Jesus to the man who would be Peter. Jesus says to him: "Simon, Simon, behold Satan has demanded to sift all of you like wheat, but

I have prayed that your own faith may not fail; and once you have turned back, you must strengthen your brothers."

Recently, I have seen wheat sifted. I have seen grains of wheat crushed to a fine powder. Surely, Simon Peter must have seen the sifting, the crushing of wheat. I would like to think that because of what he saw, those words made his blood run cold, as they did mine. I would like to think that he humbly took heart when the Lord assured him of prayer, of his returning from a fall, and of his mission to strengthen the brethren.

But as we know, Simon Peter is brash and impulsive, and he makes wild promises. He assures Jesus with these words: "Lord, I am prepared to go to prison and to die with you." We know the rest of the story. Before the sun rises, Simon Peter will deny the Lord three times.

We must be careful not to judge Simon Peter too harshly for his bravado. After all, he could not know, as we do, of two thousand years of Christians sinning and repenting. Yet, he would soon come to the painful realization that apart from God's grace, anyone can fall, because each of us has within us a most terrible strength, the strength to abuse our freedom and withhold ourselves from God.

Consider these words from the poet Elizabeth Barrett Browning. She wrote: "I too have strength – Strength to behold him and not worship him, Strength to fall from him and not to cry to him." Simon Peter will need to learn what we all already know: that apart from God's grace, anyone can fall because we are at once too weak—too weak in our love—and we are too strong—strong enough in our pride to turn away from the face of the Lord. In humility, we must start with that awful truth, and if we do not start there, we will never find, much less be consoled by, the amazing grace and comfort of the rest of what Jesus said to Simon Peter.

Jesus said, "...once you have turned back..." Jesus knew Simon Peter well enough to know that he would betray his Lord. And He knew him well enough to know that Simon Peter—whose motto could easily have been "Ready, Fire, Aim!"—He knew that impulsive Simon Peter, at bottom, loved his Lord with all his heart. Jesus knew that there would be a Saint Peter because Peter-the-sinner would repent; and He knew that there would not be a Saint Judas because Judas-the-sinner would not repent.

That is such an important lesson for us! The saints are not those who never sinned; the saints are those who never stopped repenting. And Jesus knew that Simon Peter needed to repent in a hurry, because Simon Peter would be needed to strengthen his brothers, whom Satan also wished to sift like wheat—just like us! We are not an army that can afford to shoot its wounded. We need to pick up the stragglers and the strays and the sinners of every size and shape. We need to carry and support one another as we pick ourselves up and get back into the battle. I say that and I insist on that because the great spiritual struggles of our time are getting ready to boil over.

In many ways, great and small, more and more, we will be asked to deny that we know our Lord. Let me give you just one small example, something you might not have heard of. Just last week, at Florida Atlantic University in West Palm Beach, students were given this in-class assignment. Each student was required to write the name of Jesus in capital letters on a piece of paper, was told to put the paper on the ground, and then directed to stomp on the piece of paper. One student refused. He is a devout Mormon. The university, when it learned of what had taken place in the classroom, suspended the student.

Now, all sin is a rejection of God and His Christ. We have all sinned, whether through the weakness of our love or through the strength of our pride. But soon, we may be called upon, through intimidation and threats, bribes and badgering, to separate ourselves from Christ our Lord. We are more likely to stand firm if we stand together. As

Benjamin Franklin said to our Founding Fathers, "If we do not hang together, we shall surely hang separately."

For all of our faults and weaknesses, for all of our quirks and foibles, for all of our occasional and willful blindness and deafness, we here at Ave Maria, at our core—we love the Christ of God and the Church He founded. We want Jesus to be known and loved. We want to teach and embrace what is true, good, and beautiful. God in His Providence has drawn together this band of sinners and instructed us to strengthen one another, to help one another to remain faithful, to call and carry one another to the heights of charity and sanctity. Our sins are our own, but our graces come from Christ. And the graces of Christ are more lovely than the fascination we might have with the ugliness of sin.

We must begin by letting our hearts be pierced like the Sacred Heart of Jesus and the Immaculate Heart of Mary. We must be cut to the quick, and let ourselves be shocked and overwhelmed by the truly awful fact that the Blood of Jesus, shed on the Cross, is the undeniable proof of God's most stubborn will to love us and save us.

Friedrich Nietzsche, a philosopher and a madman, gave us this challenge. He said that he would be more inclined to believe in the redeemer of the Christians if the Christians looked like they were redeemed. The best witness we can give to Christ is to have Christian joy. Only those who admit the horror of deadly sin in their lives can savor the delight of having a redeemer. Only those who are sure that their terrible sins were wiped away at a terrible cost will know the joy of living forgiven. We must admit that the proof of God's love for us is the blood-ransom paid by His Son. And we can best bear witness to the love of God by delighting in being so loved. Let's remember the words of the cleric George Herbert who wrote: "Love is that liquor sweet and most divine, Which my God feels as blood; but I, as wine."

Please, dear God, let our hearts overflow with the wine of Christian joy.

Only those who are convinced that they are loved sinners redeemed by a wildly passionate God will have the humility, charity, and courage to remain faithful during the trials that are coming our way. Only if we stand on Christ can we have any hope of echoing the words of the prophet Isaiah, and stand before the world and proclaim: "The Lord God has given me a well-trained tongue, that I might know how to speak to the weary a word that will rouse them... The Lord God is my help, therefore I am not disgraced; I have set my face like flint, knowing that I shall not be put to shame."

Humble, repentant sinners, gladly extending to others the Divine Mercy they themselves have received, joined together for the love of God and the love of neighbor, refusing to be robbed of their faith or their joy—this, I believe, is what God calls us to be here at Ave Maria. Today, in the presence of our Crucified, Risen, and Eucharistic Lord, let us say, "Yes."

May God's Holy Name be praised now and forever.

What Are You Waiting For?

Monday of Holy Week, Lectionary 257
Saint Mary's Seminary, Houston, TX, 2005

Isaiah 42:1-7
Psalm 27:1, 2, 3, 13-14
John 12:1-11

Being Irish and Catholic, I am a connoisseur of guilt. I can discriminate among various grades of guilt, knowing that old guilt is always the best, and I can savor the nuances of guilt the way that some can savor the distinctive notes of a fine wine. Being a connoisseur of guilt is not just a pastime but a lifestyle. As one who knows that everything is his fault, rarely do I miss an opportunity to immerse myself in the opportunities for brooding over guilt that present themselves every day.

And yet, there are exceptions. You may recall that several weeks ago, my Aunt Rose, my mother's sister, passed away. A few weeks before she died, she had sent me a Valentine's Day card. Somehow for some reason, I was able to put aside my penchant for procrastination and I sent her a letter thanking her. Shortly afterwards, she died.

I felt like I had dodged a bullet. Think of the zesty, galloping guilt I would have suffered if she had died before I had gotten around to writing back to her. That's the kind of guilt and regret that could last a lifetime. Hours and hours of therapy, spiritual direction, dream work, and group processes could have been spent, in vain, to reduce such guilt to a manageable size.

Now, if I were in a hurry, I would rush to say, "And the moral of the story is, don't put off an act of kindness because you never know when the person might die on you." But I'm not in a hurry and I have more to say.

Jesus said, "…you do not always have me." Mary of Bethany makes an unforgettable gesture of extravagant love by anointing the feet of Jesus with precious perfume. Had she postponed her gift by a week, she would have missed her chance to love Jesus in that way, for He would be dead soon. Windows of opportunity for love open for us, and they also close. Mary could have missed her chance forever.

I have that fact in mind as I look back to St. Patrick's Day. On that high, holy day, I was surprised to find in my mail box an envelope in my late Aunt Rose's handwriting. Puzzled, I tore open the envelope. It was a St. Patrick's Day card that Aunt Rose had bought before she died. She had written me a note inside, addressed the envelope, and put it aside in anticipation of St. Patrick's Day. My cousin included a note saying that Aunt Rose had bought the card before she died and that she wanted me to have it.

So, dear Aunt Rose kicked it up a notch. She wasn't just alert for passing opportunities for love, she anticipated opportunities for love. She planned for them. So Aunt Rose is in good company, as practical in her love as Martha, as generous in her love as Mary.

Let's resolve today that we will this day perform an act of kindness we have been postponing, and let's make plans to love again soon. If we do that consistently, we can, in our own small way, be as Isaiah says, "…a covenant to the people, a light to the nations."

May God's Holy Name be praised now and forever.

What Do You See?

Good Friday, Lectionary 40
Ave Maria, FL, 2012

Isaiah 52:13–53:12
Psalm 31
Hebrews 4:14-16, 5:7-9
John 18:1–19:42

What do we see when we look at a cross? Many years ago, I was driving with my business partner, who was Jewish, and his five-year old daughter, whose name was Leah. We stopped at a traffic light, and Leah pointed out the window and said, "That building is a church!" Her father asked, "How do you know?" She replied, "Because it has a *T* on top."

A *T* on top. Through no fault of her own, the Cross to her was just a shape, a shape in the form of the letter *T*. She looked at the Cross, but she did not see it. I want to suggest that we, like her, but for different reasons, might look at the Cross without even seeing it. I fear that the Cross has become so familiar that we are no longer shocked by it. Can the Cross become merely part of the furniture of a chapel? In the popular culture, the Cross has become a piece of jewelry, a decoration. In the popular culture, people look at the Cross and see nothing.

But the Cross of Christ should be shocking! It should be, as Saint Paul said, a scandal, a stumbling block. It should take daring to lift high the Cross of Christ. When we see the Cross, we should be startled and frightened, as if we found a ticking bomb or a child playing with a loaded gun. We must be startled and frightened and awestruck as we look upon the Cross—for the Cross of Christ has unimaginable power. On this most solemn day, this Good Friday, may we look at the Cross of Christ and see it as if for the first time.

What can we see when we look at the Cross of Christ? We have to learn to look at the Cross again and again, seeing more and more each time that we turn our eyes and hearts and minds to it.

Let us look at the Cross and say, "That's me—that's what the world has done to me." We need to be able to look at the Cross of Christ and see our own pain, our own suffering and disfigurement. We have to look at the crucified Lord and see our own wounds. We must identify each of our wounds and ask God to touch them with His healing. In this way, the Cross can become for us a remedy for sin.

If we repent of our sin without asking God for healing, we will almost certainly commit the same sins again and again. Repenting without getting healing for those wounds which are the roots of sin is like trimming the tops of weeds and then becoming surprised that the weeds grow back. You see, sin more easily takes root in places where our hearts have been wounded. If we want to be free of our habitual sins, we must find healing for our hearts.

We cannot receive healing if we do not ask for it. The first step for the healing of our hearts, essential as a remedy for sin, is to look at the crucified Lord and then to see and name our wounds so that we may offer them to God.

Let us look at the Cross again and say, "That's me—

and I did it to myself. This is what I look like when I disfigure myself by sin. I, the nearest neighbor whom God has given me to love—I have wounded and mangled myself by my sin." We have to look at the Cross and see the awful truth. I behold the crucified and see that I am destroying myself by my sin.

Let us look at the Cross again and say, "That's Jesus—Son of God and Son of Mary. He is the Christ of God—and I did that to Him." The Cross announces what my sin does to love and innocence. Tearing, shredding, piercing, defiling. The Cross reveals the portrait and sculpture and result of my sin.

Let us look at the Cross again and see God's stubbornness, His unshakeable will to love and save me. No matter how much hatred and malice I heap upon him, beyond the scorn of my indifference and lukewarmness, despite the brazenness of my ingratitude, the Cross proves that God will not give up on me. The Cross shows that no matter how low I go, no matter how far I have fallen, the roots of the Cross go even deeper. The Cross shows that God is willing to reach underneath me. His suffering and death prove that Jesus would rather go through Hell for me than go to Heaven without me. The Cross proves that God can take the very worst that the world and I can offer and arise victorious.

That's what we see when we look at the Cross.

What shall we do in the presence of our crucified Lord?

Let us be shocked—shocked to know that I—with my sin—I have murdered love.

Let us remember—remember that the Cross and the resurrection of Christ always go together as one event. The story of the Cross and resurrection of Christ shows that my sin has murdered love and that love has overcome sin.

Let us cry—cry tears of sorrow and tears of joy. It is right that we cry before our crucified Lord, for as the poet Christina Rossetti said, "Am I stone, and not a sheep, that I can stand, O Christ, beneath Thy Cross, to number, drop by drop, Thy blood's slow loss, and yet not weep?" Yes, let us cry in the presence of our brokenhearted God.

Let us, in the presence of our crucified Savior, behold the Blood of Jesus. Let us meditate on the awful fact and awesome power of the Blood of Jesus. Do we marvel at the offering of the shed Blood of Jesus? Today I cannot help but recall these words of the poet George Herbert: "Love is that liquor, sweet and most divine, which my God feels as blood, and I as wine."

In the Jewish temple, blood served two purposes. First, blood purified. Sin is death, life is in the blood; sprinkled blood washed away the deadly stain of sin. Second, blood was also used as a bond. The blood of an animal was used to seal the relationship of two parties bound by covenant. The covenant between God and Abraham was sealed by an animal's blood. The covenant between God and the Jews was sealed by the blood of the Passover lamb.

So, what about the Blood of Jesus? Look into His Heart torn open by a spear and see the Blood which is life flow from the source of life itself. See the Lifeblood of God that wipes away the curse of sin and death. And behold the Blood of Jesus Who is the Lamb of God; see His blood that binds us forever to His Father.

The Blood of Jesus protects us from despair. It would be easy to look at the Cross and cry out, "What have we done?" But we must stay at the foot of the Cross, behold the One Whom they have pierced, and cry out, "Look at what God has done for us!"

In the end, the story of the Cross is a love story. God loves us with a crucifying passion. In the presence of the Cross we may celebrate God's undefeated love for us.

In the Byzantine Church, on the Feast of the Exaltation of the Cross, the bishop gives each worshipper a sprig of fresh basil, so that he may carry with him throughout the day a reminder of the sweet victory of the Cross.

When we take our leave of this oratory, let's leave with a humble and grateful heart, with the words of the Prophet Isaiah on our lips: "By his stripes, we are healed."

May God's Holy Name be praised now and forever.

EASTER

Do You Need a Savior?

Thursday of the Octave of Easter, Lectionary 264
Ave Maria, FL

Acts 3:11-26
Psalm 8
Luke 24:35-48

Do you want to hear a story? There was a man who fell down a long flight of stairs. He landed with a thunderous crash. Then he picked himself up, dusted himself off, and looked over his shoulder and said, "I wonder what all that noise was about?"

What was all that fuss about Easter and Lent about? Oh, Easter is nice enough, alleluias and flowers and white vestments and all. But Lent—all that fasting and fish dinners and wood and nails and thorns and blood, was all that really necessary? Aren't Lent and Good Friday just a bit of melodrama, some overreacting on God's part? And if we can just ease up on Lent, then maybe we can calm down about Easter. Maybe we can turn Lent into a kind of Advent where we still wear purple, but we wouldn't have to eat fish, and then maybe we could have two Christmases a year. No more talking about death. Wouldn't that be nice?

The Scriptures today point to an important question: Do we really need a savior? Well, maybe not. After all, aren't we all just basically good people? Oh, we may have an occasional unpleasantness from time to time, but do we need to have God step in as savior? If we were God, wouldn't we be the kind of people that we'd want to have around? Isn't it true that God should be glad that He has basically good people like us on the payroll? Shouldn't He be thrilled to have the worship of nice people like us?

Now, maybe those other people, you know, the people we don't like, maybe they need a savior…but not us. And if you really get me thinking about it, I'm not too sure about all of you either. You may be up to something really awful that I don't know about, so maybe you need a savior…but do I need a savior? Ahh, there's the question. Can I believe that I am such a sinner that I need a savior?

Well, it depends on when you ask me. When I'm feeling confident and things are going my way and I've just made a bunch of New Year's resolutions, then, no, I'm not really looking for a savior.

But when I've fallen flat on my face. When I look at my broken promises. When my heart and body and mind are pulled in different directions. When I slam up against the awful truth that I can't control myself and I can't control the world I live in. If you ask me at those times, then, yes, I'll admit, grudgingly, that I need a savior.

And what about you? Can you dare admit that you need a savior? If you can look in the mirror and say, "I'm not God," then you're well on your way to admitting that you too need a savior. And as we look around our broken world and ponder the tragedies of human history, we can say that all of creation needs a savior.

Ok, fine, a savior. But why the wood, the nails, the thorns, the blood? I once saw a three year old boy spill grape juice on a white carpet. As his mother screamed in horror, he said, "Don't worry Mommy, I'll just magic it away!" Couldn't God do that with our sin? Couldn't He just magic it away? Couldn't He just snap His fingers or wiggle His nose or pull on His ear lobe to wipe away all of the sin of the world? Wouldn't it just be easier, wouldn't anything be easier than Calvary? Couldn't God have picked a simpler, cleaner, less violent, less bloody way to be our Savior?

I suppose He could have. I don't want to be seen putting limits on God's absolute power. But God always gives His best. And in choosing to save us through the Passion and Death of the Christ, He saved us the best way of all.

In the Passion and Death of the Christ, we have undeniable proof of God's love for us. As St. Paul writes in the Letter to the Romans, "While we were still sinners, Christ died for us."

In the Passion and Death of the Christ, we see a perfect example of obedience, humility, courage, and all the other virtues that we need to live holy lives. And so St. Peter writes, "Christ also suffered for us, leaving you an example that you should follow in His steps."

In the Passion and Death of the Christ, we have motive to refrain from sin. As St. Paul tells us in 1 Corinthians, "You are bought with a great price: glorify and bear God in your body."

In the Passion and Death of the Christ, we see that human nature has an unforeseeable dignity. Just as human nature was deceived and ensnared by the devil, so too it is in the human nature of the Christ that the devil is overcome and death is conquered. So Saint Paul tells us in 1 Corinthians, "Thanks be to God who has given us the victory through our Lord Jesus Christ."

So, do we need a savior? Yes. Do we need a Crucified and Risen Savior? That's the best kind to have.

As the Spirit opens up the word of God to us today, we learn that we have a mission. Listen again to what Jesus says in the gospel: "Thus it is written, that the Christ should suffer and on the third day rise from the dead, and that repentance and forgiveness of sins should be preached in his name to all nations, beginning from Jerusalem. You are witnesses of these things."

That's right. You and I, we are now the witnesses. We must testify that the Christ had to suffer, and then rise on the third day. We must proclaim, to all the nations, repentance and forgiveness of sins in His name. Are we ready for that? Are we ready to be witnesses and evangelists? Are we ready to convict the world of sin as we herald the divine mercy? Easter is more than colored eggs and chocolate bunnies! Today Christ says to us, "I have won the victory. Now live it and tell the world!"

Where would we start? Let's start right here at this altar, where the sacrifice of Calvary will be made present again. Let's offer our lives with Christ to the Father. And then we will receive here the first fruits of that sacrifice. We will receive the Body and Blood, Soul and Divinity of the crucified and risen Christ. Let's come to this altar and cry out in our hearts: "Lord! Enflesh yourself within me. Take deep root in me. Make me more and more your own. Lord! Seal me again in the blood of your covenant!"

With that new and victorious life within us, we can go out to the world and proclaim: "Christ has died, Christ is risen, Christ will come again."

May God's Holy Name be praised now and forever.

Can You Endure?

Second Sunday of Easter, Lectionary 45
Ave Maria, FL, 2013

Acts 5:12-16
Psalm 118:2-4, 13-15, 22-24
Revelation 1:9-11a, 12-13, 17-19
John 20:19-31

If I were a lazy preacher, and you all were an ordinary congregation, we could wrap up this homily quite quickly. I could say, "Thomas doubted and made Jesus mad; then Thomas believed and made Jesus happy. Doubt is bad; faith is good. In the name of the Father, and of the Son, and of the Holy Spirit." And then you all could reward my laziness by thinking to yourselves, "Well, that was useless, but at least it didn't take very long," and then we could get on with the rest of Mass.

But I am not a lazy preacher, and you all are not an ordinary congregation, so let's try do something better than what I just described. Let's listen again to what Saint John wrote in the Book of Revelation: "I, John, your brother, who share with you the distress, the kingdom, and the endurance we have in Jesus…"

He starts with, "I, John, your brother..." That will help us later to understand what is going on with Saint Thomas in our gospel passage. But right now let's focus on John's use of three words: distress, kingdom, and endurance.

The Greek word John used for "distress" is not easy to translate. The Greek word *"thlipsis"* is *"tribulatio"* in Latin, which gives us the English word "tribulation." In this sense, "distress" means "a crushing pressure from the outside"; think of a huge rock being placed on the body. In the New Testament, the word "distress" refers to persecution.

In the time of Saint John, as he wrote these words, the persecution and the slaughter of Christians was the policy of the Roman Empire. In our own time, in our own country, Christians are subject to distress, to pressure, to persecution. Sometimes, it appears to be almost comical. For example, this week, a certain university that calls itself Catholic told students that they could not start a Knights of Columbus council there, because the Knights of Columbus is for Catholic students, and that would be "exclusive," and being exclusive is not consistent with diversity, and failing in diversity is not consistent with the university's Catholic identity, and that is why the university cannot tolerate a Catholic organization at that Catholic university.

And sometimes, in our own country, the tribulation, pressure, distress, or persecution of Christians appears to be slow, deliberate, and grinding. I say this when I see Catholic institutions arguing in court not to be forced to pay for abortions and contraceptives for their employees.

Now in other countries, in our day, the persecution of Christians is steady, systematic, enthusiastic, and deadly. The persecution of Christians in these countries, supported by society and state, is most often seen in those places that most fervently embrace that religion so often referred to as "the Religion of Peace."

In response to pressure, tribulation, distress, and persecution, Saint John writes that in Jesus we have "endurance." The Greek word he uses is *"hupomone"*; that is not a passive, submissive, fainthearted patience. The steadfast endurance John speaks of here is filled with a spirit of fortitude and heroism, and can turn suffering into glory. This steadfast endurance admits the pain but prefers to think of the honor of remaining faithful until the end.

Saint John saw his own Christian community in distress. He saw that they desired to enter into the *"basileia,"* that is, the kingdom of God, upon which they had set their hearts and for which they were risking their lives. John knew, as we should, that the only way from affliction to glory was through a stubborn and conquering endurance. Remember that Saint John heard Jesus say, "Anyone who endures to the end will be saved." And surely he must have known that Saint Paul preached that if we endure with Christ then we shall reign with Him.

The way to endurance is by way of union with Christ. He Himself endured until the end and was victorious over sin and death. (That is why we celebrate Easter, by the way.) Because He endured and triumphed, He can enable those who follow Him to achieve the same endurance and reach the same goal.

How shall we endure with Christ to the end? Saint John and Saint Thomas show us how. We shall endure with Christ by enduring with each other. Remember, Saint John began with these words: "I, John, your brother…" In other words, John is saying, "I am with you and going through the tribulations with you."

Saint Thomas found it harder to believe in the resurrection because he withdrew from the community of believers. He missed out on what God was doing among His people. God can do more good with us when we are together as friends in the Lord. We are more likely to stay with Christ when we stay together.

The predators we meet, predators both physical and spiritual, look for isolated individuals to prey upon. It is easier for the enemy to pick us off one by one than if we are standing together.

So, what shall we do about the instruction we have received from the Word of God this evening? Well, let's face the facts, and the facts are these:

First, as Christians, we have enemies, both secular and spiritual, who hate us precisely because we are Christians. Some of our enemies want us silent, and some of our enemies want us dead.

Second, as Christians, we are not helpless, because our help is in the Name of the Lord, Who made Heaven and Earth. God our Lord gives us His Holy Spirit, the same Spirit by which He raised Jesus from the dead, and He gave us each other.

Third, as Christians, our mission is to spread, endure, and triumph. Our vocation is to finally share in the glory of the Lord in the home of our Heavenly Father.

In light of these three facts, we can see that we have work to do. We have to deepen our bonds with Christ, and we have to deepen our bonds with one another. If we do that, if we are able to draw our strength from Christ and with one another, then before the whole world and the entire company of Heaven, we can echo the words of the Psalm we heard this evening:

"I was hard pressed and was falling, but the LORD helped me. My strength and my courage is the LORD, and he has been my savior."

May God's Holy Name be praised now and forever.

Never Mind!

Second Monday of Easter, Lectionary 267
Ave Maria, FL, 2009

Acts 4:23-31
Psalm 2
John 3:1-8

What if God looked at Adam and Eve after the fall and said, "Ah—never mind! It doesn't matter that you ate from the Tree of Good and Evil. Let's just forget it ever happened. It's not a big deal. Just try not to do it again, ok?"

Would we really want to live in such a world? A world wherein our actions don't matter? A world wherein character has nothing to do with destiny? A world wherein nothing was ever demanded of us? In such a world, could there be such a thing as real success if there is no chance of real failure? Would we really want to live in a world wherein our words and our deeds count for nothing?

If we think about that for a while, surely, we would agree that such a world would not be worth very much, certainly not worth our time and effort. And how could we claim to have any dignity in such a world where excellence and depravity were equally matters of indifference?

But we don't live in such a world. We live in a moral world, a world with a purpose, a blessing, and a fulfillment to be achieved. In this moral world, when we sin, which is simply to betray God, ourselves, and our neighbor, when we sin—what have we done? When we sin, we cheat creation and we cheat our Creator. When we sin, we strangle the notes that we are meant to sing in the symphony of praise and thanksgiving that all creation owes God. When we sin, we decide that there will be one less person seated at the table of the eternal banquet God is preparing. How can that not matter? How can that not count? When we sin, we choose to tear a hole in the fabric of the universe. When we sin, we inject the cancer of annihilation into creation. How can any of that be undone and set to rights with even a divinely spoken, "Oh, never mind"?

Someone had to re-build the bridges to God that we have burned with our sin. Someone had to defeat the power of eternal death that we had brought upon ourselves. Someone had to overcome the horror with love. Only the Christ, who is true God and true man, could do what needed to be done.

Jesus said: "The Son of Man must be lifted up, so that everyone who believes in him may have eternal life."

Jesus was lifted up on the cross, so that when I look at him, I may see the human cost, and the divine cost, of my sin. Jesus, Son of God and Son of Mary, Jesus Christ crucified, is the human and divine cost of my sin, and He chose to pay the price. He chose to pay the price for my sin because He, for reasons I will never understand in this life, He chose to pay the price for my sin because He thinks I'm worth it.

And He paid the price for your sin because He thinks you're worth it too.

Now that the Son of Man has been lifted up on the cross, now that the Christ of God has been raised from the dead, now that we know that the price of sin has been paid and the gift of glory has been offered, what shall we do? How shall we live? We can walk away and return to our routines as if nothing happened, telling ourselves we live in a cartoon world wherein nothing matters; or, we can resolve now to live our lives in such a way that Christ will be assured that what He suffered was not in vain, and that the gift He offers us will not be wasted. We know that the folly of the Cross defeats the wisdom of the world. Let's pray for each other today, that we may choose wisely and live faithfully.

May God's Holy Name be praised now and forever.

Have You Ever Been Amazed?

Third Sunday of Easter, Lectionary 48
Ave Maria, FL, 2013

Acts 5:27-32, 40b-41
Psalm 30:2, 4, 5-6, 11-12, 13
Revelation 5:11-14
John 21:1-19

When was the last time that you were amazed? Not merely surprised, but truly amazed. Saint Thomas Aquinas said, "Amazement comes from the inability to see the whole; therefore God cannot be amazed." In other words, amazement is shown when you say, "I sure didn't see ***that*** coming!"

To be a disciple of Christ is to be a person who is frequently amazed. Let me give you three Scriptural reasons to be amazed. First is the single most important sentence in the Bible: "He is risen!" Saint Paul makes clear that if Jesus is not risen from the dead, then Jesus is a fraud, His mission is a failure, and our faith is a farce. Nonetheless, not even the apostles expected to find an empty tomb. So, when they met the Risen Lord, they were amazed.

Here is a second Scriptural reason to be amazed: "The

Lord is risen, and He has appeared to Simon!" I think Saint Luke may have forgotten to write down the really amazing part of that exclamation, which is: "...and when the Risen Lord met Simon, He didn't kill him!" The wonder of it all! Jesus proves that He is the shepherd of the sheep and not the hunter of the sheep by seeking out Simon Peter and embracing him, His most boastful and most repentant betrayer.

And now a third Scriptural reason to be amazed: "Feed my sheep." These words of Jesus to Simon Peter are amazing and fascinating because they indicate how the Lord deals with sinners. The Lord gives Simon Peter a great mission, a mission by which he will glorify God. This mission the Lord Jesus entrusted to a repentant sinner.

I am thrilled to talk about these words of the Lord with you because I am a sinner, because I am a loved sinner, and because I am a priest. I am a sinner—I have shaken my fist in the face of a holy God and yelled, "My will be done! Not yours!" I am a loved sinner—God pursued me and washed me clean in the Blood of His only begotten Son. I am a priest—called by God and ordained by the Church to be a sacramental servant of the Divine Mercy, bringing hope and healing to sinners just like you and me.

I say that the words of Jesus to Simon Peter on the shore of the Sea of Tiberias are amazing because they show that the way the Lord forgives sin is not to merely forgive. First, for God, there is no such thing as "*mere* forgiveness," because His forgiveness comes at a terrible cost to Himself, the Blood of His only begotten Son, to ransom us from sin and death. Second, for God, there is no such thing as "*mere* forgiveness," because God does not *only* forgive us. As we see with Simon Peter, the Lord does so much more than forgive. When the Lord forgives us, He also offers us opportunities for reparation, restoration, and elevation.

Why is reparation an important part of divine forgiveness? When we sin, we tear a hole in the fabric of creation. Sin is an act of violence against the truth, goodness, and beauty intended by God. Think of it this way: Sin is like driving a nail into a board. Forgiveness, then, is the nail being pulled from the board. That nail left a hole in the board. That hole needs to be filled in again. Reparation for sin is like that—it is an attempt to fill in—to make right—what sin had made wrong. We cannot offer complete reparation for our sin, however, because our sin is an infinite offense against God. But God's call to us to make reparation for our sin shows God's desire to uphold our dignity as moral agents. We see this in the exchange between Jesus and Simon Peter. On the night Jesus was arrested, boastful Simon, standing by a fire, denies that he even knows Jesus. Now, in the presence of his Risen Lord, Simon Peter, standing by a fire, receives from Jesus the opportunity to affirm three times his love for his Lord. The call to reparation for sin is an invitation by God to share in His power of healing the wounds left by sin. That is how the Lord deals with sinners, sinners like Simon Peter, sinners like you and me. He does not "merely" forgive us—He ennobles us—by calling us to reparation for sin.

I also spoke of restoration. What do I mean by that? Notice that Jesus did not forgive Simon Peter and then banish him from His sight. No! Jesus said to Simon Peter, "Follow me." Is that not amazing? Jesus said to His most boastful betrayer, "I still want you with me." Jesus shows us that His love for sinners is decisive; His choice to love us is more powerful than our choice to betray Him. The love of Christ is the final word, not sin! That is amazing!

Finally, I spoke of elevation. What do I mean by that? This, perhaps, is the most amazing element of all. Our sin, which is an infinite offense against God, Jesus forgives, at a terrible cost to Himself. Jesus forgives our sin and then honors our dignity by sharing with us His healing power by calling us to reparation for sin. Next, after we are forgiven, He offers to make us whole by inviting us to restoration, putting in place again the relationship with Him which we had broken by our sin. Then, beyond anything we could have expected, He offers us an elevation. In other words, He asks repentant sinners to come up higher in His service. We see this in the mission He gives to Simon Peter, whom He once called to be a fisher of men. Now, Jesus, Who called Himself the Good Shepherd, calls Simon Peter to be the shepherd of His flock, the Church. Jesus gives Simon Peter a new mission. He tells him, "Feed my lambs. Tend my sheep." Now we can see clearly how Divine Mercy works. Jesus forgives repentant sinners and does not condemn them; Jesus ennobles repentant sinners and does not humiliate them; Jesus embraces repentant sinners and does not banish them. And most amazing of all, Jesus trusts repentant sinners, and will give them an important mission, which is to serve His Church by seeking the lost, feeding the hungry, and protecting the vulnerable. Is that not amazing?

This Mass is a great joy for me because here and now I get to tell you a wonderful story that is perfectly true. Today I get to tell you the story of how our Crucified, Risen, and Returning Lord treats repentant sinners. I can testify that what Saint John wrote about Jesus and sinners, sinners like Simon Peter, is true, because our Lord has done the same for me. I am a sinner, and the Lord in His mercy offered to me invitations to forgiveness, reparation, restoration, and elevation. And I am amazed. And I am delighted to tell you that our Lord, the Good Shepherd offers the same mercy, the same healing, the same dignity and joy to you, and to all repentant sinners.

So, now what? What shall we do? What shall we do in response to the most amazing grace of our Lord's mercy? How shall we receive all the good that the Lord offers us? First, let us testify to all the world what God has done for us. Let us echo the words of the apostles before the Sanhedrin and declare: "We are witnesses of these things, as is the Holy Spirit whom God has given to those who obey him." Second, let us offer worthy worship to our most amazing and merciful God. Let our worship here on Earth imitate what Saint John showed us of the worship in Heaven, as we cry out: "To the one who sits on the throne and to the Lamb be blessing and honor, glory and might, forever and ever." And let the reason for our joy never be far from our minds, our hearts, or our lips. Let us live constantly the words of the psalm we heard today: "I will praise you, Lord, for you have rescued me."

May God's Holy Name be praised now and forever.

Do You Believe? How Do You Know?

Third Monday of Easter, Lectionary 273
Ave Maria, FL, 2008

Acts 6:8-15
Psalm 119
John 6:22-29

"What can we do to accomplish the works of God?" Jesus answered and said to them, "This is the work of God, that you believe in the one He sent."

There is a story of a man visiting Niagara Falls for the first time. Awed by the majestic spread of water, height, and power, he was surprised to see a wire stretched from one end of the falls to the other. He was even more surprised when he saw a woman approach him with a wheelbarrow full of bricks.

She asked him, "Do you believe that I can cross that wire with this wheelbarrow full of bricks?" He replied, "Not at all! That's crazy!" She winked at him and said, "Watch this!"

He couldn't believe his eyes as he saw the woman get up on the wire with the wheelbarrow full of bricks. She walked right across, turned around, and came back. She asked him, "NOW do you believe that I can cross the wire with this wheelbarrow?"

"Oh yes!" he said. "Now I believe!" "Do you really believe?" she asked. "Oh yes! Now I really believe!" She asked, "Do you really, really believe?" "Oh yes!" he replied. "I really, really believe!"

She winked at him, emptied the wheelbarrow of bricks and said, "Fine—if you really, really believe, then YOU get in the wheelbarrow."

Are we ready to do the work of God? Are we ready to believe in the one He sent? Saint Ignatius, in his Spiritual Exercises, gives us three tests, tests to determine whether we believe.

First, imagine this: You are offered all the goods of the world—health, wealth, long life, happiness, good reputation. All these will be yours. All these are for you—for the simple price of one freely committed mortal sin.

If you recoil in horror, and say, "No! No! Not for a mortal sin!", Saint Ignatius would say, "If you answer that way, then you can be sure that you believe."

Do want to know if you really believe? Then imagine this: You are offered all the goods of the world—health, wealth, long life, happiness, good reputation. All these will be yours. All these are for you—for the simple price of one freely committed venial sin.

If you recoil in horror, and say, "No! No! Not for a venial sin! "Saint Ignatius would say, "If you answer that way, then you can be sure that you really believe."

Do you want to know if you really, really believe? Then imagine this: Place yourself before Christ and say, "Even if I could have all the goods of the world without sin, I would accept from your hands, if you wish, the poverty that you endured, the contempt and scorn of the world you suffered, the cross that you carried, so as to be more like you."

Saint Ignatius would say, "If you can say that to Christ, then you can be sure that you really, really believe."

So, today, take some time in prayer. In the presence of Christ, put yourself to the test, and find out if you really, really believe.

May God's Holy Name be praised now and forever.

What Happens to Useless Branches?

Fifth Sunday of Easter, Lectionary 53
Ave Maria, FL, 2012

Acts 9:26-31
Psalm 22:26-27, 28, 30, 31-32
1 John 3:18-24
John 15:1-8

"I am the vine, you are the branches."

Does that mean very much to you? Not to me. I'm a city boy. I really don't know much of anything about gardens, vines, branches, or fruit. In the world I grew up in, milk comes from cartons, fish comes from cans, and fruit was made of wax and sat in a basket on my grandmother's dining room table. So when I read today's gospel, I don't get a big "Aha!"

But let me give it a try. When I sleep very soundly, sometimes I sleep on my side, and when I wake up, I've found that I've lost circulation in my arm. My arm goes numb, and I can't get it to work quite right. When I was in high school, I was of the era that required that a retreat took place while everyone sat in a circle on the floor and shared their innermost thoughts. After a while, I would lose circulation in my leg. But I wasn't aware of it until I tried to stand up, and then I would promptly fall down.

I think what Jesus is saying about the vine and branches is analogous to losing circulation in a limb. If a limb is cut off from the circulation of the blood, it can go numb, become dysfunctional, and even die. The same, I believe, is true of us, if we are cut off from the life of Jesus. We too can go numb, become dysfunctional, and even die. The difference, however, is that when your leg goes numb, you know it right away because when you try to stand up, you fall down. The frightful truth of the human condition is that it is possible for us to cut ourselves off from the life of Jesus and not even know it.

What does it look like to be united to Christ as branches to the vine, and to bear good fruit? In the end, it means to live for the greater glory of God and for the salvation of souls. If that is not our motivation and our true way of life, then we have to wonder whether we have cut ourselves off from the life of Christ.

And what does it look like to be a branch that is not drawing life from the vine? Biblical scholar William Barclay describes such Christians as "...useless branches, all leaves and no fruit." He also reminds us: "It is a first principle of the New Testament that uselessness invites disaster. The fruitless branch is on the way to destruction."

Perhaps a few examples might help. When I think of useless branches, I think of self-identified Catholic schools who invite architects and advocates of the culture of death to speak at their graduations. When I think of useless branches, I think of self-identified Catholic politicians who gladly accept donations from abortion providers. When I think of useless branches, I think of self-identified Catholic religious communities who appear to advocate for every conceivable form of "justice," with the exception of true justice for the unborn.

But I must speak with caution here. You and I must

resist the temptation to consider these images and then to pray the prayer of the Pharisee found in the Gospel of Luke: "O God, I thank you that I am not like the rest of humanity." God forbid that we ever pray such a prayer!

If we are going to be honest about looking at vines, branches, good fruit, and the life of Christ, we must humbly and fiercely look in the mirror and look within our own hearts. "Am I certain that I am united to Christ as branches to the vine? Am I certain that above all the life of Christ sustains me? Am I certain that my first wish and final hope are to be found as a fruitful disciple of Christ?" Each person here has to answer these questions for himself. No one can do it for you, and no one dare ask such questions except in the spirit of prayer.

When Pope Pius XI observed the rise of fascism in Europe in the 1930's he said, "Let us give thanks to God that we live in times such as these, for now it is permitted to no one to be mediocre." Those words were true in his time; I daresay they are even more true in our own time. In our own time and place, life is not seen as a gift of God; faith is reviled as a mere fantasy or worse; and our nation seems to be forgetting that obedience to God constitutes the first freedom. The Church needs heroes; the Church needs the kind of saints and scholars, families and religious, priests and poets, musicians and mystics—wise warriors one and all—that can be produced at a place like Ave Maria.

We must not succumb to a fear or despair that is unworthy of the faithful and fruitful Catholic. The Church has an amazing tradition of burying those who would volunteer to be her pallbearers. The Church has endured the scorn of empires; She has resisted the jihads waged by....the misunderstanders of the Religion of Peace; She has passed through a veritable Red Sea of innocent blood shed by ungodly men in the twentieth century. Let our only fear be the holy fear of failing at the task which the Lord, in His Providence, has entrusted to us in our time and place.

Now, *now*, Holy Mother Church rallies Her children around Her King. Now She calls upon Her children to take up the banner of Christ the King, and to carry it from here to eternity. Let us resolve to take up the banner of Christ, which is His Cross. Let us steel ourselves for the human and supernatural resistance we will surely face. Saint Ignatius Loyola warned us with these words: "Nothing worthy of God can be done without earth being set in uproar and hell's legions roused."

Our crucified and risen Lord is our victorious King. He calls us to join Him in defeating sin and death and to enter into His life and glory. Would it not be a waste, a tragedy, a scandal, a shame, a horror, if we do not accept His invitation to share in His passion and in His victory?

Let's listen again to the psalm we heard this morning: "Let the coming generation be told of the LORD that they may proclaim to a people yet to be born the justice he has shown." In other words, even greater than the financial debt that we Americans owe to the Chinese, we Catholics in America owe a debt to God and to future generations. Our mandate from Heaven is to lift high the Cross and to proclaim the gospel until Christ returns. How shall the next generation know Christ if He is not proclaimed? Who shall refuse to cower before the powers and principalities of this world and declare that God alone is worthy of worship? Who shall insist that God alone is sovereign over life and death? Does that call belong to someone else? To some other time? No! If not us, who? If not now, when?

Again the psalm we heard this morning teaches us the way, with these words: "I will fulfill my vows before those who fear the LORD." The Lord is faithful; He calls us to be faithful; and to those who ask He gives the spirit of fidelity. It is time to ask daily for that gift of courageous and hopeful fidelity. And God will gladly give us that gift, if we remain united to Christ as branches to the vine.

I will ask that you pray today and for each day this

week, for three graces from God, three special blessings. First, pray for union—union with Christ as branches to the vine; second, pray for union—a union of heart and mind with the Church Christ founded; third, pray for union—union with our fellow Christians who as one body will proclaim Christ to the world. If we do that, if we are in union with Christ, if we are in union with the Church, if we are in union with our brothers and sisters in Christ, then we will see these words of Jesus fulfilled: "By this is my Father glorified, that you bear much fruit and become my disciples."

May God's Holy Name be praised now and forever.

Christ's Cross and Resurrection Are Inseparable

Fifth Sunday of Easter, Lectionary 54
Ave Maria, FL, 2013
Acts 14:21:27
Psalm 145:8-9, 10-11, 12-13
Revelation 21:1-5a
John 13:31-33a, 34-35

Would you like to learn how to kill a conversation in a hurry? Would you like to learn one simple statement that will cause people to turn pale, stare at their feet, and start longing for the exit? Quite by accident, I discovered an amazing thing to do just that. It works every time. The problem is, it only works on married couples.

Here's what you do: Sit down with a married couple and say to the husband the following words: "When you got married, you stood at the altar of God and promised to love your wife so well that people will look at how you love her and say, 'Hey! See how he loves her? That must be how Christ loves His Church!'" The guy will get quiet and the wife will suddenly become fascinated and say, "Tell us more!"

Oh, but it cuts both ways. Then I say to the wife: "When you got married, you stood at the altar of God and promised to love your husband so well that people will look at how you love him and say, 'Hey! See how she loves him? That must be how the Church loves Christ!" Then it is the wife's turn to get quiet and stare at the floor.

Why are those words such conversation-stoppers? Because honest married couples—in fact, all serious Christians—know that being a faithful disciple of Christ, following the way of the Master, means not avoiding the cross. And we are all at least a bit squeamish about the cross of Christ.

Now, please be sure that I take no pleasure in making that statement. Honesty demands that I admit to you that on my own, I do not have the courage or generosity to run towards the cross. On my own, I do not have the faith, hope, or love to embrace and cling to the cross. Maybe you do—but don't worry—I won't ask for a show of hands…

Now, here you might object: "Oh, Father! Yes, the cross is scary, but there is the resurrection too! Let's not forget about that!" To which I wish to offer a resounding, "NO!" For a Christian to say, "There is the cross BUT there is the resurrection" is just plain wrong. Let me explain why.

The formula, "There-is-the-cross-BUT-there-is-the-resurrection" is what I call Blind Date Theology. Did you ever try to set up a guy on a blind date? What is the first question he is likely to ask? He asks, "Is she pretty?" Now you answer, "Everyone likes her!" But is she pretty? "She makes all of her own clothes!" But is she pretty? "She's very kind to animals!" You offer up all these unrelated qualities, good in themselves, to avoid answering the awkward question that may have an unwelcome answer. Blind Date Theology presents the resurrection as a welcome but unrelated compensation for an otherwise regrettable fact. It is like getting hit by a car and finding a winning lottery ticket when you land in the gutter. You might say, "Yes, I got hit by a car, BUT I did find a winning lottery ticket..."

If we say, "Yes, there is the cross—which no one wants—BUT, there is the resurrection, and that's kinda nice...", then we have not understood properly the Christian message. We will fail as disciples of Christ if we do not understand properly the link between His Cross and His Resurrection. First, the cross is necessary, because only by embracing and clinging to the cross can we love as Christ loves, as His new commandment requires. Only then can we love without self-seeking.

Second, the true Christian message is always to speak of the-cross-AND-the-resurrection. The two must always be spoken of together. The real excitement of the gospel, what makes the proclamation of Christ so important that the Church proclaims Him throughout the world, is that whenever Christ crucified and suffering is found, there also is Christ risen and victorious to be found. Yes, very often, Christ risen is harder to find than Christ suffering, but the cross-AND-resurrection are inseparable.

That fact, that mystery, that paradox is what makes the proclamation of Christ the most urgent task in all of human history. That's exciting, isn't it? Yes, but let's pause and catch our breath for a moment. Let's think this through together. We proclaim Christ, not simply as a concept, but as a person Who is the way, the truth, and the life. There is no way to our Heavenly Father apart from Him; there is no enduring truth apart from Him; there is no lasting life apart from Him. Therefore, our highest hope and our greatest mission is to unite with Him, to love with Him as He loves, to cling to His Cross in order to find His Resurrection, to die and rise with Him for the life of the world.

His new commandment, to love one another as He has loved us, from cross to resurrection, that is the only path to what Saint John saw in his visions of Heaven. Only an acceptance of the cross and resurrection together will lead us to the new Jerusalem, where every tear will be wiped away.

Now, again let's pause and catch our breath for a moment. We don't want bright and beautiful words about Heaven to obscure from our sight the always practical, often difficult, and sometimes delightful work that you and I have to do here and now.

As I asked myself when I looked in the mirror this morning, I now ask all of you: "How shall we live this? How shall we live the new commandment? How shall we live the truth and mystery that the Cross and Resurrection of Christ are inseparable?" If we are really going to live the new commandment of Christ, we will have to put to death our own selfishness and self-righteousness. We will have to serve each other and hope for each other in a way that will crack our hearts wide open. And we will have to yearn constantly for a deeper union, a deeper identification with Christ crucified and risen.

If we agree to do all that together—and we must—then how shall we begin? I think that we can begin with three simple steps. First, let's give each other the benefit of the doubt. In other words, let's assume that we are each well-intentioned, so let's stop throwing at each other the stones of gossip and detraction.

Second, let's forgive each other. Yes, we are all flawed and annoying. I myself am a sinner whose quirks and habits could strain the patience of Our Blessed Mother. I'm sure that Saint Ignatius Loyola would have slapped me if he had to live with me. And I am a sinner who has offended God infinitely. Yet, God, in His mysterious mercy, has not let me die in my sins. He has forgiven me my infinite offenses against His goodness, at a terrible cost to Himself. What He has done for me, He has done for you.

Therefore, I believe that we each need to look in the mirror and say: "If God can put up with the likes of me, then surely I can extend mercy to others." If we are to be united with Christ in His Cross and Resurrection, if we are to obey His new commandment, then we must learn how to forgive each other.

Our third task: Let's work to bring out the best in each other. In other words, let's be near occasions of grace for each other, rather than near occasions of sin. Let's look for and call forth whatever is good in each other. And let's protect what is good in each other by our chastity, our sobriety, and our joy.

If we begin with these three steps—the benefit of the doubt, forgiving each other, promoting the good in each other—then we will have begun well our deeper obedience to Christ's new commandment. United with Him, loving as He loves, we will pass over with Him from the cross to the resurrection, from death to life. And finally, we will see for ourselves what Saint John saw long ago, we will see the One Who sits on the throne, and we will hear Him say, "Behold, I make all things new."

May God's Holy Name be praised now and forever.

Do You Have a Motto?

Fifth Tuesday of Easter, Lectionary 286
Ave Maria, FL, 2008

Acts 14:19-28
Psalm 145:10-11, 12-13ab, 21
John 14:27-31a

"The Few. The Proud. The Marines." "Air Force: Aim High!" "Navy: It's not just a job—it's an adventure!" "Army: Be all you can be!"

Every advertiser will tell you that you have to have a catchy slogan or motto that people will associate with your product. Marketers call it branding. New York City is called "The Big Apple." Boston is called "Beantown."

For many years, signs at the entrance of Philadelphia said, "Welcome to Philadelphia, the City of Brotherly Love!" A few years ago town officials asked citizens to submit ideas for a new slogan. Having lived there, I can understand why citizens suggested slogans such as "Welcome to Philadelphia—Lock and Load!" and "Welcome to Philadelphia—Hey! That's my car!" City officials then stopped asking for suggestions.

Even religious communities have their branding. Jesuits

are renowned for their motto, "*Ad maiorem Dei gloriam*—For the greater glory of God!" More recently, young Christians have been wearing bracelets with the letters "WWJD," which stand for "What would Jesus do?" Unfortunately, I've taught at schools where the students thought that "WWJD" stood for "We want Jack Daniels!"

I learned not long ago that the WWJD bracelet-wearers started wearing a second bracelet to answer the question of the first bracelet. The second bracelet had the letters "FROG" which stand for "Fully rely on God." And that brings us closer to today's gospel passage.

What is Jesus' motto? What's His slogan? What's His branding? Notice what He says in the gospel of John: "I love the Father and I do just as the Father has commanded me." Jesus referred everything back to the Father. All that He did and said was in loving obedience to the Father. And His greatest desire is to lead us home to the Father.

What about us? Could we adopt as our own personal motto: "I love the Father and I do just as the Father has commanded me"? Do we believe that we have been given the Spirit of adoption, and so may rightly call out with Jesus, "Abba—Father!"? Do we believe that we have a Heavenly Father who loves us, who created us in love for a good purpose, which is to share His glory forever? Do we believe that we are on our way, a pilgrim people, processing slowly but surely to our Father's house?

You might well answer, "Of course we do! Otherwise we wouldn't be here." Fair enough. But our own experience will tell us that it is frightfully easy to forget our identity as children of God, and frightfully easy to forget our heritage and future as His children. We might assent with our minds and lips to Jesus' motto, but we might live as practical atheists, choosing and acting as if we had neither a divine origin nor a divine destiny. What can we do to keep ourselves from forgetting who we really are?

Here's where St. Ignatius Loyola may help. He offers

us what he called the First Principle and Foundation, which says, "Man was created for the praise, reverence, and service of God." Very simply, we are to measure everything we do in light of that standard. Whatever helps us in the praise, reverence, and service of God is good; whatever takes us away from the praise, reverence, and service of God is bad. Easy to remember, simple to apply. If we faithfully live according to the First Principle and Foundation, we will in fact do as Jesus has said: "I love the Father and I do just as the Father has commanded me."

May God's Holy Name be praised now and forever.

Only Real Love Leads to True Joy

Fifth Thursday of Easter, Lectionary 288
Ave Maria, FL, 2012
Acts 15:7-21
Psalm 96:1-2a, 2b-3, 10
John 15:9-11

In order to ensure that I never suffer from low blood pressure, every morning I read news and commentary online. Of course, the big news this morning is that yesterday the president announced his support of so-called "gay marriage." One commentator wrote that because Christians are taught to follow Christ's footsteps, the Christ who preached a life of simplicity, love, and compassion, they ought to live by these precepts. His conclusion is that the simplicity, love, and compassion demanded by the imitation of Christ entails support of "gay marriage." Now, I agree that if people profess belief in Christ, they ought to live lives of simplicity, love, and compassion. There is no reason, however, to believe that someone cannot both live a life embracing these three requirements and at the same time be against "gay marriage." The burden of proof remains on the proponents of "gay marriage" to show that it is impossible to live with these three values while insisting that marriage can only be between a man and a woman. Mother Teresa surely lived a life of simplicity, love, and compassion, and, although I did not know her personally, I find it hard to imagine that she would be a supporter of "gay marriage."

In light of today's gospel reading, let's focus on love. Jesus speaks a great deal about love, especially in the Gospel of John. Unfortunately, the word "love" has been hijacked by people with muddled thinking and little Christian culture. On their account, "love" is essentially the presence of warm feelings and the absence of painful feelings, and, speaking from a "spiritual" if not religious view, the greatest proof of the presence of love is an elevated "self-esteem."

There was a time, however, when people knew that love meant something quite different. Medieval scholars called it *amor benevolentiae*. Now, that could be translated as "benevolent love," but that translation would be accurate yet insufficient. *Amor benevolentiae* means wishing, wanting, willing, desiring, urging the best for the beloved. And there was a time when people knew that what is best for the beloved is God. The most loving thing we could do, then, is to point out to the beloved the path to God, and to offer to guide him on that pilgrim's path.

That pilgrim's path to God could be begun to be found by reason reflecting on nature, and that path is well marked out and lit by the revelation which Christ has entrusted to the Church He founded. When we use our God-given reason to reflect on our God-given human nature, when we receive wholeheartedly and clear-mindedly the Sacred Scriptures and Sacred Tradition divinely revealed to the Church, it becomes quite clear that marriage can only be between a man and a woman. This conclusion is not some arbitrary human convention or prejudice. Christ, Who is the Word of the Father, is inscribed into nature by the Father Himself, and we can read in our human nature God's plan and wisdom in making us male and female. Christ, Who is the Word of the Father, is spoken to the Church by the Father Himself, and we can hear of His plan of salvation revealed in the call of the Bridegroom to the Bride.

Now, I admit, the words I have just spoken, and the truths they point to, may, in some quarters, cause hurt feelings. So, why did I just say them? And why must you say them too? Let's listen again to Jesus' words in the Gospel of John: "If you keep my commandments, you will remain in my love, just as I have kept my Father's commandments and remain in his love." No one knows better than Jesus that obedience to the Father's commandments can be costly. Just look at the Cross.

So, why does Jesus ask us to imitate His obedience? And what does obedience have to do with joy? Again, let's listen to the Gospel of John: "I have told you this so that my joy might be in you and your joy might be complete." Aquinas said that joy is caused by love, through the presence of the beloved. The beloved of Jesus is His Father. Our beloved and our greatest good is to be in the presence of our loving God. Fidelity and love, which together constitute true obedience, is the path to joy, the path to our beloved, the path to our greatest happiness, satisfaction, and perfection. Obedience to the commands of God, which are found in nature and in revelation, obedience to the commands of God for the sake of love, in imitation of Jesus, is the only path to the joy Jesus desires for us.

So, we really have no choice but to tell the truth about God, about love, and about marriage. Telling these truths is the most loving thing we can do. I also know that telling these truths can be troublesome and costly. Therefore, let's resolve to pray today for three groups. First, let's pray for those who will be attacked for telling the truth. Second, let's pray for those who find it difficult to know and understand the truth. Third, let's pray for those who are reluctant or unwilling to accept the truth. For all three, let's pray that through God's grace, their joy may be made complete, as our Lord desires.

May God's Holy Name be praised now and forever.

Where Is Your Weakness?

Fifth Friday of Easter, Lectionary 289
Ave Maria, FL, 2008
Acts 15:22-31
Psalm 57
John 15:12-17

"Be sober and vigilant. Your opponent the Devil is prowling around like a roaring lion looking for someone to devour."

Do we believe that? I once heard a priest, renowned for being an absolute pacifist, refuse to pray for what he referred to as "our so-called enemies" because "Christians have no enemies."

Now, let's review: There are millions of people around the world, animated by religious fervor, who want all of us in this church dead because we love Jews, eat pork, drink alcohol, pray together as men and women, assert the divinity of Jesus, and worship the Triune God. So, I'd say yes, Christians do have enemies, and we really do need to pray for them. But that's a topic for another time.

I want to focus on spiritual warfare this morning. This excerpt from St. Peter's epistle reminds of me St. Paul when he wrote: "For our fight is not against flesh and blood, but against the rulers, against the authorities, against the powers of this dark world and against the spiritual forces of evil in the heavenly realms." A sobering thought.

I once gave a friend a copy of a painting depicting a child sound asleep in his bed. In the background, standing watch, was a 6-foot tall angel with a 7-foot long spear in one hand and a ball of flame in the other. I said to her, "Don't you find that image comforting?" She replied, "Not at all! If I need that kind of protection, what kind of monster is after me?"

The truth is, we are in a spiritual war, and our souls are being contested for. With God's grace, and with the wisdom of the saints to guide us, we can protect ourselves and not end up as soul food for the enemy.

This excerpt from St. Peter's epistle puts me in mind of #14 of St. Ignatius Loyola's Rules for Discernment. In that rule he writes, "The enemy behaves as a chief bent on conquering and robbing what he desires: for, just as a captain and chief of the army, pitching his camp, and looking at the forces or defenses of a stronghold, attacks it on the weakest side, in like manner the enemy of human nature, roaming about, looks in turn at all our virtues, theological, cardinal, and moral; and where he finds us weakest and most in need for our eternal salvation, there he attacks us and aims at taking us."

In other words, a chain is only as strong as its weakest link. The enemy will probe our defenses, and invade us at our most vulnerable point. So, what do we do about it? We could panic, and wait helplessly for the attack. Or, we can anticipate the attack and thereby discourage the invasion. With honesty, humility, and prayer, we can find our own weak link. It might be a habit of self-indulgence, or weakness of faith, or lack of charity, for example. Whatever it is, we have to find that vulnerable spot and reinforce it. Wherever we are weak, we need to work against the weakness, build it up into a strength, fortified with grace and virtue.

So, your spiritual homework for today is to take time out in prayer and reflection. Ask God to reveal to you your weakest point in your defense against the enemy. Prayerfully, make a concrete plan to strengthen that weak link. And then get to work, remembering that the enemy is a coward and a bully, and will not attack what is well defended.

May God's Holy Name be praised now and forever.

Will You Run Away?

Seventh Monday of Easter, Lectionary 297
Ave Maria, FL, 2008

Acts 19:1-8
Psalm 68
John 16:29-33

"Behold, the hour is coming and has arrived when each of you will be scattered to his own home and you will leave me alone."

The sad truth is that like the Apostles, we too, at one time or another, have scattered, and deserted the Lord. The truth of it, the horror of that fact, would be unbearable if it were not for the mercy of God. After the Resurrection, Jesus always greets the Apostles with the words, "Peace be with you." Who could have dared hope for such mercy?

This is a hard time of the year for a university community. We're all under stress. It's easy to panic, or to worry ourselves sick by trying to anticipate every contingency, to plan for absolutely everything that could go wrong. I recall what the philosopher Camus said: "Any idiot can survive a crisis. It's the little things that will drive you crazy." We can go mad worrying about the little things, and we can let the big things crush us. We can convince ourselves that we are fighting our battles alone, that there is no help or hope for us. And in that moment, we are scattered and we leave the Lord alone. In other words, if we want to have the faith that moves mountains, we must focus on the mountain mover and not on the mountain.

Jesus said, "In the world you will have trouble."

The poet William Butler Yeats said,

"Things fall apart; the centre cannot hold;
Mere anarchy is loosed upon the world,
The blood-dimmed tide is loosed, and everywhere
The ceremony of innocence is drowned;
The best lack all conviction, while the worst
Are full of passionate intensity."

We have a choice. We can panic and run away from the Lord. Or we can choose to remember and act upon the words of Jesus who said, "Take courage, I have conquered the world." Whatever the world can throw at us, it does not have to separate us from God. The Cross of Christ reaches beneath it all, and the Resurrection rises above it. We are on the winning side, simply awaiting the distribution of the spoils.

Let's get practical. This week, you will be fighting a battle mostly in your mind, as you take your final exams. That's why St. Paul said, "Put on the helmet of salvation" and "Hold every thought captive for Christ." We will be tempted to tell ourselves that the pain and burden are unbearable and that this misery will last forever. We will be tempted to tell ourselves to obey our fear, because God cannot be trusted. All of that is a lie. Crowd out the lies with truth. Remind yourself of all the times that God has been faithful to you in the past. That God is still in charge. Do what is humanly possible, and commend the rest to God. Stay in the present. Focus on the present grace to meet the present challenge and leave the rest to God. There's a wonderful story of Pope John XXIII. He said that before he went to bed, he'd pray, "Lord—it's your Church." Then he'd turn out the light and get a good night's sleep. Before you go to sleep tonight, bury the day in God's mercy.

My friends, we're all stressed and hurting right now. Let's promise to pray for each other in the coming days, that Christ's own peace, which Saint Paul says is beyond all understanding, may reign in our hearts.

May God's Holy Name be praised now and forever.

A Useless Gift?

Pentecost Sunday, Lectionary 63
Ave Maria, FL, 2013

Acts 2:1-11
Psalm 104:1, 24, 29-30, 31, 34
Romans 8:8-17
John 20:19-23

What is the most unexpected and apparently useless gift you have ever received? When a friend got engaged, one present she received was a set of salt and pepper shakers, in the shape of a maid and a butler, and when you used them, they played the classic Elvis Presley song "Love Me Tender." That, I suspect, is not a gift that anyone would think of asking for.

I mention this because today we at least *acknowledge*, if not outright *celebrate*, the Solemnity of Pentecost and the giving of the Holy Spirit to the Church. Can we really celebrate the giving of a gift that we do not quite understand, are not quite convinced that we need, and do not really know how to use? Can we even describe the gift of the Holy Spirit? If pressed, what would we say to anyone wanting to know about the presence and functions of the

Holy Spirit in our lives? Could we really say, "Gosh! The Holy Spirit is just great! I couldn't live without it! Sometimes I use the Holy Spirit as many as five times a day!" I am not sure that we could say even that. But I am sure that we need to rethink our attitude regarding the presence and power of the Holy Spirit in our lives. I say that because of what Saint Paul wrote about the Holy Spirit in his letter to the Romans. Let's listen to that again.

Saint Paul writes: "Those who are in the flesh cannot please God. But you are not in the flesh; on the contrary, you are in the spirit, if only the Spirit of God dwells in you. Whoever does not have the Spirit of Christ does not belong to him." So says Saint Paul.

Saint Paul makes clear that we will surely die if we remain in the flesh, if we remain in our state of fallen rebellion against God, and he makes clear that the only lasting life is new life in Christ in the power of the Holy Spirit. So we have to ask ourselves—are we more alive than dead, or are we more dead than alive? Are we more in the flesh, or more in the Spirit? I think today's Solemnity of Pentecost is a gift for us because it reminds us that until we enter the glory of Heaven, until that time, the world, the flesh, and the devil have a grip on us, and therefore we must cry out daily for the gift of the Holy Spirit.

We must cry out and proclaim to God and to the world and to ourselves that we need the Holy Spirit. We need a deeper release of the Holy Spirit. We need a generous and fragrant anointing of the Holy Spirit. We need to be caught up in the white hot heat of the Holy Spirit.

We need the Holy Spirit because life is so hard; we need the Holy Spirit because life is so good. We need the Holy Spirit because we are miserable sinners; we need the Holy Spirit because we must be saints. We need the Holy Spirit because we are foolish; we need the Holy Spirit because we must be wise. We need the Holy Spirit because we live as orphans; we need the Holy Spirit because we are adopted heirs to a Kingdom. We need the Holy Spirit because we live in darkness; we need the Holy Spirit because we are called to be the light of the world.

How shall we mark the Solemnity of Pentecost here at Ave Maria in the year 2013? We have a choice. We can mark it with a shrug of the shoulders, a polite nod of the head, and a perfunctory "thank you" to God for an apparently useless "gift"—a gift inexplicably depicted as a bird and a flame.

Or....we can try something different this year. We can begin, for a change, by admitting our need. We need the Holy Spirit because we are surrounded by human beings just like us, people who can appear to act almost like demons and nearly like angels. We need the Holy Spirit because we can drag each other into Hell or rally each other to join the long pilgrimage into Heaven. This year, for a change, we can offer heartfelt praise for the amazing gift of the Holy Spirit—the breath, fire, and peace of God that can carry us from this life to the next. This year, for a change, we can be good stewards of the amazing grace of the Holy Spirit entrusted to our care. We can do so by giving as a gift to our neighbor what we have received as a gift from God. And this year, for a change, we can mark Pentecost by making a conscious choice to live, as Saint Paul taught us, no longer in the flesh but in the Spirit.

What would our lives look like, as individuals and as a community, if we were living in the Spirit? And how shall we know? How shall we know whether we are living in the flesh or living in the Spirit? One sure sign that we are in the flesh and not in the Spirit is if there is a lack of Christian charity among us. If we lack Christian charity, then we would not look for the best in each other but rather would expect the worst. Lacking Christian charity, we would presume to know each other's intentions rather than give each other the benefit of the doubt. Lacking Christian charity, we would continue to cannibalize each other through gossip and detraction rather than defend one another's good name and reputation.

Lacking Christian charity, living in the flesh, is a luxury that we can no longer afford. I say that because I believe that storms are coming—storms more devastating and longer lasting than anything the hurricane season can throw at us. We may soon find ourselves living in a culture wherein faithful Catholics are not tolerated.

To be ready for the coming storms, we must be in the Spirit, and by the Spirit alone can we be knit together as members of the Body of Christ. I believe that we here at Ave Maria have the burden and the privilege of being called to a great mission. When the storms come, we must keep the fire burning. When the storms rage, we must ensure that the light of faith and the light of reason are not snuffed out. Anointed by the Holy Spirit, we can and must learn to live together so well that the doors of the Oratory and the library remain open, even when cold, hard winds blow against them.

We must beg God for a deeper release of the Holy Spirit within us and among us so that, knit together as members of the Body of Christ, we can continue to hand on the blessings of nature and of grace. We must learn to live together so well that even during the storms, we will know how to offer living water for Baptism and clean water for drinking. We must learn to live together so well that even during the storms, we can offer at this altar the Living Bread from Heaven and the daily bread made by our own hands. We must learn to live together so well that even during the storms, we can provide hope and healing for those wounded in soul and in body.

Anointed by the Holy Spirit, we can live together so well that we can generously and gladly perform the spiritual and the corporal works of mercy. Brought to life in the Holy Spirit, we can learn to live together so well that no one among us will ever go unloved or unfed. In the power of the

Holy Spirit, we can learn to live together so well that Ave Maria will become a community wherein body and soul may be safe. All this, I believe, is the mission, the path, the goal being entrusted to us here at Ave Maria. This great task is what the Holy Spirit can equip us for in our time and place, in our parish, university, and town. I believe this—and I expect that you believe it too.

So, now what? What shall we do to mark the Solemnity of Pentecost here at Ave Maria, in the year 2013? How shall we prove to ourselves, to God, and to the world that our Lord offered us no "useless gift" when the Holy Spirit was poured out upon the Church? Today, and for every day until the Feast of Corpus Christi, I will ask us all to focus on three tasks. I will ask us to pray, to prepare, and to provide. Let us pray for a deeper release of the Holy Spirit within and among all of us here at Ave Maria. Let us prepare to offer, to the best of our ability, the spiritual and corporal works of mercy. And let us provide for the needs, weaknesses, and potential of our neighbors. If we do that, if we learn to pray, prepare, and provide together, then we will joyfully recall these words of Saint Paul which we heard this morning: "…those who are led by the Spirit of God are sons of God. For you did not receive a spirit of slavery to fall back into fear, but you received a Spirit of adoption, through whom we cry, 'Abba, Father!'"

May God's Holy Name be praised now and forever.

Ordinary Time

Follow Me

First Monday of Ordinary Time, Lectionary 305
Ave Maria, FL, 2011

Hebrews 1:1-6
Psalm 97
Mark 1:14-20

Which emotions do we usually associate with our reading of the gospels? We may expect to feel sorrow when we read of our Lord's suffering, and we may expect to feel elation when we read of His resurrection. Less obvious, but no less real, I believe, is a feeling of envy when we read the gospels. Let's look again at today's gospel passage and see if we can't find in it at least a near occasion of envy. Mark writes: "Jesus said to them, 'Come after me, and I will make you fishers of men.'"

Aren't we at least slightly tempted to feel a twinge of envy? Jesus walks right up to Simon and Andrew and says, "Follow me." It's definitely Jesus talking to them. And His call to them is simple, obvious, and unambiguous. Just like our lives, right? Only not really….we have to discern, we have to ask, "Is it really the voice of the Lord I'm hearing? Am I hearing Him correctly? Am I being deceived?" And

Simon and Andrew did nothing to earn that clarity! They didn't make holy hours or novenas or nine first Fridays or pilgrimages to Lourdes! How come Simon and Andrew got their vocation clarity on the cheap when we've been trying so hard? Sounds like envy, doesn't it?

If we look again, we can see yet another near occasion of envy. Mark uses these words to describe the response of Simon and Andrew to the Lord's call: "Then they left their nets and followed Him." They just dropped everything at once and ran after Jesus. They didn't have to fill out an application or be interviewed or take a test or get letters of reference or submit a resume or get a scholarship or apply for a grant or pay off their student loans or ask their parents' permission. They just dropped their nets and followed Jesus. It was so easy for them and it's so hard for us! Who wouldn't envy them their freedom and availability?

Reading today's gospel passage through the eyes of envy is both very understandable and it's also very wrong. Mark did not write that Simon and Andrew had never met Jesus before. Mark did not write that Jesus was unacquainted with Simon and Andrew. Mark did say that Jesus had come to Galilee proclaiming the gospel. They must have heard Jesus preach. They must have met with Him and talked with Him and gotten to know Him. In other words, Jesus, Simon, and Andrew, all truly human, needed time to get to know each other in order to have an effect on each other.

How do we know this for certain? Listen again to what Jesus said to Simon and Andrew: "Come after me, and I will make you fishers of men." I will make you fishers of men. Not "and you will instantly become fishers of men." Jesus, truly divine and truly human, knew that humans are changed over time, not instantly. Jesus called Simon and Andrew because He knew them. Simon and Andrew were able to hear the call of the Lord so clearly, and were able to respond so promptly, freely, and fully, because they knew Him. And they got to know each other over time.

That means there is no reason to envy Simon and Andrew for the clarity or their freedom. Their clarity and freedom, while surely gifts of grace, were also the fruit of time spent with Jesus. And that's the moral of the story for us. Jesus can become known to us; we can hear His voice clearly; we can be truly obedient to His call, on the condition that we give Him time, as Simon and Andrew did.

It's a new calendar year; it's a new semester. It's time for resolutions. Let's resolve that starting this week, we will choose to give Jesus our best time and attention, so that we can know His voice and answer His call.

Saints Peter and Andrew, pray for us!

May God's Holy Name be praised now and forever.

"They Have No Wine"

Second Sunday of Ordinary Time, Lectionary 66
Ave Maria, FL, 2013
Isaiah 62:1-5
Psalm 96:1-2, 2-3, 7-8, 9-10
1 Corinthians 12:4-11
John 2:1-11

What do you think of when you hear the words "bad news"? Do you think of a doctor saying, "cancer"? Do you think of a boss saying, "fired"? Do you think of a professor saying, "failure"? What is the worst news you could be told? Would that news involve the word "death"? What if I told you that perhaps the worst news you can hear is, "They have no wine"? Would you think that I am crazy, or merely that I like wine just a bit too much?

In the Psalms, wine is spoken of as a gift from God to gladden men's hearts; wine is a sign of joy. Its presence suggests festivity and delight. If we understand wine in that way, how shall we then understand these words of Mary: "They have no wine"? Sinless Mary knows the sorrows that afflict the sinful human heart. She knows, as do we, when we are honest, that sin robs us of the joy that God intends for us.

But what is that joy? Joy is the delight one has when in the presence of the beloved. We readily speak, for example, of the joy of a newly married couple. I think that we speak easily, but most often theoretically rather than concretely, of the joy of the Christian. Now, let's be honest: Do you run into joyful Christians on a daily basis? Me neither. I'm not pointing fingers, I'm just making observations, and I began this morning's observations by looking in the mirror, and I can tell you that what I saw there did not look a whole lot like joy.

I will say it again: Joy is the delight one has when in the presence of the beloved. *Our* beloved, the beloved of each us and all of us, is God our Lord. God alone is the only hope we have of our hearts being full; only when we delight in God can we ever honestly say, "You know, it doesn't get any better than this!" Only in union with God can we rightly say, "You are truly enough for me." Any other love, any other delight, however good and beautiful, is just a pointer to the heart's fullness that God offers us when He offers us Himself. For the human soul, there is only one true, lasting joy, and that is the delight that comes from union with our beloved, the heart for which our hearts were made, which is that of God alone.

Now we can see the sorrow and, yes, the horror of the words, "They have no wine," when we understand that these words really mean, "They have no joy." Those without joy are those not united, not in contact with their true beloved, Who is God. Apart from union with God, human life has a God-sized hole that nothing and no one can fill. Not even everything and everyone could fill that hole in just one human heart.

So, let's hear those words again and shudder: "They have no wine." *They have no joy.* Their hearts are empty. Their souls can find no rest. As we look at the world around us, we can see the horrible effects of joylessness. There are people who run from one thrill to the next, one idol to the next, looking for something or someone to fill their emptiness. They run around looking for anyone or anything to at least distract them from their heartache. And, as we have been recently reminded, there are those joyless souls who thrash out in murderous rage, wanting the whole world to feel their pain and anguish.

Into this world that sometimes seems bent on suicide, into the human condition which appears to be resolutely tragic, into our world and into our human life, enters Jesus, the Christ, Who is Son of God and son of Mary. He takes on the full weight of human weakness, He takes in the full power of human malice, and breaks them in His Body on the Cross; and He transforms them as He emerges victorious from His tomb. In doing so, He opens for us the gates of Heaven, the path to our Father's Heart and our heavenly home, where already a banquet is prepared for us. And He offers to guide us by His Spirit all the way home. That is why Christians may be both hopeful for the future and joyful in the present, because God Who is the only satisfaction of the human heart has embraced us as we walk home to Him.

But, sometimes, at least sometimes, might it not be said of us, of us who are in these pews or in this pulpit, might it not be said of us at least sometimes, "They have no wine"? *They have no joy.* Friedrich Nietzsche, that acutely observant philosophical madman, said of the Christians he had met, "They should look more redeemed." Cannot the same be said of us? At least sometimes? We do not have to appear giddy all the time—I myself would find such a requirement to be exhausting—but should not our joy be evident in the way that we extend to others the divine mercy that we have received? Should not our joy be evident in the way we cheerfully offer service in gratitude for the gifts God has given us? Should not our joy be evident, at least sometimes, in the charitable way we speak of one another, we, who are made in the image and likeness of the one true God? I think it should, at least sometimes. But does it?

Now, please do not misunderstand me. Only Disney World claims to be "The Happiest Place on Earth," so I do not ask that the town of Ave Maria change its name to "Joyville." But my hard question—first asked of myself and now addressed to all present—is this: If we cannot find or show joy now, while we are still free and well fed, how shall we bear witness in times of persecution or peril?

You see, this is my concern: We are already so abundantly provided for and blessed here at Ave Maria, as citizens, as Catholics, as neighbors, and as friends. Why then are we not renowned for our joy, a joy expressed in mercy, service, charity, and compassion? If we cannot find joy in delighting in God our beloved now, what shall our Christian witness be like when hunger or harm presses against us? Now, while there is still time and opportunity, we must sink the roots of our hearts and minds into the goodness of God our beloved. Now, while we still have freedom and strength to do so, we must order our lives to embrace God our Lord Who constantly reaches out to us and calls us to Himself. Now is the time to cast down our idols, surrender our misplaced priorities, and toss aside all of our distractions, so that we might be free to give to God all of who we are, and to receive from Him all that we are meant to be.

I believe that we must not become complacent. We must not think that we have any time but today to become the community of disciples that Ave Maria can and should become. In our time, we can work now to become an oasis and a beacon, a home of faith, hope, and love in a culture that is succumbing to soul sickness and mental madness. We, as a community of Christian disciples, have been entrusted with truth and faith, a library and an oratory; we have been entrusted with land and water; we have been entrusted with neighbors and children. Among us we can decide that here the light shall not go out. We ourselves, in response to God's providence and mercy, can decide to live, study, and pray together so well, so faithfully, so gratefully, that no one here could lack what is needed for human and Christian dignity. And the measure of our fidelity, the proof of our good stewardship of all of God's blessings here, is whether we live our lives with joy.

If not today, then very, very soon, we must decide what kind of people we will become. If we want it enough to work for it, together, we can become a people made by God and made for God. Here, as citizens and as members of the Church founded by Christ, we can become, as the prophet said, Zion—God's holy people; we can become Jerusalem—God's holy city. We can become a community that people will turn to for light and refuge in times of darkness and danger. That is why I urge all here to spend some time today committing to memory the words of the prophet Isaiah that we heard today. Let's listen again to his words: "For Zion's sake I will not be silent, for Jerusalem's sake I will not be quiet, until her vindication shines forth like the dawn and her victory like a burning torch." So says the prophet Isaiah.

Therefore, we must not tire of calling all here to learn how to live together so well, so providently, so faithfully, that our lives together could only be described as a victory of the grace of God, a shining victory that people in darkness will need to see.

Our Christian discipleship, lived fully, gratefully, and joyfully, can feed, teach, and protect people who are without hope in this life, and who are without expectation of the life to come. What do I mean by that? Consider these words from G.K. Chesterton. He said, "This is something much more mystical and absolute than any modern thing that is called optimism; for it is only rarely that we realize, like a vision of the heavens filled with a chorus of giants, the primeval duty of praise." So wrote Chesterton.

That duty of praise which Chesterton spoke of is fulfilled by a heart singing for joy, it is found in worship expressed in awe at the altar and publicly proved by service in the world. Christians are to offer a song of praise, a gift of compassion, because they know that God has given them the wine of gladness, the joy of knowing that their hearts may become full to overflowing. We disciples of Christ can become, with God's grace and with one another, a community of faith that the world cannot ignore, dismiss, or forget.

I know that these words are difficult to say and difficult to hear; they are perhaps even more difficult to live. How then, concretely, specifically, shall we live these words in our own lives, as these real individuals in these pews, as this man in this pulpit? And what, exactly, would keep us from putting these words into practice? What lies, wounds, or illusions would keep us from acting on the Word of God we have heard? If we are to do what we have been told this day, then let us agree to embrace three tasks, three tasks that will make demands on us and liberate us if we embrace them. First, let's take time—time to note the lack of joy in our lives. Second, let's take time—time to consider the joy God wishes us to have. Third, let's take time—time to plan how our emptiness and God's fullness may meet. If we turn the hunger of our souls to the only thing that will fill our souls, which of course is God, then we will be made full, then we will delight in our beloved, then we will have the joy for which we were made. And then it may never again be said of us, "They have no wine."

May God's Holy Name be praised now and forever.

How Good Is Your Hearing?

Third Sunday of Ordinary Time, Lectionary 68
Ave Maria, FL, 2012

Jonah 3:1-5, 10
Psalm 25:4-5, 6-7, 8-9
1 Corinthians 7:29-31
Mark 1:14-20

Do you want to hear a story? In the early 20th century, a group of Anglican missionaries decided that they would imitate Jonah, and call towns and villages to conversion. They decided to go to rural China to carry out their plan. They went from place to place, standing in the center of gatherings of people. They attracted a lot of attention, because, in rural China in the early twentieth century, these missionaries of the Church of England were clearly rare, foreign, and exotic. Then they would read John 3:16 out loud and ask if anyone wanted to be baptized. They never got any takers. The missionaries would leave, disheartened, wondering why Jonah was able to call the entire city of Nineveh to conversion, and they could not get one single convert.

These well-intentioned missionaries overlooked one

factor. The Chinese people they met in China spoke Chinese; the missionaries were announcing the gospel in English. They were announcing something that no one but they themselves could hear, understand, and act upon.

That story got me to thinking about hearing. I've seen parents stand at the edge of a playground occupied by dozens of screaming kids, and they can pick out the voice of their own child and filter out the words and yells of all the other kids. I don't know how they do that; it must be a grace that you get when you bring a child into the world.

Not only can parents hear children in a way that I cannot, they can understand what the child says in a way that I am unable. To me, every child's cry sounds the same. I'm the kind of person who thinks that if the baby burps we should call 911. Not so for the experienced parent.

When I'm visiting with my sister in Orlando, it is inevitable that one of her little girls will be screaming at any given moment. When I hear my little niece Brigid yell, "AAAAAHH!!", I jump up, ready to respond to a life-and-death crisis. And my sister will say, "It's ok, she's just mad because she's not getting her way." A few minutes later, and Brigid will yell, "AAAAAHH!!", and I jump up, ready to respond to a life-and-death crisis. And my sister will say, "It's ok, she's just cranky because she's overtired." And a few minutes after that, little Brigid will yell, "AAAAAHH!!", and I, thinking I've finally figured out how this game is played, I just sit there. But my sister is on her feet in an instant, running to her daughter while yelling at me, "How can you just sit there? She's crying because she's hurt!" But it all sounds the same to me—the cry of anger, the cry of cranky, and the cry of pain are indistinguishable to me. But that shouldn't be surprising to anyone, because I don't live with a bunch of crying preschoolers, and have never had the need to know how to speak toddler. I don't have much need to learn what little kids are saying by their screams and cries, so I'm not much use to them when they do scream and cry.

I can hear them, but I can't interpret what they say, because I don't understand them. And because I can't understand them, I can't act on what they say.

Hearing, understanding, acting: These words bring us to the account of the conversion of the city of Nineveh by the preaching of Jonah. Whatever language the people of Nineveh spoke, Jonah spoke it too. They could understand Jonah. But even more importantly, they understood at least something about God. They must have understood something of God's sovereignty, goodness, justice, and mercy, because when Jonah preached God's warning, the people repented. Because they could hear and understand rightly, the people of Nineveh could act rightly when God spoke to them through Jonah.

Hearing, understanding, acting: These words also bring us to Jesus' calling of the fishermen in the Gospel of Mark. We would be mistaken if we think that Peter and the others had never heard Jesus before He called them out of their boats. Some of them were disciples of John the Baptist and would have witnessed the baptism of Jesus. They all would have heard Jesus preach in Galilee. And although they did not yet know the full truth about Jesus, they heard something from Him that touched their mind and hearts so deeply, that they understood that they must drop everything when He called them by name. They could understand already that Jesus was sent by God, and they understood, perhaps only dimly then, that Jesus was more than just another prophet. They heard, they understood, and they acted.

All right then—what about us? All this talk about hearing and Nineveh and Galilee and fishermen—what does this have to do with us? Well, now it is our turn. It is our turn to join the ranks of those who hear, or join the ranks of those who do not hear. It is our turn to join those who understand, or join those who do not understand. And perhaps most significantly, it is our turn to join those who act, or join those who do not act. For as Jonah spoke to the people of Nineveh, as Jesus of Nazareth called the apostles, so now Jesus Christ the Risen Lord speaks to us.

Christ Who is the Word of the Father is always speaking to us. Are we alert enough to hear and wise enough to understand? In each sunrise, can we hear Christ say, "Behold! I make all things new!"? In the Sacred Scriptures can we hear Christ say, "I am the way, the truth, and the life!"? In the Eucharist, can we hear Christ say, "Take and eat"? In our neighbor, can we hear Christ say, "I thirst"? And in the silence of our heart, can we hear Christ say, "Follow me"?

Christ Who is the Word of the Father is always speaking to us. Can we hear Him? If we hear Him, do we understand Him? If we understand Him, will we act on what He says? Today, and for each day this week, I ask that you will pray for three graces, for three special blessings. First, pray for alertness, that you might hear Christ when He speaks to you. Second, pray for wisdom, that you might understand Christ when He speaks to you. Third, pray for obedience, that you might act when Christ speaks to you. If we do that, if we pray and live to hear, understand, and act, then we will be telling the truth when we join the psalmist and pray: "Teach me your ways, O Lord."

May God's Holy Name be praised now and forever.

The Sin Against the Holy Spirit

Third Monday of Ordinary Time, Lectionary 317
Ave Maria, FL, 2011
Hebrews 9:15, 24-28
Psalm 98
Mark 3:22-30

If I were the mortal enemy of scrupulous people, I would wish to torment them constantly and allow them not a moment's peace. And one of the ways I would torture such poor souls is to beat them about the head and shoulders with these words of Jesus: "Amen, I say to you, all sins and all blasphemies that people utter will be forgiven them. But whoever blasphemes against the Holy Spirit will never have forgiveness, but is guilty of an everlasting sin."

If I were the mortal enemy of scrupulous people, I would lay the groundwork by convincing them that at any moment, they could unintentionally, accidentally, commit a mortal sin. I would convince them that God, in His inscrutable Providence, had spread puddles and pockets of invisible grave matter everywhere, and that at any moment, a deed, a word, a thought might trip them up and land them head first into a pool of grave matter, thereby committing a mortal sin, and leaving their salvation in peril.

If I were the mortal enemy of scrupulous people, I would want to nail shut their escape hatch, which is the door to the confessional. I would tell them about a sin so horrible that it cannot be forgiven. And—best of all—no one really knows what that sin is! It has such a vague name, "the sin against the Holy Spirit," that it can be taken to refer to anything or everything! What could be better for driving a scrupulous person insane than an unforgiveable sin that has no definite description? Any thought, word, or deed, done or undone or partly done or unconsciously done could qualify as the unforgiveable sin!

But since I am not the mortal enemy of scrupulous people, and am, in fact, a pastor of souls who also has pity on beleaguered spiritual directors and confessors, I will dare to take up the question of the sin against the Holy Spirit referred to in today's gospel.

We must begin by remembering that Jesus could not have used the phrase 'the Holy Spirit' in the full Christian sense of the term. The Spirit in all His fullness did not come until Jesus had returned to His glory. It was not until Pentecost that there came to men and women the supreme experience of the Holy Spirit. Jesus must have used the term in the Jewish sense of the term. Now in Jewish thought the Holy Spirit had two great functions. First, He revealed God's truth; second, He enabled that truth to be recognized. That will give us the key to this passage. The Holy Spirit enabled men and women to recognize God's truth when it entered their lives. But if people refuse to exercise any God-given faculty they will in the end lose it. If they live in the dark long enough they will lose the ability to see. If they stay in bed long enough they will lose the power to walk. If they refuse to do any serious study they will lose the power to study. And if people refuse the guidance of God's Spirit often enough they will become in the end incapable of recognizing that truth when they see it. In their eyes, evil becomes good and good evil. They can look on the goodness of God and call it the evil of Satan.

There is only one condition of forgiveness and that is penitence. As long as people see loveliness in Christ, as long as they hate sin, they can still be forgiven. But if people, by repeated refusals of God's guidance, have lost the ability to recognize goodness when they see it, if they have gotten their moral values inverted until evil to them is good and good to them is evil, then, even when they are confronted by Jesus, they are conscious of no sin; they cannot repent and therefore they can never be forgiven. That is the sin against the Holy Spirit.

The good news of the today's gospel, then, for scrupulous souls and for everyone else, is that as long as any desire for God is alive in our hearts, then we have not committed an unforgiveable sin, we have not blasphemed against the Holy Spirit.

But it is not enough to say that. To stop there is to leave the door open to the idea that Christian discipleship is primarily about sin management. No! Christian discipleship is above all about growing into the image and likeness of Christ. If we allow God to form us into the image of His Son, and strive to take on His mind and heart and will, then sin will inevitably get crowded out. If above all we seek to love as Christ loves, to love those whom Christ loves—that is, everyone—then we can have a bright hope for the happiness of heaven, and we can echo each day the words of today's psalm: "Sing to the LORD a new song, for he has done wondrous deeds."

May God's Holy Name be praised now and forever.

Why Are Christians Persecuted?

Fourth Sunday of Ordinary Time, Lectionary 70
Ave Maria, FL, 2011

Zephaniah 2:3, 3:12-13
Psalm 146
1 Corinthians 1:26-31
Matthew 5:1-12a

Would you be surprised if I told you that I'm still thinking about Christmas? This past Christmas was extra special for me, because I was able to watch my two year old niece, named Teigan, as she for the first time encountered Christmas with some understanding. She knew that Christmas had something to do with someone named Jesus, and she knew Christmas had something to do with birthdays and babies. And she must have seen some image of "swaddling," even if she didn't know what swaddling meant. I say that because Teigan took her favorite doll, which wore bright pink pajamas and was given the highly original name of "Dolly," and she wrapped Dolly in a blanket and called the doll "Baby Jesus." I will be keen to see how much more she understands of Christmas next year, when she is three years old.

Watching Teigan encounter Christmas got me to thinking about who Jesus Christ is for us, not in terms of theology or of dogmatic formulas, as important as they are, but who Jesus Christ is for us in a very practical, everyday way. Who we believe Jesus Christ really is for us can be seen in how we live with Him in our daily lives.

For example, Jesus Christ can be for us our expletive, if we shout out His name after we hit our thumb with a hammer. Christ can be for us our insurance agent, whom we call upon when we want protection for something we cherish. Christ can be for us the clerk at the complaint desk of the customer service department, as we berate Him whenever our egos are bruised.

But there is a problem in viewing Christ that way. If Jesus Christ for us is merely on call, useful when we need Him and forgettable when we don't, then the Beatitudes of Saint Matthew's Gospel don't make a lot of sense. Let's listen again to this line in particular: "Blessed are you when they insult you and persecute you and utter every kind of evil against you falsely because of me. Rejoice and be glad, for your reward will be great in heaven." If Jesus is just a convenient tool, if He is just some celestial concierge we call upon to set things right and then dismiss Him when we're done with Him, then being persecuted for His sake seems unlikely and rejoicing in being persecuted for His sake seems bizarre.

Only if Christ is the archenemy of Satan, only if Christ is the first cause of all true human joy and fulfillment, only if Christ is the completion of our Heavenly Father's will for us, only then would the world and its prince of darkness wish to insult, slander, and persecute His followers. In other words, it simply doesn't make sense for the disciples of Christ to be hated if Jesus is just some Handy Heavenly Helper.

So we have to ask ourselves some difficult questions: Who is Christ, really, if His disciples can rejoice over their inevitable persecution? And do we know Christ well enough to be the kind of disciples worthy of persecution? Are we united with Christ well enough to be able to rejoice over persecution for the Kingdom of Heaven? If we wish to know and love Christ, the true Christ, as He has revealed Himself and as the Church proclaims Him, then we would do well to turn to the words of Saint Paul. Let's listen again to these words to the Corinthians. Paul wrote: "Christ Jesus, who became for us wisdom from God, as well as righteousness, sanctification, and redemption…"

Paul teaches us that Christ is the wisdom of God. Jesus Christ is the expert in human life. If we wish to live wisely, if we wish to live our human vocation well, if we want to get right what it means to be human, we must turn to Jesus Christ, and learn to think as He thinks, love as He loves, and obey as He obeys.

Paul teaches us that Christ is our righteousness. We can receive from Jesus what we need most, which is a right relationship with God. That right relationship is a gift from Christ, won for us by His Cross and Resurrection, and offered freely to all who would receive it. Christ is the bridge we must walk if we wish to proceed to the home of our Heavenly Father.

Paul teaches us that Christ is our sanctification. Only the pure can hope to stand before God. We cannot achieve that purity by human efforts to remain sinless, no matter how hard we try. Only receiving Christ, only being washed in His shed Blood, can prepare us for the union with God for which we were made.

Paul teaches us that Christ is our redemption. Only Jesus Christ, Who is Son of God and Son of Mary—only He can redeem us from past sin, from present helplessness, and from future fear. Only Christ crucified and risen, only Christ our victorious King, can liberate us from slavery to self and slavery to sin.

That's a lot to remember, isn't it? Memory alone won't

help us to remember it, especially when we need to remember it most. The best way to remember what Saint Paul taught us in today's Scriptures is to live it. To help us live what Paul has taught, I will ask you to pray today and throughout the week for three graces, for three special blessings.

First, pray to see, to see Jesus Christ as He truly is. Second, pray to see, to see ourselves as Christ sees us. Third, pray to see, to see the path we must walk with Christ to the home of our Heavenly Father.

If we do that, if we pray to see rightly Christ, ourselves, and our path, then we can join the Psalmist and proclaim to God and the world: "The LORD gives sight to the blind; the LORD raises up those who were bowed down."

May God's Holy Name be praised now and forever.

MARRIAGE AND CELIBACY

Fourth Sunday of Ordinary Time, Lectionary 71
Ave Maria, FL, 2009

Deuteronomy 18:15-20
Psalm 95
1 Corinthians 7:32-35
Mark 1:21-28

Well, this morning I'm going to do something that I've never done before from the pulpit. I'm going to start a homily with a quote from a Broadway musical. In the play "Annie Get Your Gun," the characters Annie Oakley and Frank Butler sing a duet called "Anything You Can Do." They sing back and forth against each other, "Anything you can do I can do better. I can do anything better than you. No, you can't! Yes, I can." On and on, back and forth.

That song came to mind as I read today's passage in First Corinthians. The passage seems like the basis of a squabble between the vocation of marriage and the celibate vocation, a squabble conducted with only slightly more dignity than making faces and saying "Nyah, nyah, nyah." With a little bit of confusion, a chip on one's shoulder, and a generous helping of ignorance, how might one hear the following words? "An unmarried man is anxious about the things of the Lord, how he may please the Lord. But a married man is anxious about the things of the world, how he may please his wife, and he is divided. An unmarried woman or a virgin is anxious about the things of the Lord, so that she may be holy in both body and spirit. A married woman, on the other hand, is anxious about the things of the world, how she may please her husband."

One can read that and say, "According to Saint Paul, the score is Celibacy–2, Marriage–0. Let the celibates do the happy dance, and let the married sulk. Tune in tomorrow for another episode of 'Why Catholics Hate Sex'." That's one way to read Saint Paul.

Do I exaggerate? Let's see. I recently read in an online Catholic journal an article on how to promote religious and priestly vocations. The author had a noteworthy suggestion. He suggested that we need to speak more openly about the unique blessings and joys of celibacy. In response to that suggestion, many readers posted indignant replies, asserting that even hinting that celibacy may afford goods not offered by marriage is highly offensive. Cue the music: "Anything you can do, I can do better. I can do anything better than you. No, you can't! Yes, I can…" On and on…

Really, that's not helpful. Rather than bickering about who has cornered the market on holiness, all of the faithful, regardless of their vocation, need to come to terms with the words of Saint Paul and begin to apply them to their lives and to the culture. We can do that with the aid of a handy little maxim of Scripture scholarship, namely, "Text without context is pretext for proof text." In other words, read in context, the words of Saint Paul cannot be used as a bludgeon against marriage or against those who honor celibacy. Let's take a look.

When Saint Paul wrote First Corinthians, he did so aware of the Mosaic law releasing a newly married man from the obligation of military service for one year. The intention and wisdom of that law are obvious. With that in his mind, Paul wrote First Corinthians while there was still the lively expectation that Jesus was coming back any minute now, so why start something that you're not going to be able to finish, with the end of the world right around the corner?

By the time Paul writes the Epistle to the Ephesians, the expectation that Jesus will return any minute has begun to recede. Paul instructs us that it looks like we're going to be here for a while, so we need to get on with our lives, while waiting in joyful hope for the Lord's return, whenever He may come. In that context, Paul writes the profound meditation on marriage in Ephesians chapter 5, depicting Christian marriage as an icon of the relationship between Christ and His Church.

Contrary to the claim that Paul and those influenced by him disdain marriage, which one might think if one reads First Corinthians ignorantly, we see that in God's providence Christian marriage is a vocation of beauty and dignity, and a great school of holiness. But if that's the case, now we have *another* problem, namely, if marriage is so good, then what could be good about celibacy? Indeed, there are some in Church circles who refer to celibacy as "part of the problem," requiring of the Church, "structural change." Or, as one priest told me when I was a student, "Nobody *chooses* celibacy—you just put up with it."

I want to be as clear as possible. Marriage and celibacy are complementary vocations. The Church needs both vocations, and needs more of both vocations. In fact, the whole world needs the witness of sacramental marriage and consecrated virginity. Indeed, in this New Reign of Herod, when practices contrary to life, chastity, marriage, and family are being written into law, married couples and vowed celibates need to ally themselves as witnesses to life, truth, mystery, and destiny.

Here's what I mean: The celibate points to the destination, the married point to the path. The celibate reminds us that every human love is incomplete, and our full happiness will be found only in our resurrected life in union with the Communion of Persons which is the Trinity. The celibate reminds us that there is life and an order of fruitfulness beyond this life. The married couple reminds us that the path to our destiny, the way home to the heart of God, is through mutual self-sacrifice, offering oneself to the beloved as a gift and receiving the beloved as a gift.

Aristotle said that bravery is found where bravery is honored. I believe that chastity will be found where chastity is honored. Where chastity is honored, there we will find both joyful and confident married couples and celibates, each in their own way helping us towards the glory for which God has made us.

Ok, nice words. But what shall we *do*? What shall we do now? At least three things. First, we need to pray. We need to pray for the grace to live the call to chastity with both internal and external purity and fidelity, whether we are single, married, or celibate. That is the path to the heart of God. Second, we need to study. I urge you to get a copy of a little book by Steven Kellmeyer with the unlikely title of "Sex and the Sacred City." It is a brief meditation on the theology of the body, and it is the most concise account of the harmony of marriage and celibacy I know of. Third, we need to act. We need to act to let confused Christians as well as the benighted and besotted world we live in know of God's plan for men and women. Write a letter to the editor, send an email to a friend, start a blog, form a reading group, call your senator, but do something, *something* to get the word out. We need to tell the truth that the body is sacramental, that sex is sacred, that male and female are complementary and not merely incidental; we need to tell the truth that no culture survives without strong marriage and family life and that celibacy reminds us that our destiny is not in this world but in the world to come.

If we so pray, study, and act, then perhaps in our own

time we will hear the words of today's gospel: "All were amazed and asked one another, 'What is this? A new teaching with authority! He commands even the unclean spirits and they obey Him.'"

May God's Holy Name be praised now and forever.

Salt and Light

Fifth Sunday of Ordinary Time, Lectionary 73
Ave Maria, FL, 2014
Isaiah 58:7-10
Psalm 112:4-5, 6-7, 8-9
1 Corinthians 2:1-5
Matthew 5:13-16

Do you want to hear a story? When my Italian grandmother, Teresa Formisano, made sauce for pasta, she was very careful to add just the right amount of salt. The curious thing about her adding salt was that she did not use a measuring cup. She would take the salt shaker in her right hand, spread the fingers of her left hand over the pot, and then pour salt back and forth, through her open fingers. Somehow, it worked. She was very careful about adding salt, because she knew that sauce without salt was inedible.

I think of Grandma seasoning with salt because of the gospel passage we just heard, wherein Jesus tells His disciples that they are called to be the salt of the earth and the light of the world. I will get to light in a moment, but for now, let's reflect on salt. We know that in the time of Jesus, salt represented purity, it was used for the preservation of food, and it was used in cooking to enhance flavor. I said before that Grandma knew that sauce without salt was inedible. What happens to the earth when Christians fail to be the salt of the earth?

Let me give you just two examples. A few months ago in a large city in Argentina, there was an annual conference of self-described "radical feminists." One night, these women decided to attack the local cathedral, in order to express their hatred for the Church and their enthusiasm for abortion. These women arrived at the cathedral, angry, shouting, not fully clothed, their bodies painted with obscene and blasphemous words and images.

Now, let's think about this for a moment. This took place in Argentina. That means it is almost a certainty that most if not all of these women attacking the cathedral were baptized Catholics. What happened, and what failed to happen, in the lives of these young women between the time of their baptism and their arrival at the cathedral that night?

This is not an isolated case. One night last week, in Madrid, a Cardinal arrived at the cathedral. A group of women who describe themselves as "sextremists," yelling obscenities, half-clad, painted in blasphemous words and images, attacked the Cardinal. They shouted and did things which I would not repeat in polite company, and certainly not in the presence of the Blessed Sacrament. This took place in Spain. So again I must say that it is almost a certainty that most if not all of these women attacking the cathedral were baptized Catholics. What happened, and what failed to happen, in the lives of these young women between the time of their baptism and their arrival at the cathedral that night?

The answer to that question is simple—no salt. There was no salt in their lives. The salt of Christian discipleship, the salt of disciples called to be the salt of the earth was not in their lives. Salt for purity, salt for the preservation of the faith, salt to help them savor the grace of God—that salt was not in their lives. Yes, I know that somewhere along the way, they used their own free will and made their own choices. To what degree these young women are responsible for the state they are in now is up for God to decide. But it must be true, it simply must be true that at some time in their lives, disciples of Christ failed to be the salt of the earth for these young women in Argentina and Spain. Whether family or friends, schools or parishes, it must be true that some disciples of Christ were not the salt of the earth that these young women needed and deserved. Somewhere in their lives, the salt had lost it savor. And look at what happened.

What about light? Jesus called His disciples to be the light of the world. There seemed to be a lack of salt during those dark nights in Argentina and Madrid—was there any light? In that city in Argentina, a group of young men heard that the cathedral was about to be overrun and desecrated. These young Catholic men, men with spine and spirit, ran to the cathedral, surrounded it, and locked arms with each other. There they stood, reciting the Rosary, refusing entrance to the vandals. The young women were enraged. They began chanting, *"El aborto es sagrado! La iglesia es basura! El aborto es sagrado! La iglesia es basura!"* "Abortion is sacred! The Church is garbage!"

These brave young men did not give ground. They were screamed at, spat upon, and hit. They had paint dumped on them. The vandals used black markers to draw on the faces of the young men. But they did not break ranks. They did not yield. They would not surrender the cathedral to those intent on desecrating it. These young men—these brave and good young men—I believe that they would be recognized and welcomed as brothers in Christ and comrades-in-arms by the likes of Charlemagne, the Knights of Malta, and Saint Edmond Campion and Saint Maximillian Kolbe. Chesterton would have written a poem about them. These young men were light in the midst of furious darkness; they were a bright line between sin and grace that declared, "This far and no farther!"

Was there also light that dark night in Madrid? Yes. When the Cardinal was attacked, men from within the cathedral rushed to his aid, and they shielded the Cardinal as the screaming young women threw verbal and physical filth at him. Amidst the chaos and the screaming, during that storm of shadows, there was one point of light.

A young woman emerged from within the cathedral. She stood at the doorway, framed in light from within the church. This small woman, seeing and hearing the ungodly rage of the assailants, began to sing. She started to sing the Salve Regina. As the shrieking women around her violently rejected the maternity of their womanhood, this one small woman invoked the Blessed Mother. As these enraged women assaulted a successor to the apostles, this one woman sang the praises of *the* woman, the woman whose heel is destined by God to crush the head of the serpent.

Was there light in the darkness that night in Madrid? Oh, yes. Yes indeed. Caravaggio would have painted that woman singing outside of the cathedral. One small light pierced the darkness, and the darkness did not overcome it. Why do I tell you these things this morning? I tell you because the gospel demands that we be indelibly clear about what life looks like when salt loses its savor, and that we be indelibly clear about the power of light to withstand the darkness. And I tell you this because now it is our turn. It is our turn to be the salt of the earth and light of the world because we cannot afford to do otherwise and because our Lord has commanded us to be salt and light.

How shall we do it? To be salt and light requires three commitments: prayer, preparation, and proclamation. What about prayer? Well, let's start by resolving to pray for those poor lost souls in Argentina and Madrid. Let's spiritually adopt them, and intercede for them; let's pray for their deliverance from evil and their restoration to reason and to grace.

We need to pray for ourselves. We need to breathe in the Spirit of God so that we can answer the Lord's call to be salt and light. We need to fast and sacrifice so that we can be the worthy stewards of the True, the Good, and the Beautiful that our Lord calls us to be. In prayer, with and for each other, let's resolve today that we will be salt and light so that no one in our care will be lost to the Lord.

Consider these words from the great nineteenth century British preacher Charles Spurgeon, who wrote: "If sinners be dammed, at least let them leap to hell over our bodies. If they will perish, let them perish with our arms about their knees. Let no one GO there UNWARNED and UNPRAYED for."

My friends, let's resolve here and now that we at Ave Maria will be, with God's grace, salt and light, in our community, parish, and schools. Especially, let's resolve that no one entrusted to our care will perish for lack of the salt and light we could have provided for them. We cannot afford to lose anyone.

Let's resolve today, here and now, to be salt and light, so that it will nearly impossible for any child of ours, any student of ours, to become the next Nancy Pelosi, the next Joe Biden, the next Kathleen Sebelius, the next Andrew Cuomo, or the next Ted Kennedy—God rest his soul. We cannot afford to raise a generation of traitors to the faith. We cannot afford to finance so-called Catholic institutions that embrace and cultivate such traitors.

Let's be salt and light together, locking arms like the young men in Argentina, invoking the Mother of God like that young woman in Madrid. Let's pray and pray and pray—with and for each other; let's pray for the lost and the nearly-lost; and let's pray especially for the young, that none of them go without the Christian salt and light that they need us to be.

I said that our second commitment to be salt and light was preparation. Here and now we must resolve to prepare for hardship, persecution, and chastisement. We must prepare by ordering our lives, equipping ourselves for the spiritual and corporal works of mercy. As salt and light, we must be provident stewards of the True, the Good, and the Beautiful. And so we must be ready to nourish and defend the bodies and souls of our families and neighbors and of all entrusted to our care.

The third commitment to be salt and light is proclamation. We must proclaim Christ and His gospel. We must proclaim that we will not compromise with darkness. We must proclaim that one way or another we will be faithful until the end. We cannot fail to do otherwise. We must be faithful until glorious victory or glorious death, until Christ returns to judge the living and the dead, and the world by fire. It must be so.

Salt of the earth and the light of the world. Prayer. Preparation. Proclamation. That seems like an awful lot of work, doesn't it? Is all that really necessary? Yes! Yes! It is what Christ commands! To be salt of the earth and the light of the world—that is our vocation! We dare not shirk. We dare not shrink back. We dare not ignore the seal and the summons Christ Himself has set upon us! Lives are at stake! Souls are at stake! The honor of the Bride of Christ is at stake! The glory of God is at stake! Let us be the humble, holy heroes our Lord calls us to be. What could be better than that?

We know what the Lord commands. We know that our vocation is to be the salt of the earth and the light of the world. We have always known it. Since the moment of our baptism that call has been echoing in our souls. We are liars, cowards, and traitors if we ignore it. We may become martyrs if we answer that call, but we will surely be welcomed into the company of Heaven, into the home of our Father, if we answer the Lord's call to be the salt of the earth and the light of the world.

Isn't all this just too much to take in all at once? Yes, very likely it is. So, as we prepare to offer ourselves with Christ at the altar, as we prepare to receive His Body, Blood, Soul, and Divinity, let's resolve to leave this holy place keeping in mind three points for prayer. The three points are these—imagine, desire, act. Imagine living fully as the salt of the earth and the light of the world; desire to live the good that you have imagined; act as the salt and light that you are called to be. If we do that, if we imagine, desire, and act as the salt of the earth and the light of the world, then lives will be saved, and souls will be saved, and—best of all—God will be glorified.

And remember this, remember this: both Heaven and Hell are watching, and both are waiting for us.

May God's Holy Name be praised now and forever.

Let Go

Sixth Friday of Ordinary Time, Lectionary 339

James 2:14-24, 26
Psalm 112
Mark 8:34—9:1

"Whoever wishes to save his life will lose it, but whoever loses his life for my sake and that of the Gospel will save it."

What could that mean? What do you think of when you hear about losing or saving your life? I think of drowning. I don't swim, so I have a great fear of drowning. In America, we have people called lifeguards at beaches and swimming pools. Their job is to rescue people who are starting to drown.

Being a lifeguard is a dangerous job. When the lifeguard comes near a drowning person, the person in danger may panic. He may be so eager to be rescued, so eager to be drawn out of the water, that he actually works against the efforts of the lifeguard.

If I were drowning, I would try to climb on top of the lifeguard and stand on his shoulders so that I could get out of the water as quickly as possible. But if I'm screaming, and climbing with my arms waving and my legs kicking, the lifeguard will have a hard time getting ahold of me. He will find it difficult to get his arms around me and take me to safety. He may have to knock me unconscious so that I will stop struggling and making things worse.

In order for the lifeguard to rescue me, I must relax; I must let go of my life, lose my life into his hands. That's my only hope, because I can't swim.

Most of us, when we think of losing our lives, we think of dying, perhaps dying as martyrs for the faith. Not many of us will be called upon to be martyrs in that way. But I believe that we are all called upon to let go of our lives into God's hands, lose our lives into God's hands. Like the drowning man who can't swim, the only way to be rescued from this "adulterous and sinful generation" is to let ourselves go into God's arms.

We struggle against God very often. We insist on doing things our way rather than His. We can resist His invitation to grace by trying to save ourselves. That will never work.

The best place to lose your life, the best place to let go of your life into God's hands, is right here at this Eucharist. We can lay down our lives with the sacrifice of Christ to the Father. We can put our bodies into the bread, our souls into the wine, and be offered up with Christ to the Father in a perfect sacrifice of praise. If we relax into the arms and heart of God, we will find rest for our souls, and we will save our lives.

May God's Holy Name be praised now and forever.

Why Should We Proclaim the Christ?

Twelfth Sunday of Ordinary Time, Lectionary 96
Ave Maria, FL, 2013

Zechariah 12:10-11, 13:1
Psalm 64:2, 3-4, 5-6, 8-9
Galatians 3:26-29
Luke 9:18-24

Do you want to hear a story? One of the ways that I know for sure that God is merciful is that I have not had to take a math class since I was sixteen years old. I was never good at math. I found math to be a form of torture and humiliation. I remember, when I was in junior high school, being afflicted by those dreaded "word problems." You remember those, don't you? They'd go like this: "John is six feet tall; Mary is five feet tall; how old is the gorilla?" What....? I'd slide down in my seat and pray, "Please don't call on me, please don't call on me..." In any math class I ever took, I was never the one raising his hand and crying out, "Oh! Oh! I know this one! Pick me! Pick me!"

I mention this because of the surprise quiz we heard Jesus drop on the apostles in today's gospel reading. Jesus asks, "Who do you say that I am?" Now, had any students from Ave Maria been there, I'm sure they would have jumped up and down and yelled, "Oh! Oh! I know this one! Pick me! Pick me!" And of course, the Ave Maria student would have given Jesus chapter and verse of all the relevant Scripture passages, quotes from the various councils, creeds, and catechisms, defining precisely all of the dogmas pertaining to Jesus of Nazareth as the Christ of God. And that would be a very fine thing.

Now, if I were a lazy preacher, and you were an ordinary congregation, I could drone on, "And that's why everyone should memorize doctrines, because we never know when Jesus will give us a quiz...In the name of the Father...." And in reply you would drone, "Yes, Father, amen...." Then you could turn to each other and whisper: "Well, that was useless...but at least it didn't take very long..." But—I am not a lazy preacher, and you are not an ordinary congregation, so let's try to do a little better than that.

I could say that while it is all very well and good to know who Jesus is, it is also at least as important how we say who Jesus is. In other words, many people will know the truth about Jesus Christ only by what we Christians reveal of Him through our joy and our charity. And it would be a very fine thing to be reminded of that fact. But, I think we need to do something a little bit different in today's homily.

Yes, we have to know the answer to the question from Jesus: "Who do you say that I am?" And, yes, we have to be alert to how we answer that question not just with our words but with our lives. But today, I want to focus on a deeper question, namely, this: "*Why?* Why should we proclaim Jesus of Nazareth as the Christ of God?" You might answer, "We should proclaim Him the Christ because it is true!" Yes, that's right. But why else should we proclaim Him the Christ?

And you might answer, "We should proclaim Him the Christ so that God may be glorified!" Yes, that's right too, but unless we start to get very specific, we will run the risk of treating the glory of God as an imprecise, ineffectual, and ultimately forgettable pious abstraction. So, how shall we begin to get it right?

Let's recall that Saint Irenaeus said that "the glory of God is man fully alive." That is where we need to start. We must proclaim the most practical truth, the truth that Jesus of Nazareth is the Christ of God, for the sake of our life in this world and for the sake of our eternal life in the next. Jesus reveals to us, in His words and deeds, in His living and dying, the fullness of human life lived in response to the call of our loving Heavenly Father. If we are to live our human vocation in this life and in the next, we simply must live the imitation of Christ for the sake of union with Christ. A failure to be Christlike is a failure to be fully human, both in time and in eternity.

What do you make of that claim? Well, you might say, "Yes, yes, Father. That's fine. But it all seems more than a bit abstract doesn't it? Can you show us what a truly Christlike human life looks like?" That is a good question. We can answer it by turning to history, and in doing so, we can find some very practical lessons for our own day-to-day living here in Ave Maria.

When the Roman Empire collapsed, eaten away by moral corruption, bankrupted by manic spending, and overrun by barbarians, many people thought the world had come to an end. And who could blame them? All that was thought to be enduring and reliable came crashing to the ground. The light of learning was snuffed out, the rule of law became the law of the jungle, and beauty was replaced by the beast.

Except among the Christians. The Christians, unlike the barbarians, did not cannibalize each other. The Christians, unlike the barbarians, created art and did not destroy it. The Christians, unlike the barbarians, built libraries rather than burned them. Above all, the Christians loved their neighbor for the love of God. The Christians after the fall of Rome ensured that the truths of the faith, the life of learning, and all the necessities for a fully human life were preserved and handed on, and we, eighteen centuries later, are their beneficiaries, their heirs.

Because the Christians proclaimed Jesus of Nazareth as the Christ of God, because they did so both in season and out of season, welcome and unwelcome, faithful until death, even when the world seemed to end with the fall of Rome, neither the light of faith nor the light of reason was snuffed out. Across oceans and centuries, countless generations have been able to live their truly human vocation, to live fully alive for the glory of God, because Christ, Who is true God and true man, has been proclaimed, loved, and imitated. Now, now more than ever, it is our turn to do the same. It is our turn, right here at Ave Maria, to make Christ known and loved by the witness of our words and deeds, so that the light will not go out, even as shadows fall around us.

History shows repeatedly that wherever Christ is not known and loved, humans do not become what God calls them to be. Instead, they debase, abuse, and consume one another, both physically and spiritually. Wherever Christ is not known and loved, culture corrodes human dignity and tyrants usurp human freedom. If you take an honest look at the past and a sober look at the present, you will see this truth for yourself. The truth is this: Wherever Christ is not known and loved, human life in this life and in the next is in peril, and has no sure safety.

We live in a time and culture when Christians are asked to be silent and to be invisible. We are asked not to notice that the walls are crumbling and that the barbarians are on the move. In our time, torches are being lit, not to illumine but to burn and to purge. And we, we ordinary human beings at Ave Maria, we are being called by Christ and the Church He founded to respond to the growing darkness, just as the Christians were called to do at the fall of Rome.

Our call now is to make disciples of Christ, to form a profoundly and thoroughly and authentically Catholic community. For a truly Catholic community will keep open the doors of the church and the doors of the library, even when the storms of rage and bigotry beat against them. A truly Catholic community will ensure that the Bread of Life for the soul and bread made by our own hands can be shared with the hungry. A truly Catholic community will ensure that the living waters of Baptism and water safe to drink can be shared with the thirsty. A truly Catholic community will ensure that the precious, vulnerable, glorious human soul, mind, and body will be given a safe haven. This is what we are called to build here; we here at Ave Maria are called upon to build such a Catholic community. What a tragedy, what a scandal, what a horror, for us, our children, and the future, if we do not answer the call!

Ok, so, now what? How shall we do all that? We need to do three things, starting today, and ending only when God calls us home. We need to get holy, we need to get smart, and we need to get busy.

We need to get holy in a hurry. The recipe for that is simple: Conversion, study, and love.

We need to get smart in a hurry. The recipe for that is simple: Learn about what is going on in the world, learn what your family and neighbors need, learn how to meet those needs.

We need to get busy in a hurry. The recipe for that is simple: Act on what you believe; act on what you know; act on what you hope.

We must order our lives and our community around making Christ known and loved. For the love of God and for the love of our neighbor whom Jesus has commanded us to love, we must forget ourselves, take up our cross, and follow him. If we do that, then lives will be saved, and souls will be saved, and, best of all—God will be glorified.

May God's Holy Name be praised now and forever.

No Excuses

Thirteenth Sunday of Ordinary Time, Lectionary 99
Ave Maria, FL, 2013

1 Kings 19:16b, 19-21
Psalm 16:1-2, 5, 7-8, 9-10, 11
Galatians 5:1, 13-18
Luke 9:51-62

What do you do when you want to distract yourself from performing some onerous or unpleasant duty, but you still want to maintain the illusion of productivity and perhaps even the appearance of intellectual curiosity? I go to the Amazon web site and search for book titles.

Recently, I went to Amazon and typed in the words "No Excuses." In a split second, the web site produced 122,730 books with the words "No Excuses" in the title. Apparently, human beings have an unlimited ingenuity for making excuses, and, in response, have displayed remarkable ingenuity in writing books that offer to guide one away from the habit of making excuses.

That got me to thinking. What if we could live our lives without excuses? What if we lived our lives just doing the right thing when and as it needed to be done, without a second thought? These questions cross my mind as I read the gospel we just heard today. In our gospel passage for today we see Jesus dealing with three cases of hesitations, excuses, and second thoughts—all forms of vacillation.

Perhaps the most familiar form of vacillation is procrastination, that is, putting off until a later date what ought to be done now. Christian tradition has always taken a dim view of procrastination. Consider these words from Saint Augustine: "God has promised forgiveness to your repentance, but He has not promised tomorrow to your procrastination." The 19th-century Scottish preacher Edward Irving is even more alarming. He wrote these words: "Procrastination is the kidnapper of souls, and the recruiting-officer of Hell." Taking Augustine and Edward Irving together, we can see that procrastination depends upon a tomorrow that may never come, and can rob us of eternity.

That fact forces us to ask ourselves some hard questions. First, what have I allowed to become more important than my Christian duty? Second, what do I fear more than disappointing Christ? Third, what if I lived my Christian discipleship without making use of excuses?

Jesus Christ calls us *now*. To each of us He says: "I am on my way; I am going to the cross, to resurrection, and to glory—*come with me now.*" And He waits for our answer, but He will not wait forever.

Please God, let not our final answer to Christ be hesitation, excuses, and procrastination! Please God, let not our final answer to Christ be the bitter fruit of a divided heart!

Anyone who is sane, just, and loving will run to Christ when He calls. But we live in a culture that is insane, unjust, and self-centered. That means that we have some very important choices to make, and we need to make them today.

We must choose to put Christ and His call to us first.

We must choose to resist distractions, illusions, and excuses. We must choose to prove our love above all by deeds, and not merely by words. We must choose, with an undivided heart, to set our hand to the plough and not look back.

If we do that, if we say "yes" to Christ every time He calls us closer to Himself, He will prove Himself to be faithful. And then we can stand before God and the world, and cry out the words of the psalm which we heard today: "You will show me the path to life, fullness of joys in your presence, the delights at your right hand forever."

May God's Holy Name be praised now and forever.

WHY DOESN'T GOD DO SOMETHING ABOUT EVIL?

Fifteenth Saturday of Ordinary Time, Lectionary 394
Ave Maria, FL, 2012

Micah 2:1-5
Psalm 10:1-2, 3-4, 7-8, 14
Matthew 12:14-21

One of the problems for a preacher who watches the news closely is that sometimes you have to rewrite your homilies in a hurry, in light of something that has taken place in the world and that is on everyone's mind.

That is the case today, as, like you I'm sure, I am thinking about the awful shooting spree in the movie theater in Colorado that happened this week. That massacre left about a dozen dead and over fifty wounded. We naturally recoil when we think of such monstrous evil, of such a senseless waste of human life. Like everyone else, we are asking, "Why?" And because we are people of faith, as we ask that common question, we turn to God.

The Scripture passages we heard this morning say out loud what may be rumbling in our hearts. From the psalmist we hear: "Why, O LORD, do you stand aloof? Why hide in times of distress? Proudly the wicked harass the afflicted, who are caught in the devices the wicked have contrived." This psalm asks what we are asking. Surely, we too, since we heard the news of that mass murder, we have been asking, "Where was God in all this? Could God do nothing about this?"

Perhaps the murderer thought that God would be blind or silent. Again we hear from the psalmist: "The wicked man boasts, 'He will not avenge it'....'There is no God,' sums up his thoughts....His mouth is full of cursing, guile, and deceit; under his tongue are mischief and iniquity. He lurks in ambush near the villages; in hiding he murders the innocent; his eyes spy upon the unfortunate." The writing of the divinely inspired author of this psalm shows that God does know the wickedness that can fester in the human heart.

"All right then," you might say. "God *knows about* evil—but does He *do* anything about it?" A time like this can and should rob us of any form of a naive faith. Any thought that faith in God provides a magic bubble around ourselves, our loved ones, our town, or our nation must be surrendered, or horrors like the one at Aurora, Colorado, will scandalize us and keep us from a mature faith in the living God. It is time to put aside any inclination to wish for a simpler world wherein we can blissfully sing "He's Got the Whole World in His Hands" and then walk about assuming that we are immune to the evils of this world.

Our only sane option, our only faithful option, is to turn to the Cross and to make a decision about who Jesus Christ really is. Either all that the Church proclaims about the Cross and Resurrection of Christ is completely true, or we have no hope and life is a bad joke that probably should not have happened. Those are the only honest options we have. Either we insist constantly to the world that nothing is beyond the redemptive reach of the Cross and Resurrection of Christ, or we should just fall silent and admit to ourselves that we Christians are frauds. And I should take these robes off and start looking for honest work.

While we still suffer from the nausea of yet another mass murder, let's call to mind Saint Mary Magdalene. When Mary Magdalene went to the tomb, she did not expect it to be empty. She thought that the crucifixion had defeated Jesus. And *still* she went to Him! We, therefore, we who proclaim Christ crucified, risen, and returning, we must—we simply *must*—enter into the mystery of suffering, evil, and death, and the deeper mystery of hope, in the company of our scarred and glorious Christ the King.

The first and final step of entering into the most sacred mysteries is to approach the altar and receive the Body, Blood, Soul, and Divinity of the Christ of God, Who is the Son of Mary. We must approach with desperate confidence Jesus, Whom Mary Magdalene believed she would never see again. We must come to the altar and admit that during this present darkness, words fail, sight fails, and our only hope is to embrace our Lord Who suffered everything and Who conquers all.

May God's Holy Name be praised now and forever.

Goals and Feelings

Twenty-Second Thursday of Ordinary Time,
Lectionary 434
Ave Maria, FL, 2011

Colossians 1:9-14
Psalm 98
Luke 5:1-11

Have you ever gone fishing? Not me. I'm a city boy; as far as I know, fish come from cans. So I find myself at a disadvantage having to preach on today's gospel passage. I don't know why Peter and his buddies were fishing all night rather than in the morning after a good night's rest, which would have been my first choice. And I don't know how unreasonable it was of Jesus to ask Peter and company to put out their nets one more time. But I do know something about human nature, and about the nature of Christian discipleship, and I think that this gospel passage, along with today's reading from Saint Paul to the Colossians, has a lot to teach us.

What can we notice first about today's gospel? Jesus says to a boatload of tired and discouraged fishermen, "Put out into deep water and lower your nets for a catch." After working all night and in vain, would we have agreed to try again? Notice Peter's reply: "Master, we have worked hard all night and have caught nothing, but at your command I will lower the nets." What is important is what Peter did *not* say. Peter did *not* say: "Master, I don't feel like it. I don't feel like putting out into the deep. I'll get around to it when I'm in the mood to try again." He didn't say that. Peter didn't wait for his feelings to catch up with his goal. He acted for the goal rather than delay his actions until such time as his feelings for the goal might show up.

Why is that important? It's important because this semester, there will be many times when you don't feel like doing your duty or taking advantage of an opportunity; if you're a student, you might not feel like studying or doing your homework; if you're a parent you might not feel like dealing with your needy child, and I don't think a parent ever feels like changing a diaper; if you're a professor you might not feel like grading essays. Saint Peter shows us the way forward. Peter acted for the *results* he wanted (more fish) and not on what he *felt* like doing. He kept his eyes on the prize and acted accordingly.

That's what we can learn about human nature from today's readings; what can we learn from them about discipleship? Once Saint Peter realizes that Jesus is a holy man of God, he says, "Depart from me, Lord, for I am a sinful man." It is natural, in the presence of light and holiness, to recoil, when one is covered in filth and sin; it is natural—it is also a mistake. Peter's response is indicative of a view of discipleship that emphasizes what I call "sin management." According to sin management, we somehow get it into our heads that what God is most concerned about is our sin, and that somehow we have to purify ourselves before we dare present ourselves to God. Wrong, wrong, wrong.

Yes, God hates sin. And God deals with our sin through Jesus at a terrible cost to Himself. But Jesus doesn't rub the disciples' noses in their sin. Instead, He lifts them up to the great mission He gives them: "Do not be afraid; from now on you will be catching men." Jesus will prepare them to receive the mission that the Father has in store for them. And the disciples leave their old way of life behind to follow Jesus, and *that* is the heart of discipleship. True discipleship is not "sin management," whereby we try to purify ourselves to make ourselves worthy to be in the presence of God. True discipleship is following Jesus, gladly. That is why Saint Paul writes these words which we heard today: "...with joy [give] thanks to the Father, who has made you fit to share in the inheritance of the holy ones in light." He delivered us from the power of darkness and transferred us to the Kingdom of his beloved Son, in whom we have redemption."

May God's Holy Name be praised now and forever.

Do We Have Enemies?

Twenty-Third Wednesday of Ordinary Time,
Lectionary 439
Ave Maria, FL, 2013

Colossians 3:1-11
Psalm 145:2-3, 10-11, 12-13ab
Luke 6:20-26

Do you and I have any enemies? I think we do. And I think that our worst enemy is ourselves. I am my own worst enemy, and you are your own worst enemy. I say this because of the words of Saint Paul we heard today. Saint Paul urges us to "put to death…the greed that is idolatry." The Greek word that Saint Paul uses for greed is *pleonexia*, which is not easy to translate. It might be understood as a ruthless and relentless selfishness that can never be satisfied. And then we divinize that selfishness by making it an idol to which we offer sacrifice in the hopes of getting more and more. That idolatrous greed, that diabolical selfishness, left unchecked, can destroy the world and deny us the happiness of Heaven. We know that, but I wonder how vigorously we daily pursue the war against our own worst enemy, which is the idol of our selfishness?

On this date of September 11, I will ask again: Do we have any enemies? If we are honest, I think we must admit that we do.

There are people who hate us because we won't take down the crucifix. There are people who hate us because we will not leave the tabernacle empty. There are people who hate us because we kiss the pages of the Gospel and not another book.

These people may threaten us, but we will not remove ourselves from the source of human life and everlasting life; we will not withdraw from the living and life-giving God, the Word-made-Flesh Who dwells among us still.

Christ calls us to extend mercy; He gives us the grace to do so. He also gives us the grace and solemn obligation to resist evil, to stand against hate, and to uphold the culture of life against the culture of death, in both its secular and sectarian guises. Christ calls us, the Church blesses us, and our nation, civilization, and world need us.

In this time, which in God's Providence is *our* time, in this time, we are called to be peacemakers and watchmen and heralds and prophets and teachers and warriors, and above all to be strong in God's strength and victorious in His victory.

In this, the time and place that God has given us, we cannot afford to be lukewarm, partially committed, or insufficiently prepared.

Let us resolve today that we will begin to work as never before as neighbors and citizens, as scholars and as students, and above all as people who are baptized and so consecrated for resurrection. Let's all resolve to work to form a people who will stand unafraid with clear eyes and uplifted hands as Christ comes to restore all things to our Heavenly Father.

We must embrace the noble Christian tradition of protecting what God has entrusted to our care. Remember what G.K. Chesterton said: "The true soldier fights not because he hates what is in front of him, but because he loves what is behind him." We, as individuals, and especially as a Catholic community, must put ourselves between those who hate Christ and those who embrace Him.

Consider this quote from the Office of Readings from Volume IV of the Liturgy of the Hours: "We are warriors now, fighting on the battle field of faith, and God sees all we do; the angels watch and so does Christ. What honor and glory and joy, to do battle in the presence of God, and to have Christ approve our victory."

Those beautiful and haunting words point to our vocation to be a community of vigilant discernment and militant intercession as we read the signs of the times. Reading the Word of God, let's prepare ourselves for what is coming next.

Preparing, but not with a sense of fear or with a sense of despair. Preparing with a sense of lively obedience, with a sense of solemn duty, and with a resourcefulness born of a commitment to ensure that our children, our nation, and our civilization will continue to stand, and that the faith of the Church founded by Christ will be handed on to the next generation.

With God's grace, we can choose who will write the pages of our history, whether it will be written by our enemies standing upon our graves and the smoldering ruins of our culture, or whether it will be written by our children who learn in our schools and pray in our churches.

And at all times, let us take heart. Even in our struggles, especially our struggle against our own sin and against the powers of this present darkness, let us recall these words of Jesus that we heard today: "Blessed are you when people hate you, and when they exclude and insult you, and denounce your name as evil on account of the Son of Man. Rejoice and leap for joy on that day! Behold, your reward will be great in heaven."

May God's Holy Name be praised now and forever.

"Oh Well, I Guess You Had to Be There…"

Twenty-Fourth Tuesday of Ordinary Time,
Lectionary 444
Ave Maria, FL, 2012

1 Corinthians 12:12-14, 27-31a
Psalm 100:1b-2, 3, 4, 5
Luke 7:11-17

You may know that I like stories. I like to tell stories, and I enjoy hearing stories, especially good stories that are well told. Of course, that means that I find it especially disappointing when a storyteller fails in his task. One sign that a storyteller has failed is when he finally shrugs his shoulders and says, "Oh well, I guess you had to be there…." That's an indication that the storyteller did not connect his audience to his story. In other words, the story, as told, was so remote, so obscure, so hard to express in a way that the audience can grasp, that the storyteller finally admits his failure to bring his audience into the story and signals his surrender by saying, "Oh well, I guess you had to be there…."

I mention this because I fear that we might treat today's gospel passage in the same way. I fear that we might hear the story of Jesus showing compassion in a profound and miraculous way, and find no connection to the story. In other words, we may think that the people in the story, the people around the young man raised from the dead, were very excited and their lives were changed…but…that was so long ago and far away, and Jesus doesn't act like that anymore, so when we hear this gospel passage, we just shrug our shoulders and say, "Oh well, I guess you had to be there…."

If today's gospel passage is merely a tale of long ago and far away, a story with no connection to us, no message for us, if it offers us nothing to hold onto and carry with us, then we will go away sad, empty, and hungry, when in fact Christ wishes to give us joy, to make us full with His own abundance. So, let's have another look at this gospel passage.

This translation says that He "was moved with pity" for the widow. Others say that Jesus was "being moved with mercy towards her." Some say, "his heart went out to her." I think that the best translation says that "When the Lord saw her, He was moved to the depths of His heart for her." Could we dare believe today that when the Lord looks at us, and sees our need, that He is moved to the depths of His heart. Could we dare believe that His heart has boundless compassion, mercy, and pity for us? Could we dare believe that He looks upon us and says, "I can't do nothing—I must do something for this person!"? Could we dare believe it?

There is nothing else to do with a dead body but to get rid of it and move on. That is what the widow was doing with her son, and who could blame her? But what about us? Are there parts of our lives that we have decided are dead? Are there causes and dreams we have just given up on? Have we resigned ourselves to habits of sin that cannot be defeated? Have we lowered our sights because we believe that the Lord does not care to help us reach our goals? Have we shut down whole sections of our heart because we can no longer find any life within us? I won't ask for a show of hands, but I have to believe that each of us could say "Yes" to at least one of those questions. Now, here comes the really hard question: Could we dare believe that Jesus, the Christ of God, in His compassion, wishes to raise to life in us what we thought was dead? Can we allow ourselves to have hope that the risen Lord Jesus could bring His victorious life to what we thought was dead and lost? Could we allow ourselves to believe that Jesus can offer us not only His pity but also His power?

As the shadows loom larger over our world, as we suffer daily defeats and disappointments, as we tire of beating back our fears for yet another day, it is time to turn to Christ, and ask Him to share His life, His victory, with us.

If our celebration of the Eucharist is to be honest, authentic, and not mere empty habit, then we must learn again to pray with empty hands, with highest hopes, and deepest gratitude. And when we receive what God our Lord wishes to give to His trusting children, then we can join the psalmist and cry out, "We are his people: the sheep of his flock."

May God's Holy Name be praised now and forever.

A Vow of Silence?

Twenty-Fifth Wednesday of Ordinary Time,
Lectionary 451
Ave Maria, FL, 2012

Proverbs 30:5-9
Psalm 119:29, 72, 89, 101, 104, 163
Luke 9:1-6

A certain religious whom I know well said not long ago, "I was about to resolve not to talk to stupid people anymore, but since I am surrounded by stupid people I was afraid that folks would infer that I had taken a vow of silence."

That memory comes to mind as I read these words we just heard from the Book of Proverbs. Let's listen to them again: "Put falsehood and lying far from me…" Now, I just have to ask, "If I could no longer hear lies, would people assume that I have gone deaf?"

I ask that question because I believe that we are surrounded by lies. Falsehood and dishonesty are not new; they are as old as the Garden of Eden. But nowadays we are bombarded by lies 24/7, by every form of intrusive media: we are lied to in print through newspapers, magazines, and books; we are lied to electronically through television, radio, the internet, even our phones. And we all know people who repeat to us in person the lies they hear. If God were to answer our prayer to "Put falsehood and lying far from me," would we each end up on a deserted island, living as a hermit?

Now, more than ever, I believe, the disciples of Christ are called upon to know the truth and to tell the truth. We must know the truth Who is Jesus; we must know what is taking place in our world which is in rebellion against God and His Christ; and we must tell the truth—always with charity, but always the truth.

In the gospel reading for today, we see Jesus sending out the Twelve to proclaim the truth. They are to travel light so as not to be distracted by what is not essential. They are to do the Lord's work, with the Lord's power and authority, and not their own. Just like us.

What would our lives look like if we firmly believed that our vocation is to know and tell the truth, to proclaim the Kingdom of God? What would our lives look like if we firmly believed that we must rely on the Lord's strength and not our own? What would our lives look like if we firmly believed that we must put aside all distractions that keep us from obedience to God's command? Each of us has to answer that question in his own way, but as I look in the mirror, I have to suspect that our lives would look rather different from how they appear right now, if we took to heart Christ's command to proclaim the Kingdom of God.

Today, let's approach the altar hungry for the truth Who is the person of Jesus; and then let's go out into the world determined to serve the truth Whom we have met here. If we do that, then we can echo the words of the psalmist and say, "Your word, O LORD, is a lamp for my feet."

May God's Holy Name be praised now and forever.

"It Is Not Good for the Man to Be Alone"

Twenty-Seventh Sunday of Ordinary Time,
Lectionary 140
Ave Maria, FL, 2012

Genesis 2:7-8, 18-24
Psalm 128:1-2, 3, 4-5, 6
Hebrews 2:9-11
Mark 10:2-16

Do you want to know a secret? I come from a mixed marriage. My mother was a woman and my father was a man. Now, as you can imagine, that inevitably led to some conflict and misunderstanding, but ultimately I am grateful for having had the opportunity to have grown up in a household that celebrated such diversity. And I only wish more young people today could grow up in a home environment as multi-cultural as mine was.

It is odd, and sad, is it not, that the words I just spoke could be perceived as a joke today, but twenty years ago, those words would have been unintelligible. People back then would have said, "What does he mean, 'mixed marriage'? What other kind of marriage is there?" Oh, how times have changed…

As we look down at the texts of today's readings, and then look up at the world around us, I think we can see that today the Scriptures give us three tasks. We must offer compassion for those who have suffered from divorce; we must offer encouragement for those struggling in marriage (and if you're married, you are struggling); and we must offer preparation for the young to assume the responsibilities of marriage.

Our Church, our nation, and our world suffer because of the sorry state of marriage today. Weak marriages lead to weaker families. Weaker families lead to children unprepared to become adults. And when the next generation of Peter Pan-like children come of age but refuse to grow up, they will distract themselves from their failures by turning to pornography and promiscuity, which lead inevitably to disease, abortion, and a further erosion of human community. The readings we just heard offer us a way out of the mess that we are in.

Where shall we start? Well, at the beginning, of course. In the beginning, God chose to share His own overflowing life and love with human beings, those of His creatures made in His image and likeness. God is Trinity; God is a community of persons in love. Because we are made in the image and likeness of God, our only chance at fulfillment is to learn how to give ourselves as a gift to another, to learn how to receive worthily the gift of another, to learn how to make that exchange of gifts fruitful and life-giving. That way of covenant love, which may be lived in various ways, ought to be most readily apparent in marriage.

If we are to begin at the beginning, let's go to the Book of Genesis, where we find these words: "The Lord God said, 'It is not good for the man to be alone.'" Why not? It is not good for the man to be alone because that is not how he was made; isolation is not what he was made for. He was made in the image and likeness of God Who is a community of love. To be in isolation is for man unnatural, inhuman, and ungodly.

So, what does God do for the man? Again, we read in Genesis that God said, "I will make a suitable partner for him." That is a very important sentence, now more than ever, when we are drawn into discussions about defending or attacking what is called "traditional marriage," by which is meant the marriage of one man and one woman. I think it is a mistake to call that marriage, which of course is true marriage, by the name of "traditional marriage." That name gives opponents of true marriage the opportunity to dismiss marriage as mere tradition. It allows them to say, "Well, it used to be a tradition for men to wear powdered wigs and silk stockings, and that tradition, happily, has fallen away. The 'tradition' of heterosexual marriage is also a mere tradition that may just fall away—and the sooner, the better."

The tortured logic of the opponents of true marriage shows us why it is better to refer to true marriage as "natural marriage." The design of marriage for man and woman was put into nature by God. That means that the glory of natural marriage is that it has a supernatural origin. God decides what marriage is, and we tamper with divine definitions at our peril.

God created the woman, and in the Book of Genesis we read, "He brought her to the man," like a father walking his daughter down the aisle of the church on her wedding day. What an act of trust! This passage of Scripture shows us that men must build their lives around becoming worthy of the trust that God invests in us when He brings women into our lives.

Let's turn again to the Book of Genesis. Man's response to God's gift of woman is so beautiful. Man cries out, "At last!" He knew that he was incomplete. He knew that he could not be the giver and receiver of love that God intended him to be as long as he was in isolation.

When reading these words, "At last!", I thought of the

song played at my sister's wedding reception. She and her husband danced to song entitled "At Last," sung by jazz artist Etta James. I think it is easy to hear the lyrics and imagine them being sung by the man made by God. Etta James sang these words: "At last, My love has come along, My lonely days are over, And life is like a song... I found a dream that I could speak to, A dream that I can call my own, I found a thrill to press my cheek to, A thrill that I have never known...At last."

Unfortunately, beautiful words by themselves are never enough. We know that the man and the woman in the garden did not live happily ever after. They, like all of us, have the same problem, namely, the gap between our calling and our falling. Our human vocation is to love as God loves; our human tragedy is that our ability to love is crippled by our selfishness. Where there is selfishness, the growth of love is always stunted; and if selfishness is left unchecked, love will die.

By the death of love, I do not mean the end of romantic emotions; most of you know as least as well as I do how fickle romantic emotions are. By the death of love I mean an unwillingness, perhaps even the inability, to give oneself as a gift, and to receive the gift of another. This death of love comes from, as Jesus said, "...the hardness of your hearts." A hard heart is a soul closed up like an angry fist, unable to do its natural work, and unable to receive God's grace.

So, that's the problem—what shall we do about it? We, as a community of faith, need to do three things. First, let's offer true Christian compassion to those whose lives have been ripped apart by divorce, by directing them to the example and person of Christ, "Who loved His own until the end."

Second, let's encourage married couples, who struggle in their daily lives together, and remind them that the grace they need is always available to them from the God Who called them to their particular form of the human vocation of love.

Third, let's prepare our young people for the vocation of Godly love, whether lived in marriage, the consecrated life, or the single life. Let's teach them that mere sentimentality can never attain the heights of sacrificial love for which they were created. Let's teach them that the best way to prepare for true love is by means of chastity of body, mind, and heart. And let's make undeniably and unforgettably clear to them the horrors that come from promiscuity and all forms of impurity.

If we become a community of faith that can offer such lessons of compassion, encouragement, and truth by how we speak and how we live, then we will be able to teach the world "…why a man leaves his father and mother and clings to his wife, and the two of them become one flesh."

May God's Holy Name be praised now and forever.

How Much Does Heaven Cost?

Twenty-Seventh Sunday of Ordinary Time,
Lectionary 141
Ave Maria, FL, 2013

Habakuk 1:2-3, 2:2-4
Psalm 95:1-2, 6-7, 8-9
2 Timothy 1:6-8, 13-14
Luke 17:5-10

How much does Heaven cost? The Jesuit author Father John Powell wrote about staying in a German monastery while speaking at an academic conference. He said he returned to his room in the monastery and was horrified to discover an elderly nun on her hands and knees, scrubbing the already-spotless floor with a brush. He tried to tell her in his halting German that what she was doing was not necessary. He wrote that she snarled at him in German, *"Der Himmel ist nicht billig, Vater!"* ("Heaven isn't cheap, Father!") Father Powell wrote that he believed there would be a special place in Heaven for such hardworking souls, but he also said the nun's attitude could be dangerous, and I agree.

I think the nun's attitude could be dangerous because of the words of Jesus we heard this morning: "When you have done all you have been commanded, say, 'We are unprofitable servants; we have done what we were obliged to do.'" That nun was right, that Heaven isn't cheap, and Jesus makes it clear that Heaven is also not for sale.

Is that statement good news or bad news? Well, if you were planning to earn Heaven, if you were planning to show up at the pearly gates and demand entrance because you had accumulated a favorable account in God's ledger, then these words of Jesus are very bad news. Jesus makes clear that we can't earn Heaven; God can't be bribed, and no matter how well we think we have served God, we always serve at a net loss to God.

However, if you wish to be loved freely, as a child is loved; if you wish to receive love graciously and with wonder, as a lover does; if you believe that gratitude is the best gift that you can give God, then the words of Jesus today are very good news indeed.

We cannot earn Heaven; we cannot repay God so that we are even. But we, who are made in the image and likeness of God, can show that we are grateful to God. How? God is truth, so in gratitude let us love and then tell the truth. God is beauty, so in gratitude let us love and make what is beautiful. God is goodness, so in gratitude let us love and do what is good. God is infinite mercy, so in gratitude, let us be merciful.

We will never be God's profitable servants. But we can be His grateful children; we can be His good stewards, and, with His grace, we can be credible witnesses and attractive icons of the living God. How then, shall we live?

Ok. Let's begin by agreeing then that we cannot earn Heaven and that we cannot put God in our debt. Let's agree that we can never honestly say that God is fortunate to have such high-performers like us on His payroll. And let's agree that we can be His beloved children, His adopted heirs, His good stewards, His credible witnesses. Let's agree to all that. But that agreement is nothing but a stack of empty words, if we do not also agree to put those words into practice, together, concretely, daily.

Remember these words that Saint Paul wrote to Saint Timothy, which we heard this morning: "I remind you, to stir into flame the gift of God that you have...God did not give us a spirit of cowardice but rather of power and love and self-control... Guard this rich trust with the help of the Holy Spirit that dwells within us." So says Saint Paul.

Let's examine these words from Saint Paul, and use them as guides for putting into practice the mandate we have from the gospel passage we heard this morning. First, Saint Paul urges us to fan into flame the gift of God that we have. The spark of Christian life within us is fanned into flame through the fire of prayer. The fire of prayer is not merely "saying our prayers" (although saying our prayers is good); the fire of prayer is not merely being faithful to our "prayer time" (although fidelity to prayer time is good); the fire of prayer is the passionate love of God absorbed by us in prayer and used as fuel for living the Christian life. If we pray and then do nothing, if we pray and then do not repent, worship, witness, and serve, then we know that we have not found the true fire of prayer. I will say it again: The fire of prayer is the fuel for our Christian life. What good does it do to sit behind the wheel of the car and just make engine noises? The purpose of the car is fulfilled when it is put in gear and we put the pedal to the metal. It should be obvious to us that we are not living the Christian life unless we are living it zealously and fully. So, to use Saint Paul's words to Saint Timothy to guide us in our living of today's gospel passage, we must begin by seeking the transforming fire of prayer as the fuel of our discipleship.

Saint Paul instructed Saint Timothy that God did not give us a spirit of cowardice. That's good news, because we finite and fallen humans are afraid of so many things. We are afraid of failure, of humiliation, of loss, of rejection. But there is only one final failure, humiliation, and loss: and that is to be a Christian who does not become a saint. There is only one final rejection, and that is not being recognized by Christ as one of His own. The world cannot give what Christ offers; and the world cannot take away what Christ gives. Why then, are we afraid?

Saint Paul told the young Timothy that God gives us a spirit of power. That spirit of power is not a spirit of bullying or domination. That spirit of power is related to the fire of prayer. The spirit of power is the ability to get the job done, the ability to remain faithful until the end, the perseverance to overcome every obstacle. We are on the winning side. Christ offers us a share in His victory! How could a sane man not run towards Christ?

The young Timothy was taught that he, like us, was given a spirit of love. That spirit of love enables us to imitate Christ, to give and not to count the cost, to strive to bring about the best for the beloved, despite all our human weakness. How could a sane man not run towards Christ?

Perhaps the hardest lesson of all is that God gives us a spirit of self-control. The world will tell us that self-control can bring only a loss of freedom and a loss of joy. But true followers of Christ know that the opposite is true. Self-control protects us from illusion, compulsion, and addiction. Self-control frees us to love and serve and enter the joy of the victorious Christ. How could a sane man not run towards Christ?

Saint Paul urges his pupil Timothy to marvel at the great gifts God has given him, and then to turn to the Holy Spirit for guidance in the preservation, use, and growth of these gifts. That wise and guiding Holy Spirit can be found in prayer, the sacraments, and the authentic teaching of the Church. We cannot live our Christian discipleship well without the guidance of the Holy Spirit.

If we commit to the Spirit-filled discipleship of gospel-living described in today's readings, what would life here in Ave Maria look like? I think that we would measure the quality of our prayer by the good work that our prayer leads us to do. I think that we would extend mercy that is undeserved, as God has shown undeserved mercy to me and you. I think that we would prepare to feed the body, mind, and heart of our neighbor, in imitation of God's provision for my own body, mind, and heart, and for yours. And we would ask for help. I think that we would ask for help of God and of our fellow Christians to do all that God asked of us, not to earn Heaven—which we can't—but simply to express gratitude to God. I think that we would ask for help of God and of our fellow Christians to work together to proclaim Christ to a world that is dying from lack of faith in Him. That is what I think we would do if we were Spirit-guided disciples of Christ here and now at Ave Maria. So…let's do that. Let's commit to living together here as Spirit-guided disciples of Christ, for the good of our neighbor and for the greater glory of God.

If we do that, if we are fueled by the fire of prayer to perform the spiritual and corporal works of mercy, if we do so gratefully, joyfully, and courageously, then we will fulfill the words of Saint Paul, when we bear our "share of hardship for the gospel with the strength that comes from God."

May God's Holy Name be praised now and forever.

Are You Hiding Anything?

Twenty-Eighth Friday of Ordinary Time, Lectionary 471
Ave Maria, FL, 2011

Romans 4:1-8
Psalm 32
Luke 12:1-7

Let's listen again to these hard words of Jesus: "There is nothing concealed that will not be revealed, nor secret that will not be known." Do those words make you sweat a bit? They make me sweat. Anyone who is over the age of five has things in his past that he regrets and is ashamed of, things that he does not want anyone else to know about. That's just part of the human condition—we want things we have hidden from others to remain hidden. So, from that point of view, it is understandable that we find these words of Jesus to be unsettling. But I think there is another reason why these words of Jesus can be profoundly unnerving.

There are things we hide from others; what of the things we hide from ourselves? Do we want those things to be revealed?

And what about things that are hidden from us because we are too blind to see them? Do we want those things to be revealed?

Let me give you an example. Before he became Pope John XXIII, Cardinal Roncalli worked for the Vatican diplomatic service. One evening, he was at a formal embassy dinner. Seated next to him was a young woman who was immodestly dressed; indeed, some said that she was scandalously dressed. And everyone was waiting to see how the Cardinal might respond. At the end of the meal, Cardinal Roncalli reached into the fruit basket in front of him, and handed the young lady a piece of fruit. She politely declined. The Cardinal insisted that she take the fruit. The young lady replied, "Your Eminence, I don't understand." The Cardinal answered, "You see, my dear, it was not until Eve bit the apple that she knew that she was naked." The Cardinal had revealed to her what she was too blind to see. The revelation was painful of course, but, if received properly, that revelation could be an occasion for repentance and mercy.

What about us? What are we hiding from ourselves? What are we too blind to see for ourselves? Only God knows for sure, but let me make some suggestions about areas of our lives where we may be hiding, or delusional, or even blind.

If we watch the news these days, it seems that we are surrounded by people who think that life owes them a living. And if we are honest, and look within our own hearts, we may think that nice people like us, people who go to church and put an envelope in a basket, deserve from God protection from the inconveniences of life, followed by a comfortable afterlife. To these I might say, "Oh really?"

Let's listen again to some puzzling words from Jesus. He says: "Are not five sparrows sold for two small coins? Yet not one of them has escaped the notice of God. Even the hairs of your head have all been counted. Do not be afraid. You are worth more than many sparrows."

What is Jesus saying? Is He saying, "Hey, God likes

sparrows, so He must be crazy about you! If God cares for stupid little birds, then you can kick back and relax, because God has got you covered." Is that what Jesus saying? No. Not at all. God loves us passionately, infinitely, and wants us to have what is best for us, namely, Himself. God will surely provide what we need to reach His heavenly home, where a banquet is prepared for us. But in this life, there are no guarantees. Neither the world nor the government nor the devil himself can guarantee us a comfortable life, sufficient employment, safety, good health, justice, or fairness. If our final hope is in anything that can be secured in this life, then we are blind, and we need a revelation, however painful that revelation might be.

Our vocation as stewards is to be lived in this life. Our goods, our abilities, our civilization and culture, all the needy and weak who are in our care, have been entrusted to our stewardship in this life. But our home is not in this world; our home is in heaven with the Father who made us and calls us to Himself. If we make this world our home, we will be cruelly disappointed. And, if we betray those goods and people who are entrusted to our stewardship in this life, we will find no joy in the life to come.

So, what are we to do? We here at Ave Maria, we a community of faith and family and friendship, a community of students and scholars and disciples—what are we to do? We must pray to see, and we must learn to teach others to see. We must ask that our blindness be healed, our illusions yanked away from us, our delusional denials rendered impossible. If the real truth of who God is and who we are is placed before our eyes and hearts and minds and hands, then we here can do great things for the greater glory of God, for the service of our neighbor, and for the help of our nation and civilization.

If we are finally stripped of our illusions, what could we do? Let me make some suggestions, and then it is up to you to meet and pray together and get more specific than what I can do here. If we embrace the truth about ourselves and about God, I think we could say the following to each other.

We can be hungry, so let us help each other prepare for famine. We can be thirsty, so let us help each other prepare for drought. We can be vulnerable, so let us help each other prepare for danger. We are Christians, so let us help each other prepare for persecution. We are mortal, so let us help each other prepare for death. We are immortal, so let us help each other prepare to meet God face to face.

If we do that, then we can become salt of the earth and light for the world, and we can someday join the psalmist and say to God: "I turn to you, LORD, in time of trouble, and you fill me with the joy of salvation."

May God's Holy Name be praised now and forever.

Disintegration or Consummation?

Twenty-Eighth Saturday of Ordinary Time,
Lectionary 472
Ave Maria, FL, 2010

Ephesians 1:15-23
Psalm 8:2-3ab, 4-5, 6-7
Luke 12:8-12

If you had to make a list of the three most annoying hymns every composed, what would be on your list? On my list, number three would be "Sing a New Church into Being," number two would be "Gather Us In," and number one would be "He's Got the Whole World in His Hands."

Why does that rank as number one in my "Book of Forbidden Hymns"? I think of "He's Got the Whole World in His Hands" as the musical version of the most offensive phrase ever spoken, which is, "Don't worry—I just know everything's going to be ok!" I have never been an advocate of any account of God that urges us to be passive and helpless because we can count on God-the-Magician to undo reality and bring about a happy ending as long as we think cheerful thoughts about how God's goodness is proved by our being spared any discomfort.

I think of these things as I look at the world, and then look at the writings of Saint Paul. He shows us that Christian hope is not wishful thinking. He also shows us that the power of God must not be thought of as the magical reworking of a cartoon world but rather as the Divine Goodness bringing to perfection even the mess we have made of His creation. In other words, as biblical scholar William Barclay said, "If the Christian message is true, the world is on the way not to disintegration but to consummation."

Let's listen again to this morning's passage from the Letter to the Ephesians. Saint Paul wrote these words: "May the eyes of your hearts be enlightened, that you may know what is the hope that belongs to his call, what are the riches of glory in his inheritance among the holy ones." Saint Paul packs so much into just that one sentence! When the eyes of our hearts are enlightened, we will see that we are not orphans stranded and abandoned in a broken world—no! We are heirs to the glory of God. His delight is to share the fullness of His Life with us. We are called to make our way to the home of our Heavenly Father, where a banquet is prepared for us.

Now, you might be thinking, "Yes, yes, very nice—but how can we be sure? How do we know that what you are saying is not merely wishful thinking?" That's a very good question, and Saint Paul has an answer. Let's listen again. Saint Paul writes that he wants us to know "…what is the surpassing greatness of his power for us who believe, in accord with the exercise of his great might, which he worked in Christ, raising him from the dead and seating him at his right hand in the heavens." We can see that Saint Paul is praying that we can have a new appreciation of the power of God, and the most resounding proof of the triumphant power of God is the resurrection of Jesus from the dead. The resurrection of Jesus proves that God will bring His purposes to fulfillment and that evil and death cannot have the last word. God's providence cannot be defeated by human events. The resurrection of Jesus proves that nothing and no one can defeat God. Saint Paul would say that we Christians must rejoice, because the Spirit of God Who raised Jesus from death is the same Spirit that is given to us. This means that we are not helpless, we must not be hopeless, even though, sometimes, we *are* clueless.

Jesus said, "Pray always." From this day forward, in good times and in bad, may our constant prayer join the eternal prayer of the company of Heaven, and may we all pray together, "You have given your Son rule over the works of your hands."

May God's Holy Name be praised now and forever.

Are You Ready?

Twenty-Ninth Tuesday of Ordinary Time, Lectionary 474
Ave Maria, FL, 2012

Ephesians 2:12-22
Psalm 85:9ab-10, 11-12, 13-14
Luke 12:35-38

What is Jesus talking about here, when He speaks of being ready for the master's return? Is He talking about being ready for His return in glory, or is He talking about being ready to face Him when death comes? Either way, we are presented with a problem. Even though for centuries many people have made a nice living from predicting the imminent return of Christ, in fact no one knows but our Heavenly Father. Jesus Himself said so.

On the other hand, most of us, most of the time, do not know when we are going to die. Consequently, many people urge us, either in person or through the agency of Hallmark Greeting Cards, "to live each day as if it were your last." I am not so sure that is a good idea. This summer, one of my former students sent me a birthday card which read, "I used to live each day as if it were my last, but people got tired of me screaming, 'I'M GOING TO DIE! I'M

GOING TO DIE!" And I don't think that's a helpful way to approach the subject.

We Christians know two facts: 1) Death comes for us all; 2) Jesus Christ will return in glory. And if we are honest, here is a third fact: There is not very much we can do to avoid facts 1 and 2. In light of that, how shall we live?

Saint Ignatius Loyola asks that we be guided by what he calls "the First Principle and Foundation," which is this: Man is created for the praise, reverence, and service of God. That is the end for which we are made. We are to evaluate everything in terms of whether it helps or hinders us to achieve the end for which we are made. Consequently, whether we have a long life or a short life, whether we are rich or poor, sick or healthy—none of these are finally decisive. What matters is that we live our lives such that all that we do helps us to live for the praise, reverence, and service of God.

The Church has always taught that the simplest, most reliable way of living a holy life pleasing to God is to do the duties of our state in life, and to do those duties to the best of our ability, and with great love. For me, that is to live as a Jesuit priest, with a particular job here at Ave Maria. For some of you, your call is to live here as a spouse and parent; for many of you, the present call is for you to live as a student. And if we are honest with ourselves, even if our daily duties are not the stuff of high drama, living them daily, faithfully, and lovingly is both simple and the stuff of great heroism—easy to know, hard to do.

We cannot be prepared for every possible contingency. We cannot study for our exams while also preparing for nuclear war and economic collapse and invasions from creatures from outer space. We can, however, always, be faithful stewards of the people, duties, truths, and goods entrusted to our care. Then, whether the Lord comes for any one of us in death, or comes for all of us in His triumphant return, we can be found vigilant, and therefore

pleasing to Him. And what could be better than that?
May God's Holy Name be praised now and forever.

Why Call God "Father"?

Twenty-Ninth Thursday of Ordinary Time,
Lectionary 476
Ave Maria, FL, 2010

Ephesians 3:14-21
Psalm 33:1-2, 4-5, 11-12, 18-19
Luke 12:49-53

Did you notice in this selection from his letter to the Ephesians that Saint Paul calls God "Father"? What are we doing when we call God "Father"? Well, I suppose that the answer to that question depends upon whom you ask.

If you ask Sigmund Freud and his followers, you will be told that calling God "Father" is a sign of our probably unhappy relationship with our own human fathers. If you ask angry feminists, you will be told that calling God "Father" is a sign of our hatred of women. If you ask a representative sample of the adherents of "the Religion of Peace," you will be told that calling God "Father" is a sign of our lack of reverence for God's transcendent, inscrutable, unapproachable majesty. If you ask overly sentimental Christians who espouse self-esteem as the Fourth Person of the Holy Trinity, you will be told that calling God "Father" is a sign of our admirable need to be constantly hugged and affirmed. If you asked Greco-Roman pagans, you would be told that calling God "Father" is a sign of a nation's origin rooted in the paternity of Zeus or Jupiter.

But if you asked Jesus and Saint Paul, you would be told that calling God "Father" is a sign of our blessedness as children of the glorious, creating, and sovereign Lord of the universe. We would be told that we could rejoice because the always transcendent and majestic God is more than merely approachable. In fact, God our Heavenly Father runs to us, as the father in the parable of the prodigal son runs towards his wayward and returning son. If you asked Jesus and Saint Paul, you would be told that calling God "Father" is a sign of our status as adopted children and heirs to the heavenly kingdom of God. If you asked Jesus and Saint Paul, you would be told that calling God "Father" is a sign of our status as brothers and sisters in Christ, bound together by the shed Blood of Jesus, the waters of baptism, and the seal of the Holy Spirit.

If we call God "Father" as Jesus and Saint Paul have taught us, then we may have hope in this life and hope for the next life. We would be eager to see the holy fire promised by Jesus set ablaze around us and within us. And we would pray unceasingly these words of Saint Paul, words of humility, wonder, and joy: "Now to him who is able to accomplish far more than all we ask or imagine, by the power at work within us, to him be glory in the Church and in Christ Jesus to all generations, forever and ever."

May God's Holy Name be praised now and forever.

"It Can't Happen Here"

Thirtieth Monday of Ordinary Time, Lectionary 479
Ave Maria, FL, 2012

Ephesians 4:32–5:8
Psalm 1:1-2, 3, 4, 6
Luke 13:10-17

Did you ever read a book and say, "Well, I'm glad those days are over with"? When you read a history book, and find an account of, say, slavery, you might say, "Well, I'm glad those days are over with." (But they're not.) If you turn to science fiction, and read an account of, say, the genes of embryos being subjected to manipulation in the laboratory, you might say, "That could never happen!" (But it has.)

What do you say when we read today's gospel account? Jesus is being attacked because He held human life and health to be sacred, and cherished human dignity more than arbitrary man-made rules. In other words, when human ideology was trumping human identity, Jesus was attacked for His rejection of such monstrous and systematic evil. When you read this gospel, are you inclined to say, "Well, I'm glad those days are over with"? But they are not! Let me give you an example.

In England, there is a committee called "N.I.C.E.", the National Institute for Health and Clinical Excellence. Not long ago, doctors told a British woman who had just given birth, "Your child was born prematurely. If only he had been born 12 hours later, he would have qualified as 'viable' under the standards set by the people of N.I.C.E., and we could have treated him and saved his life. But because he was born 12 hours too soon, under the standards set by the people of N.I.C.E., he is not viable, so it is not worth treating him and we must let him die." Now, are you inclined to say, "That could never happen!"? But it has happened. Are you inclined to say, "But that could never happen here!"? Are you sure of that? I'm not.

The moral of the story is this: the greatest defense of the sanctity of human life, the firmest foundation for the dignity of human life from conception to natural death, is the unshakeable conviction that man is made in the image and likeness of God. Moreover, the Incarnation of Christ gives the human body and human life an identity and a destiny that no philosophy and no other faith could conceive of. Consequently, human health, indeed, human safety, depend very much upon committed Christians being vocal and active in all spheres of public life, preserving, protecting, and promoting the sanctity of human life.

Biblical scholar William Barclay wrote, "In Christianity the individual comes before the system... Christianity alone guarantees and defends the value of the ordinary, individual man or woman. If ever Christian principles are banished from political and economic life there is nothing left to keep at bay the totalitarian state where individuals are lost in the system..." You might recall those words as you prepare to vote.

The truth of those words is seen in the actions of Jesus. He defends human life against any human ideology that reduces or dismisses the preciousness of those made in the image and likeness of God. Dare we do any less?

When we are confronted by politicians, philosophers, scientists, economists, or cultural opinion makers who urge us to put aside the person and example of Jesus, we must rebuke them, and take courage by recalling the words of the psalm we heard today: "Blessed the man who follows not the counsel of the wicked."

May God's Holy Name be praised now and forever.

The Problem of Pain

Thirtieth Tuesday of Ordinary Time, Lectionary 480
Ave Maria, FL, 2011

Romans 8:18-25
Psalm 126:1-6
Luke 13:18-21

Saint Paul offers us a vivid image with these words: "We know that all creation is groaning in labor pains even until now…"

How do you measure pain? My mother had a very precise standard for measuring pain. For my mother, labor pain was the gold standard of pain. When my father's appendix burst and he nearly died and spent six weeks in intensive care, my mother assured me, "Of course, I feel sorry for your father, BUT IT WASN'T LABOR PAIN!"

I do not know how to measure pain, but I do know that too much pain can be a clue that something is wrong. For example, when you are breaking in a new pair of boots, you expect that they will pinch a bit; but if you put on the boots and pass out from the pain, then you may well suspect that something is amiss. Likewise, too little pain can be no good. For example, if your exercise routine doesn't make you sweat and burn, then you will likely gain no benefit from it. Regarding exercise, a Marine told me, "Pain is just weakness leaving the body." I hope someday to work up the courage to put that to the test.

I do know that in this life, pain is inevitable. From toothache to heartache, pain cannot be completely avoided. But *misery* is avoidable, because misery is a choice. Despite our best efforts, pain will befall us, but we are made miserable only if we choose misery. When the pain of life prompts us to sulk and sink into self-pity and selfishness rather than turn to God, then we are choosing misery. And we will rightly be held accountable for our choices for or against misery.

Saint Paul consoles us with these words: "I consider that the sufferings of this present time are as nothing compared with the glory to be revealed for us." Speaking as someone who has been to hell and back more times than he count, I can tell you that life in this world offers us a very stark choice: Either that what the Church proclaims about the Cross and Resurrection of Christ is completely true, or that life is a bad joke that probably shouldn't have been told. These are the only honest options we have—anything else is merely the illusion of sitting on the fence.

Worship only makes sense if we are convinced that creation is fundamentally good and that God's purposes will be fulfilled. That is why it is right for us to come to the altar today and echo these words of the Psalmist: "The LORD has done marvels for us." Let us choose to worship God and refuse misery.

May God's Holy Name be praised now and forever.

"Lord, Will Only a Few Be Saved?"

Thirtieth Wednesday of Ordinary Time, Lectionary 481
Ave Maria, FL, 2012

Ephesians 6:1-9
Psalm 145:10-11, 12-13ab, 13cd-14
Luke 13:22-30

I'm going to speak as a professor for a moment. What if I said the following to you? "I could tell you how many people are likely to pass the exam, or I can tell you how to pass the exam." If you had to choose just one, which bit of information would you prefer to hear from me? Surely, you would prefer to be told how to pass the exam. That seems obvious, doesn't it? Not really. What we just read from the Gospel of Luke suggests that it is not so obvious.

People ask Jesus, "Lord, will only a few be saved?" Notice they did not ask Him, "Lord, how can we be saved?" Fortunately, Jesus tells them, in this passage and in others, how to be saved. He says, "Strive to enter through the narrow gate." In the Greek language of the New Testament, "strive" has the same roots as the word "agony." Striving to enter the narrow gate is a struggle that will demand of us all that we have and all that we are.

Ok, but what will that struggle look like? Striving, struggling to enter through the narrow gate is a life lived loving God and loving our neighbor as ourselves. Ok, well, how do we do that? The Church has always had a direct and simple answer to that question. The Church offers a reliable formula for holiness and salvation, but, for some reason, people don't seem to like it. The answer is this: Do the ordinary duties of your state in life, to the best of your ability, and with great love. That's it. Granted, not necessarily a recipe for high drama, yet harder than it first appears, because the world, the flesh, and the devil will try to get in our way.

So, how do we keep on striving, day in and day out? How can parents change one more diaper or prepare one more meal? How can professors go out and give another lecture? How can priests write one more homily when they'd rather sleep in? (Present company excepted, of course.) Again, the answer is very simple: Gratitude.

When every other source of motivation runs out, when every other resolution to do the right thing fails, when every act of the will falters, there is always a reason to be grateful. When we are mindful of how generous and merciful God has been on our behalf, then our hearts will expand with gratitude and drive out every excuse or encumbrance that would keep us from holiness.

How do we cultivate a habit of gratitude? Again, it is maddeningly simple; I say it is maddening because it so simple that we have no excuse not to do it, and fallen human nature loves excuses above all else. We need to take 5 minutes each day and just count our blessings. That's it. Count our blessings, and then act as truly grateful people act. That is the path to holiness; that is the means of striving to enter through the narrow gate, day by day, until we meet God face to face. Only living as a grateful people can we truthfully proclaim the words of the psalm we heard today: "Let all your works give you thanks, O LORD, and let your faithful ones bless you."

May God's Holy Name be praised now and forever.

Unrequited Love

Thirtieth Thursday of Ordinary Time, Lectionary 482
Ave Maria, FL, 2012

Romans 8:31b-39
Psalm 109:21-22, 26-27, 30-31
Luke 13:31-35

Let's look at two points in today's gospel readings. When Jesus is warned that Herod wants him dead, Jesus replies, "Go and tell that fox..." Why did Our Lord choose to call Herod a fox? In the Jewish culture of that time and place, a fox was thought to be the most sly of the animals; it was thought to be the most destructive of the animals, and perhaps most important, to call a man a fox was to suggest that he was a worthless and insignificant man.

That statement of Jesus about Herod makes me wonder three things. First, is there a powerful public figure today who might merit the term "fox"? Second, if there were, would we have the courage to name him a fox? Third, if there were such a fox wielding public power, what would true Christians be obliged to do about it? But perhaps that is topic better suited for another time and place.

Let's focus now on some of the most poignant words

of the gospel. Jesus said: "Jerusalem, Jerusalem, you who kill the prophets and stone those sent to you, how many times I yearned to gather your children together as a hen gathers her brood under her wings, but you were unwilling!" Jesus is speaking of unrequited love. Now, love that is neither received nor returned has produced a great deal of bad adolescent poetry and a lot of good country music, but unrequited love reaches unfathomable depths of tragedy when the generous lover is God and the heartless beloved is you and me.

We can see the gift of God rejected when a child is aborted; we might even begin to imagine how the gift of God is spurned when a child intended by God is contracepted. But I wonder if we have the moral imagination, the humility, the courage, to countenance the barbaric cruelty inflicted upon the heart of God when we who have been given the gift of life and the gift of grace fail to receive and reciprocate to God the offer of His most intimate love.

Whenever my friends tell me they are expecting a child, I tell them immediately that a precious gift they can give to their child is to tell him, in words and in deeds, "You are worth my time." How much more is that true of our relationship to God! Yes, I am thinking of the smallness of time and heart we offer to God in prayer, but not only that—I am thinking also how little of time and heart we offer to God moment by moment, breath by breath, none of which we deserve or can earn, as we go about our busy day, doing what we think are vast and urgent things, without a thought for the presence of God.

God constantly hovers about us, eager to offer us all that we truly need, eager to offer the gift of His very self, and we take little or no notice. Instead, we slog through our day as orphans, as practical agnostics if not convinced atheists, as if there is no Paternal Providence for us. Perhaps we think the offer of God to us is too good to be true, perhaps we think we do not deserve it so we should not seek it, perhaps we are determined to save ourselves. I do not know. Each has to puzzle that out for himself. But I do know, because Jesus said so, that He yearns to embrace us, and our scorn of Him causes Him grief.

God always respects our freedom. Our "yes" to Him cannot be real if we cannot say "no" to Him. In His goodness, He allows us to choose. In His justice, He allows the consequences of our choice to come to us. We know that because Jesus said, "Behold, your house will be abandoned." Of course. A soul without Christ is like a body without a soul—it is empty and lifeless. But God, in His mercy, does not give up on us. We know that because Jesus said, "But I tell you, you will not see me until the time comes when you say, *'Blessed is he who comes in the name of the Lord.'*" Until the moment of death, we can receive and reciprocate the love of God by embracing Jesus of Nazareth as the Christ of God, the anointed one who comes in the name of the Lord.

Let's choose today to confess that we are not yet aflame with the Love of God as we ought to be. Let's resolve today to receive gladly the love of God that is constantly offered to us. Let's act today to prove our gratitude by our grateful love of God and neighbor. If we do that, then we shall see the Lord, for we will be able, finally and honestly, to cry out, "Blessed is he who comes in the name of the Lord."

May God's Holy Name be praised now and forever.

Promises

Thirty-First Sunday of Ordinary Time, Lectionary 151
Ave Maria, FL, 2011

Malachi 1:14b–2:2b, 8-10
Psalm 131:1-3
1 Thessalonians 2:7b-9, 13
Matthew 23:1-12

Do you want to hear a story? When I was a very little boy, having not yet reached the age of reason, but knowing that life offered more opportunities when Mommy wasn't looking, I got into all of the kitchen cabinets I could reach and pulled the labels off all of the cans. For about three weeks after that, every meal was accompanied by a side dish of "surprise."

Labels and names are a kind of promise, a promise that protects us against unpleasant surprises. They let you know what to expect. When I read a label that says "Bordeaux," I get my hopes up in a way that I don't when the label says "Budweiser." And I get very cranky when the contents don't live up to the promise made by the label.

God takes promise-making very seriously. And He takes betrayal of promises very seriously. If we had any doubt of that, we need only turn to the Scripture passages we just heard this morning. Through the prophet Malachi God tells us that when we break our promises we betray Him and we betray one another. Let's listen again to these words from the prophet Malachi: "Have we not all the one father? Has not the one God created us? Why then do we break faith with one another, violating the covenant of our fathers?"

God makes clear to us there that we bring disaster upon ourselves when we break faith with Him and one another. Through the prophet Malachi God says: "...this commandment is for you: If you do not listen, if you do not lay it to heart...I will send a curse upon you and of your blessing I will make a curse."

And from the Gospel of Matthew we hear that Jesus really doesn't like it when people take the oath of office, enjoy the trappings and privileges of office, but break faith with their duties and the people they had sworn to serve. In the time of Jesus, the culprits most obviously guilty of such hypocrisy were the Pharisees. Jesus warns us against such hypocrites when He tells us: "...do not follow their example. For they preach but they do not practice. They tie up heavy burdens hard to carry and lay them on people's shoulders, but they will not lift a finger to move them. All their works are performed to be seen."

The Pharisees are long dead, but their spirit and practice live on in the hypocrites and the promise-breakers of today. If we read the Scriptures, and we obey Jesus' command to "read the signs of the times," we can begin to connect the dots.

When I read these Scriptures and look at America, I see politicians who take an oath to defend the Constitution and then betray their oath in word and deed, and I can say, "God does not like that."

When I read these Scriptures and look at America, I see Catholic clergy and religious who reject the Church's teaching while accepting the Church's paycheck, and I can say, "God does not like that."

When I read these Scriptures and look at America, I see universities calling themselves "Catholic" where condoms are more widely distributed than Holy Communion and I can say, "God does not like that."

And what about us? What about we here at Ave Maria? What about this community of family, friends, and neighbors? This gathering of disciples and scholars? Well, if you haven't figured it out already, all of us here are imperfect, all of us here are sinners, and, in our better moments, we know that we are loved sinners. And we loved sinners are trying to do something that so many academics and politicians and modern-day Pharisees don't quite understand: here, we are trying to keep our promises. We are striving to keep faith with the faith of the Church; we are striving to live within the heart of the Church and to radiate the splendor of the truth; we are striving to hand on the best that we have received from grace and nature. We are here, as a town and as a university, because we have seen elsewhere the terrible consequences of broken promises.

Martin Luther King said, "Injustice anywhere threatens justice everywhere." We are here at Ave Maria because we believe that infidelity anywhere threatens fidelity everywhere. And because it seems that these days fidelity is threatened everywhere, we have built Ave Maria so that fidelity can have a safe place to live here and now, so that fidelity can go on to grow everywhere and always. We are here because we know that our Church and our nation and our world do not need more hypocrites, do not need more false advertising, do not need more broken promises, do not need more Pharisees. Yes, here we make mistakes; yes, here we are all sinners; yes, here we imperfectly give our imperfect selves to the task. Mindful of our faults, we nonetheless focus more on Christ, Who is the source and summit of all of our striving. And because Christ loved us first, we choose to love those who are here in our care: our students, our colleagues, our families, friends and neighbors, our visitors—indeed, all of our brothers and sisters in Christ. And we live and work as we do here, so that the blessings of our faith and culture may be handed on to future generations elsewhere.

At our Holy Mass today, we have a great and urgent task. Today, if we are to be faithful to what God has entrusted to us, we must pledge ourselves to our Heavenly Father and to one another. With Christ we must place ourselves on the altar of sacrifice, and ask for our Father's blessing. We must do this because we are called to die and rise with Christ for the life of the world. We can keep our promises, we can avoid being Pharisees, only if we are a community that draws its strength from Christ, crucified and risen, Who is given to us in the Eucharist.

Today, let's resolve that this week we will meet as disciples and as neighbors and as colleagues, and talk and pray about how we shall keep our promises to God and to one another. Let's plan concretely how we can more and more become a repenting community of faith, hope, and love. Faith—embracing all that Christ has revealed to the world through His Church. Hope—striving to receive the victory God will give to those who persevere until the end. Love—protecting and providing for those in our care, and handing on the faith and the civilization entrusted to us.

If we do that, if we with God's grace help each other to keep our sacred promises, if we become the community of faith, hope, and love that God intends, then lives will be saved, and souls will be saved, and best of all—God will be glorified.

May God's Holy Name be praised now and forever.

Time

Thirty-First Tuesday of Ordinary Time, Lectionary 486
Ave Maria, FL, 2012

Philippians 2:5-11
Psalm 22
Luke 14:15-24

This parable is a painful reminder of how easy it is to build one's life around misplaced or distorted priorities. What is especially painful is that we must admit that we have infinitely more resources for distracting ourselves from God than did the people in the time of Jesus.

In the parable the invited guests made their excuses, and people's excuses do not differ so very much today. The first man said that he had bought a field and was going to see it. He allowed the claims of daily work to displace the claims of God. It is still possible to be so immersed in this world that we have no time to worship, and even no time to pray. To counter that temptation, we might ask ourselves, "What am I like when I don't pray?" If we are honest, I am sure we will not like the answer. Then we should look for a book by Bill Hybels called, "Too Busy Not to Pray."

The second man said that he had bought five yoke of

oxen and that he was going to try them out. He let the claims of novelty displace the invitation of Christ. It often happens that when people acquire new possessions they become so taken up with them that the claims of worship and of God get crowded out. It has been observed that it "is perilously easy for a new game, a new hobby, even a new friendship, to take up the time that should be kept for God." Our culture has produced people with thumbs swollen from texting and incapable of holding Rosary beads. Our culture has produced people with eyes bloodshot from watching television and who will not take time to gaze upon the Eucharistic Lord. Our culture has produced people with ears deafened by the "music" jammed into them, but who cannot hear the call of the Lord or the cry of the poor.

The third man said, "I have married a wife, and therefore I cannot attend." The Book of Deuteronomy declared that a newly-married man is absolved of military and public duties for one year. No doubt that very law was on this man's mind. It is one of the tragedies and absurdities of life when good things crowd out the claims of God. But the happiness of home and family were never meant to be used selfishly. Love of God and love of neighbor must be at the heart of every marriage and every home. For a family to say, "We are too busy trying to be happy to have time for God," is a very strange thing.

What does a culture look like when it becomes too busy, too distracted, or too selfish to have time for God? You might end up with a culture that puts pleasure above all else; you might end up with a nation that chooses to incur debt rather than accept discipline; you might end up with religious groups that prefer human praise to divine approval. You might end up with a people whose only hope of not living on their knees as slaves is to spend time on their knees in prayer.

May God's Holy Name be praised now and forever.

INNOCENT BLOOD

Thirty-First Friday of Ordinary Time, Lectionary 489
Ave Maria, FL, 2008

Philippians 3:17–4:1
Psalm 122
Luke 16:1-8

From time to time, I have taught a philosophy course called "God and the Problem of Evil." I hope to teach it again soon. Each time I teach it, I begin the semester with a quote from Dostoyevsky's novel, *The Brothers Karamazov*. Dostoyevsky writes:

"Imagine that you yourself are building an edifice of human destiny that has the ultimate aim of making people happy and giving them finally peace and rest, but that to achieve this, you are faced inevitably and inescapably with torturing just one tiny baby, say that small fellow who was just beating his fists on his chest, so that you would be building your edifice on his unrequited tears—would you agree to be its architect under those conditions? Tell me, and don't lie!"

I tell my students that whatever we say about the problem of evil, we must be answerable to Dostoyevsky and that tearful child. Otherwise, our words are empty.

Now imagine this. Imagine a nation hearing the words of Dostoyevsky and saying, "Yes! Let us build such a world! Let us build an edifice of human destiny that will make us happy, free, prosperous, unburdened, and joyful. And let us not be satisfied with building it on the unrequited tears of one innocent child. No, let us build our great earthly city on the blood of innocent children—the blood of countless innocent children, as many children as it takes to secure our freedom and our joy. Without apology, without shame, without regret, let us become drunk on the blood of our young! So let it be, by the power of choice. Our will be done!"

Imagine living in such a nation. What would the sane people do? More specifically, what would true followers of Christ do in such a nation? I think, if Christians were to live in such an imaginary nation, they might recall the words of Saint Paul that we just heard: "For many, as I have often told you and now tell you even in tears, conduct themselves as enemies of the cross of Christ."

Such hypothetical Christians, in such an imaginary nation, committing to memory those words of Saint Paul, would also do well to recall the stinging words of Christ from today's gospel passage: "For the children of this world are more prudent in dealing with their own generation than the children of light." In other words, Christians in such an imaginary nation would have to admit that their country could have come to such a sorry state only if there had been a previous catastrophic failure in teaching, wisdom, and holiness for at least a generation. If all who called themselves Christian were true followers of Christ, if Christ had been made truly known and loved in their land, then such an imaginary nation would never have come to such a sorry state. And Christians would have to admit, with Jesus, that the children of this world have been much more effective, much more bold, much more clever than the children of light.

If there were such a nation gone mad, what would the Christians there have to do? They would have to point to the Eucharistic altar, and declare to God, themselves, and the world: "The resistance starts here! The resistance starts now!" Only a sanctified people who are ready to die and rise with Christ for the life of the world could overcome such dark madness. Such Christians would leave the altar, and go out into the world, committed to prayer, fasting, and penance. Then they would work really hard to get really smart really fast, because they would know that any delay, any loss of nerve, any hesitation, means that more innocent blood would be shed. They would know that they have to become more effective, more daring, more clever than the children of this world. They would know that unless they become saints, scholars, poets, warriors, and heroes, lives will be lost, souls will be lost, and worst of all, God will not be glorified.

But, this is all just a story, isn't it? There could never be such an imaginary nation, could there? So there would never really be a need for such sanctified Christians, right? Besides, it's Friday—the weekend has begun, and who has the energy to think about such unpleasant things? Still, just in case....just in case there could ever be such an imaginary nation in fact, just in case there might be a need for a church of the faithful remnant who can become leaven in the bread, we might wish to follow the instructions of Saint Ignatius Loyola. Following his instructions at the start of his Spiritual Exercises, today, place yourself before the crucified Jesus and ask yourself these questions: "What have I done for Christ? What am I doing for Christ? What shall I do for Christ?"

May God's Holy Name be praised now and forever.

Generosity

Thirty-Second Sunday of Ordinary Time, Lectionary 155
Ave Maria, FL, 2009
1 Kings 17:10-16
Psalm 146
Hebrews 9:24-28
Mark 12:38-44

What is the strangest item you ever received in the mail? Before I was a Jesuit, while living in northern Virginia, I found in my mail box an envelope from one of the many so-called "televangelists" who were seen so often on television in the 1980s. In the envelope was the outline of a hand, along with a collection of stamps listing different prayer intentions. Among the intentions were "cure for cancer," "find a good job," "find a Christian spouse," and the one that interested me the most, "100-fold return on tithing."

I was instructed to select five prayer intentions and to stick them onto the fingertips of the drawing of the hand. Then I was to place my fingertips on the prayer intentions attached to the fingertips of the illustrated hand, and pray for each of the intentions. I was instructed to mail this item to the televangelist, along with a suitable "faith-based love offering," because, according to the enclosed letter, "God loves a cheerful giver" and "God cannot be outdone in generosity." Upon receiving my prayer intentions on the hand, the televangelist would place his hand on the same prayer intention stamps I had just prayed over. Immediately, I was promised, ***immediately***, God would grant those five prayer requests. I could be certain this would happen, wrote the televangelist, because in Matthew 18:19, Jesus said, "Amen, I say to you, if two of you agree on earth about anything for which they are to pray, it shall be granted to them by my heavenly Father."

Do you see how that works? We would both pray in agreement on the five prayer intentions, and then God must, MUST grant my requests, because of Matthew 18:19. "God said it, I believe it, that settles it—and God is stuck with it." At root, this whole venture was not an invitation to faith; it was an invitation to magic. The televangelist was telling me, in not so many words, that my actions, with his collusion, could ***obligate*** the divine power to act on my behalf. That is magic, not faith; that is presumption, not hope!

How different that magical view is from the proper understanding of divine generosity. The scholastics had a lovely phrase in Latin, *"Do ut des"*—"I give so that you might give." In other words, Divine generosity does not give so as to oblige the one who has received the gift. Rather, the Divine giver gives so that the one who receives the gift can have the joy of giving a gift also.

Let me illustrate: When I was a little boy, my father had a garden, and the best flowers in the garden were the tiger lilies. I was about 4 years old, and my father clipped a tiger lily, handed it to me and said, "Give it to Mommy in the kitchen." I took the flower and marched into the kitchen announcing: "Mommy, look what I got for you!!" I was very proud of myself, as if I myself had made the flower. So, not only was there a gift for my mother, my father had given me the gift of being able to give a gift. The moral of the story is that creation is rooted in generosity. It is rooted in benevolence. True generosity gives a gift without any strings attached. How very much unlike the scheme cooked up by that awful televangelist!

Now let's look again that the gospel passage we just heard. Jesus notes that the widow made a full return, a wholehearted and practical response to God's generosity to her, and her return was based not upon the abundance of her resources, but instead based upon the abundance of her gratitude. Jesus praises the poor widow.

And what about us? What does our gratitude and generosity in response to God look like? Now, let me reassure you that I am not going to ask you to reach for your wallets. I am not going to ask you to participate in a divine pyramid scheme by telling you that "no one can outdo God in generosity." I am not going to tell you about how much your parish needs, in the words of many desperate pastors, your "time, talent, and treasure," although it surely does. And I am not going to be like many pastors and suggest that if you have only one to give of "time, talent and treasure," please let it be treasure.

Now in fairness, it is not surprising that pastors with bills to pay have their hands out. After all, Saint Teresa of Avila said that "God, Teresa, and fifteen gold coins can do very much more than just God and Teresa." Yes, that is true, but even that honest observation by Saint Teresa, a most practical saint, is not quite right. You see, our proper model of generosity is not the poor widow from today's parable; our proper model of generosity is Christ Himself.

Christ gave Himself completely; He poured Himself out absolutely to the Father. Our vocation as Christians is to become Christ-like, to imitate Christ in His act of complete self-donation to the Father. How shall we follow the Lord's example and make a complete gift of ourselves to our Heavenly Father? Well, that does not happen all at once. It is a process.

And that process begins here. Here, in this holy place, at this Holy Mass, we can unite ourselves with Christ in His gift of Himself to the Father. Be sure about why that is so important. We will not have true and full gratitude, with generosity as the first fruit of gratitude, unless we have the vivid and unforgettable experience of being completely poured out with Christ to the Father, and, like Christ, finding ourselves completely received by the Father.

Only when we are certain that the fullness of joy can be found by uniting ourselves to Christ in the perfect sacrifice of praise, only when we are certain that a loving union with the Father is our only hope of enduring fullness—only then can we understand and live with gratitude and generosity.

Yes, nice words. Uplifting words. Gratitude, generosity, fullness, Christ, Father. But how can they be more than just words for us? How can these words become fact and flesh and faith in our lives? We begin by uniting ourselves with Christ in His Eucharistic sacrifice to the Father. Offer your body with the Body of Christ in the bread offered to the Father. Offer your soul with the Blood of Christ in the wine offered to the Father. Then come forward and receive the first fruits of that sacrifice as you receive here the Body, Blood, Soul, and Divinity of Christ, given to you under the appearances of bread and wine.

Only those who have been given in the Eucharistic sacrifice to the Father, only those who have received the fruits of that Eucharistic sacrifice will be able to be properly grateful and generous.

I will ask you to pray today and every day this week for three graces, for three special blessings. I will ask you to pray for answers to these three questions. First question: "What have I received from God?" Second question: "Do I desire the gift of gratitude?" Third question: "How shall I prove my gratitude with generosity?" If we live and pray with such honesty, then we can join the psalmist whom we heard this morning and cry out, "The LORD keeps faith forever, the LORD sets captives free."

May God's Holy Name be praised now and forever.

MILLSTONES AND BLINDNESS

Thirty-Second Monday of Ordinary Time, Lectionary 491
Ave Maria, FL, 2011
Wisdom 1:1-7
Psalm 139:1-10
Luke 17:1-6

What is the most evil show on television? Some have suggested a program now in its fourth season, called "Toddlers and Tiaras." It's a program about beauty pageants for very young girls, girls so young that they are barely potty-trained. But they have their hair and nails done; they sit in the chair quietly while make-up artists make them look like tarty teens; these girls cry about their weight and talk about diets; and their parents dress them up in provocative costumes that sometimes include padded bras.

And Jesus said: "Things that cause sin will inevitably occur, but woe to the one through whom they occur. It would be better for him if a millstone were put around his neck and he be thrown into the sea than for him to cause one of these little ones to sin." Of course, these little ones haven't reached the age of reason, and so cannot sin, but they are being set up for misery and neurosis and eating disorders and worse. And opening such doors for little girls and then shoving them through is a terrible sin.

How can parents be so stupid? These words from the Book of Wisdom give us a clue: "...perverse counsels separate a man from God...into a soul that plots evil, wisdom enters not." Or, said more simply: "Stupid gets what stupid wants."

Separating ourselves from the wisdom of God by following our own wisdom is a spiritual and moral disaster. Encouraging innocent youth to follow a wicked example is even worse. And remaining silent while the little ones are lied to, twisted, and seduced is perhaps worst of all.

So again, I ask: "How can parents be so foolish?" But I ask that question cautiously, lest we be tempted to pray the prayer of the Pharisee and say, "Lord, I give you thanks that I am not like other men." While we are rightly horrified by the dangerous and sinful blindness of those crazy parents, we must sober ourselves up and wonder what blind spots we ourselves have. What of our own behavior is scandalous and evident to others that we have blinded ourselves to? And when have we deafened ourselves to the cries of those who suffer moral violation?

Perhaps the employee paid for a full day's work who spends his workday on Facebook has blinded himself to the scandal of his behavior. Perhaps the husband who spends the weekend watching football on television while neglecting his wife has blinded himself to the scandal of his behavior. Perhaps the student who accepts a scholarship for his studies but does not bother to study has blinded himself to the scandal of his behavior.

If we look at the world around us, and we notice willful moral blindness and culpable moral deafness, we may take a moment, shake our heads, beat our breast, and say, "There but for the grace of God, go I." But that is not enough. We must turn to the Lord in prayer, and ask Him to open our eyes and open our ears, so that we might know clearly where we stand in need of repentance and mercy.

Such a prayer, at once humble and brave, will be very pleasing to God, for then we will pray as we have heard the Psalmist pray today: "Guide me, Lord, along the everlasting way."

May God's Holy Name be praised now and forever.

"HER VALUE IS FAR BEYOND PEARLS"

Thirty-Third Sunday of Ordinary Time, Lectionary 157
Ave Maria, FL, 2008

Proverbs 31:10-13, 19-20, 30-31
Psalm 128:1-5
1 Thessalonians 5:1-6
Matthew 25:14-30

If I were a mind-reader, I think I could hear the students in the church saying, "Uh oh…We're in trouble now. The parable of the talents, a microphone, and Father McTeigue. We're about to get a savage spiritual beating for not being diligent students." That would be a good inference on their part, but today I want to do something different.

Let's listen again to some of today's reading from Proverbs: "When one finds a worthy wife, her value is far beyond pearls. Her husband, entrusting his heart to her, has an unfailing prize." Dad loved to quote this in honor of Mom. Were they just words, or did he really mean them?

Let's see. I asked him once about something that happened to him when he was single. He said he couldn't remember. I asked him, "Because it happened so long ago?"

He replied, "It's hard for me to remember anything about being single. Life apart from your mother doesn't make sense to me." Mere sentiment? Or did he really mean those words? Let me tell you a story.

In the fall of 1989, my mother needed heart surgery. The night before surgery, we dropped Mom off at the hospital. Dad and I went home, and planned to get up very early the next morning to be with Mom. When we woke up, we found out that the refrigerator had given out during the night. Water was all over the floor, and the food had spoiled.

This was a crisis. I said to Dad, "We can't tell Mom about this. You know how she is. She has a personal relationship with all the appliances—this will be like a death in the family for her. Let's not tell her, and while she's in surgery we'll just get another refrigerator." Dad agreed, and we went off to the hospital.

We got to the hospital, and walked down the hall to Mom's room. I was ahead of Dad. Suddenly, he shoved me out of the way, ran into the room ahead of me and yelled, "Sue! The refrigerator died and we lost all the food." I thought to myself, "Great, Dad. Just like we had planned!"

Then my mother sat up in bed and yelled, "Don't get a refrigerator until I get out of the hospital. I know you! You'll go to some little store and pay top dollar! Wait for me and then we'll go to Sears!"

I thought I was going to lose my mind. How could this be happening? So I said, "Mom! They are going to crack you open like a lobster and poke you in the middle with sharp objects, and your obsessing about the refrigerator? And Dad! You! I thought we had a deal!"

He turned to face me, shaking, his face red, with tears in his eyes and yelled, "You don't understand! Your mother is the only woman I've ever loved! I can't lie to her!"

Mom survived the surgery, but then had a stroke. And then a mastectomy. And then another stroke. Dad spent the next 15 years taking care of Mom, 24 hours a day. He loved her not just with words, but with his whole life.

Given Mom's health history, we were surprised when Dad died first. What pained me most about Dad's death was not Dad's death but Mom's grief over Dad's death. At the funeral home, as we watched them close the casket for the last time, Mom broke free of my arm, dragged her crippled body to the casket, knelt down and said, "I love you, I love you, I love you."

About a month later, Mom told me, "Every night, before I go to bed, I say a prayer that I can dream about him. And if I dream about him that night, then the next day isn't so bad."

Could anyone dare say that theirs was a merely human love? I couldn't. Clearly, the love of God was caught up in their love for each other.

How did that happen? How did they inspire in one another and express such long, faithful, even costly devotion?

Theologically, we could say that they belonged to Christ, as baptized, and, belonging to Christ, they could give themselves to each other in sacramental marriage. They stood hand in hand at the altar of God, and promised to love each other in such a way that people would look at them and say: "Oh! That must be how Christ loves His Church! That must be how the Church loves Christ!" And they knew full well that such an exalted standard was beyond the reach of human efforts, and could be reached only with the help of God's grace.

Let's be clear: They could give themselves to each other in sacramental marriage, faithfully, for a lifetime, only because they first belonged to Christ through Baptism.

How to prepare for such a vocation? How to prepare to receive such truly amazing grace? The answer is just one word. Can you guess what it is? PURITY. Purity of body, mind, and heart. Purity is to be undivided. Purity is a two-sided coin. On one side, it means to give oneself only to what God has provided for; on the other side, to receive into oneself only what God has provided for. The pure, Jesus said, shall see God, and only those who can see God can see God in another and in themselves. Only the pure can see the beauty, the sacred dignity, the majesty and terrible vulnerability and fragility of a human being made in the image and likeness of God. Only the pure can give themselves wisely and completely. Only the pure can receive another wisely and completely. Purity is protected by union with Christ.

Ladies, if with God's grace you commit absolutely to purity of body, mind, and heart, your purity will first tell the world that you are nobody's fool, nobody's toy, and that will drive away the players, and will get a good man's attention. If you are committed to purity, your feminine dignity will shine as a beacon that can guide a worthy man to you; if you are committed to purity, your feminine dignity will be a melody that only a good man can hear and which a good man will never forget. If you are committed to purity, your feminine dignity will be a poem which a good man will want to sing as the anthem of his beloved. Ladies, please, strive to be the kind of woman whom a good man wants to find, love, and serve.

Young men, if with God's grace you commit absolutely to purity of body, mind, and heart, you will have the weapons and armor needed to fight the good fight of becoming a man of honor. If you are committed to purity, your honor as a true man of God will be a powerful call to a noble woman, who will know she can entrust her heart, soul, and body to you. If you are committed to purity, a good woman will know that you have the freedom to offer up your whole life for her, as her husband and protector. If you are committed to purity, a good woman will trust you enough to help perfect you as a man by agreeing to confer fatherhood on you, as the mother of your children.

Gentlemen, please, strive to be the kind of man whom a good woman wants to find, love, and honor.

God's promise to the young men and women here, most of whom will be called to marriage, is that all the goodness, beauty, and joy I have just described, is precisely what God wants to give them, if only they will cooperate with His grace. And the path to being ready to receive that grace is purity of body, mind, and heart, a purity protected by union with Christ.

Now, I feel compelled to address one objection. Some folks here might be thinking, "You know, Father, I'm married and my marriage doesn't look, sound, or feel like what you described. My marriage is about dishes, diapers, duties, tuition, taxes, and television. The drama, the poetry, the music, the amazing grace, the zesty passion you described—it's just not there, at least not now."

Briefly, I can only say that the drama, the poetry, the music and the magic, the sacramentality are to be found primarily in the everydayness. Yes, there are peak experiences, there are honeymoons and second honeymoons and bouquets of roses and moonlit nights. But the meeting of nature and grace, the surrender of laying down one's life, the humility and joy of receiving the gift of another, that will happen mostly in the crucible of everyday life. Pray for the eye of the artist, the ear of the musician, the heart of the poet, pray for the grace to love as God loves, fully, freely, faithfully, and fruitfully. With God's grace, the daily duties and chores, seemingly only mundane, can lead to sacraments, stories, songs, music, joy, and ultimately to the happiness of heaven.

The blind do not see, the deaf do not hear. But we are in the light and we have heard God's call. Saint Paul told us this morning: "For all of you are children of the light and children of the day. We are not of the night or of darkness. Therefore, let us not sleep as the rest do, but let us stay alert."

Therefore, all of us, single, celibate, or married, can today rightly pray for three graces, three special blessings. First, pray for purity of body, mind, and heart, for only the pure shall see God. Second, pray for a deeper union with Christ, for only those united to Christ can give themselves to others. Third, pray to be alert, alert to all those opportunities for love and joy hidden in our daily duties. If we do that, if we pray for purity, union, and alertness, then one day we will hear from our Lord's lips the words we have always ached to hear, words without which our lives will have been a failure: "Well done, my good and faithful servant. Come, share your master's joy."

May God's Holy Name be praised now and forever.

The Day and the Hour

Thirty-Third Sunday of Ordinary Time, Lectionary 158
Ave Maria, FL, 2009

Daniel 12:1-3
Psalm 16:5, 8, 9-10, 11
Hebrews 10:11-14, 18
Mark 13:24-32

"He knows when you are sleeping; he knows when you're awake. He knows when you've been bad or good, so be good for goodness' sake! Oh, you'd better watch out, you'd better not cry, you'd better not pout I'm telling you why…"

And who is coming to town? That's the question! And when is he coming to town? That's the other question! That's the question Jesus points to this morning as He says to us in today's gospel passage: "But of that day or hour, no one knows, neither the angels in heaven, nor the Son, but only the Father."

However, these words of Jesus have not stopped people from speculating about and even predicting with startling precision the day and the hour of the return of Jesus. An Evangelical Christian named William Alnor wrote a book called *Soothsayers of the Second Advent*, wherein he criticized his fellow evangelicals who predicted with undue confidence the return of Jesus. In that book he noted that the bestselling book in 1988 among Evangelical Christians was called *88 Reasons Why He Is Coming Back in '88*. He also noted that the following year the bestselling book among Evangelical Christians was called *89 Reasons Why He Is Coming Back in '89*. Presumably the 89th reason for His coming back in '89 was that He did not come back in '88.

Again, let's remember that Jesus said no one knows the day or the hour. But how then do we live so that we are mindful that the day and the hour are nonetheless surely coming? Make no mistake: there *will* be a consummation of all creation. And we can be sure that the quality of our lives and the content of our souls will be revealed—totally. In response to that revelation, God will ratify the choice we have made, whether it be the choice for Him or the choice against Him. Either God will say "yes" to our "yes" to Him, or God will say "yes" to our "no" to Him.

But before that fullness of time, when both we and God are fully revealed, we can be sure that other days and other hours will come. Days and hours are coming that will force us to disclose to ourselves, to God, and to the world the very real difference between fidelity and infidelity, the very real difference between bearing true witness to Christ and bearing false witness to Christ.

A day and an hour may be coming very soon, when we may be required to give tax dollars to pay for abortions. And then our fidelity or infidelity will be revealed.

A day and an hour may be coming very soon, when priests will be dragged out of the pulpit in handcuffs for speaking the Word of God, a word redefined as "hate speech." And then our fidelity or infidelity will be revealed.

A day and an hour may be coming very soon, when we will be required to acknowledge definitions of marriage that are contrary to nature and contrary to the Word of God.

And then our fidelity or infidelity will be revealed.

Change is coming. It will be change you can believe in, because it will be change that you cannot avoid. And on that day, in that hour, true Christians will be revealed before God and the world. And so will false Christians also be revealed.

On that day and in that hour, those who claim to be Christian will be revealed as faithful or as fraudulent, as confessors or as cowards, as heroes or as heretics.

Be sure of this: No matter where we may live or hide, no matter how we may hope or dread, no matter what we may reveal or conceal, we will each of us be put to the test. And this test can only have two possible results—either fidelity unto death and glory, or infidelity unto death and damnation.

We all know that we shall be put to the test. This is not news. Yes, from time to time, we may wish that it were not so. But if we have the slightest shred of spiritual maturity, we know that trial, death, and consummation are coming for each of us and for all of us.

So, what shall we do? How shall we live, knowing that the days and the hours of trial and revelation are coming to us and coming for us? We have four options. The first option is denial, in which case we may take up the world's invitation to distract ourselves from our fears, our infidelities, and our hopelessness. But such distractions cannot last. A second option is to become Pelagians, trying to save ourselves by our own will and wit. But none of us are so strong and wise as to be able to save ourselves. A third option is pious magic, by which we try to manipulate Divine favor by an endless devotionalism that is divorced from love of God and love of neighbor. But God is not fooled by such false piety.

The only option, the only way to respond worthily to the hours and the days of trial that are coming is discipleship. Discipleship is a way of love and obedience in service to a master. While I was working in Southeast Asia, an orphan I cared for said to me, "Father, I know what is obedience. Obedience is to listen and to do. If you do not listen, how can you obey? And if you do not do, then it is not obedience."

We who are disciples of Christ, how shall we express our love for Him? We can express our love for Him by offering Him obedience. True disciples of Christ will obey His command to eat His Body and to drink His Blood, will obey His command to baptize all nations, will obey His command to love God and to love our neighbor as ourselves.

Humble, hopeful, wholehearted Christian discipleship—in other words, love and obedience for our master, Jesus the Christ, which will result in a joyful union with Christ—that discipleship and union are the only way to be prepared for the day, the hour, the trials, and the consummation that are surely coming for each of us and for all of us.

Our love, our obedience, our consummation can begin right now at this altar. Let us join the sacrifice of our lives to the sacrifice of Christ offered to our Heavenly Father. Let us approach the altar, sure that if we are poured out with Christ in sacrifice to the Father, then we can be filled up with the victorious Christ whom the Father has raised from the dead.

Let us resolve to leave this place of prayer sure that we are on a mission, a mission to be holy, to be heralds, and to be hopeful. If we live and pray so as to be faithful to that mission, then we can be sure of a share in the victory of Christ, and we can make our own the promise we heard this morning from the Letter to the Hebrews, whose author assured us with these words: "For by one offering he has made perfect forever those who are being consecrated."

May God's Holy Name be praised now and forever.

Honesty, Clarity, and Courage

Thirty-Third Sunday of Ordinary Time, Lectionary 159
Ave Maria, FL, 2013

Malachi 3:19-20a
Psalm 98:5-6, 7-8, 9
2 Thessalonians 3:7-12
Luke 21:5-19

When I was a young boy, I enjoyed reading stories about good versus evil. Good guys fighting bad guys—especially if the good guys had swords—I thought was a formula that was hard to improve upon. As I got a little older, I started reading comic books, and was thrilled by superheroes who would save the day. If only ordinary people could hold on long enough for Superman to come to the rescue, then all would be well.

In high school, as I became more serious about the Catholic faith, Jesus was presented to me as kind of a superhero. All we had to do, it was suggested to me, was to avoid mortal sin, wait for Jesus to return, and then He would clean up all the mess in the world and get rid of the bad guys. My friends assured me that this belief rested upon the authority of the Scriptures, such as the passage from the prophet Malachi we just heard. Let's listen to it again: "Lo, the day is coming, blazing like an oven, when all the proud and all evildoers will be stubble, and the day that is coming will set them on fire, leaving them neither root nor branch, says the LORD of hosts." That seems to settle the matter, doesn't it? God is coming to mow down the bad guys, so all we have to do is keep our own sin on a short leash, and all the evil, injustice, and falsehoods in the world will be mopped up by God.

Now, that view has a certain appeal, especially if one is inclined to be scrupulous rather than courageous, but in fact it is not right. The proof of that is found in the Sign of the Cross, by which we begin and end all of our prayer and worship. The Classics scholar John Senior wrote: "It is a dangerous thing to make that sign because it says: I commit myself to that death. Catholics do not trace the descent of the Dove upon themselves, or the Star of Hope, or any other sign." So says John Senior.

Anyone who marks himself with the Sign of the Cross is declaring before God and the world that he will not be a passive bystander in the fight against the powers of darkness. The Sign of the Cross tells us that the only way you can triumph is to be willing to lose everything, up to and including your life—otherwise evil will have dominion over you. Yes, our Lord will win in the end, but the multitudes of Christians who have died before us will remind us that Jesus Christ returning in glory *before* you die is not guaranteed.

What about hope? Yes, hope is a virtue, but wishful thinking is neither a virtue nor a strategy. Hope is the choice to make oneself available to God without reservation, ready to greet Him and cooperate with Him when and as He chooses to come to us. Wishful thinking is the delusion that all will be well even if I do nothing, because I'm such a lovely person. Our wishful thinking is Satan's fondest wish.

Our Scripture readings at this Mass call us to

courageous action against evil until the Lord returns. Courage is like a debt that must be paid. If we do not act courageously now against evil, then a future generation, perhaps even our own children, will have to pay our debt with interest. If good people had resisted Hitler when it was easier to do so, then American soldiers storming the beaches of Normandy would have been unnecessary. When one generation cowers, another generation pays the price.

For the love of God and for the love of neighbor commanded by God, we must act courageously against sin and evil, starting with the sin that resides in our own heart. I will begin my campaign against sin by first looking in the mirror. I suggest that you do the same.

The Culture of Death rages against the Culture of Life. The State has declared that the Church is unwelcome. Those who should know better brand as "Christian" what no Apostle would recognize. We see all of that in the world. What shall we in our little town do?

I ask you today, and for every day this week, to pray for three graces, three special blessings. First, pray for honesty—so that we might admit the root of sin within our own heart. Second, pray for clarity—so that the evil around us might be truly seen and named. Third, pray for courage—so that marked with the Sign of the Cross we will remain faithful until death. If—and only if—we live such graces, then we take to heart this promise of our Lord: "By your perseverance you will secure your lives."

May God's Holy Name be praised now and forever.

How to Write a Letter

Thirty-Fourth Wednesday of Ordinary Time,
Lectionary 505
Ave Maria, FL, 2012

Revelation 15:1-4
Psalm 98:1, 2-3ab, 7-8, 9
Luke 21:12-19

A few days ago, I did something that I haven't done in a long time—I wrote a letter. Not an email, a letter. And I didn't type it. I wrote it out by hand. It took me a long time to do so, because I have the handwriting of an 8-year old, and for the letter to be legible, I had to take my time. Writing the letter slowly caused me to think about what I would say. I wanted the letter to be worthy of my time and effort, and worthy of the reader's time and effort.

What if you had to write a letter today? What if you had to write a letter to a person who was frightened, discouraged, having doubts about the faith, and perhaps even feeling abandoned by God? How would you write such a letter? I think that we would want that letter to be truthful, of course, and a source of hope, and especially, also memorable, even unforgettable. The best letter does no one any good if it can't be remembered.

I think of these things as I read the Book of Revelation at this time of the liturgical year, at this time in the history of our nation, and at this time in the history of our Church in America. At this time, I suspect that we all know people who are frightened, discouraged, having doubts about the faith, and perhaps even feeling abandoned by God. We don't want such people to suffer unnecessarily, we don't want them to lose heart, we don't want them to lose their way.

What shall we say to them? We might say to them what the Book of Revelation has been telling the Christian people from the beginning. We would say to them that God alone is sovereign, that God alone is greater than any earthly power, that God can use human individuals and communities, as well as the elements and forces of nature, to reveal His mercy and His justice, and to save the people He has made for Himself.

We might say to our frightened and discouraged friends, as the Book of Revelation has said long before us, that God is in the business of ending slavery. God is in the business of breaking political, economic, moral, cultural, and spiritual chains. God does so because He knows that the highest good of humanity is for a free people to worship freely the living God. In 1986, the Congregation for the Doctrine of the Faith wrote the following words: "When God rescues his People from hard economic, political and cultural slavery, he does so in order to make them, through the Covenant on Sinai, 'a kingdom of priests and a holy nation' (Ex 19:6). God wishes to be adored by people who are free."[1] Those are simply the words of theologians used to explain in prose what the Book of Revelation spoke of in the theology of poetry. They echo the words spoken by our

---

[1] *Libertatis conscientia*, 44

Lord in our gospel passage for today. The Lord's promise is this: His faithful people need not be overcome by fear; His faithful people will not be defeated; His faithful people can rely on His divine wisdom and not on their own.

Today, when it seems that it is getting colder and darker all around us and perhaps even within us, let's recall the letter that God wrote to us through the Book of Revelation. Let's listen again to the Word-made-Flesh Who speaks to us through the gospels. And then let's speak that word to those around us who may be frightened or discouraged. If we do that, then we can help our Lord gather a holy and hopeful people, and echo the words of the psalm we heard today: "Great and wonderful are all your works, LORD, mighty God!"

May God's Holy Name be praised now and forever.

Saints & Solemnities

Now It's Our Turn

Memorial of Saints Edmond Campion,
Robert Southwell, and Companions
Ave Maria, FL, 2009

Isaiah 53:3-7
Psalm 16:5, 8, 9-10, 11
Luke 17:11b-21

Where were you 15 years ago today? On this day in 1994, I was living in London. I had joined a group of pilgrims who wished to honor the Elizabethan martyrs. We met at the jail in central London where Catholic priests, who by definition were enemies of her majesty and her government, would be kept until their day of execution. We walked along the streets of London, following the path that the doomed priests rode in carts, on their way to a place in London called Tyburn, where they would be hanged, drawn, and quartered.

We marched quietly, carrying a few signs and banners. I was surprised by the anti-Catholic bigotry and ugly words that were yelled at us by passersby. Finally, we arrived at Tyburn. That place of horror, where the martyrs suffered tortures I would not dare to speak of in the presence of children, is now simply a traffic circle, not even marked by a statue.

Edmond Campion, like so many other young British men, fled the persecution of the Church in England, not to save his life but to prepare to help save the souls of his countrymen. He went to Rome and joined the Society of Jesus, studied theology in Vienna, Prague, and the Low Countries. Then, like so many before and after him, he returned to his homeland, sure that he would eventually be betrayed and suffer horrific violence and death. He was eventually captured by a spy and taken to London in chains, bearing on his hat a paper with the inscription, "*Campion, the Seditious Jesuit.*"

Campion was sentenced to death as a traitor. He answered: "*In condemning us, you condemn all your own ancestors, all our ancient bishops and kings, all that was once the glory of England—the island of saints, and the most devoted child of the See of Peter.*" Then he sang the "*Te Deum.*"

Before his execution, he wrote a letter to Queen Elizabeth and her senior counselors. This letter was called "Campion's Brag" by his detractors. In this letter, he challenged the queen, her counselors, and the entire faculties of Oxford and Cambridge to a debate regarding the truth of the Catholic faith. He assured the queen that even if she rejected his request, his faithful countrymen would not despair of her salvation or of the re-conversion of England. He spoke of students preparing to defend the faith in England, and urged her to "…hearken to those who would spend the best blood in their bodies for your salvation. Many innocent hands are lifted up to heaven for you daily by those English students, whose posterity shall never die, which beyond seas, gathering virtue and sufficient knowledge for the purpose, are determined never to give you over, but either to win you heaven, or to die upon your pikes. And touching our Society of Jesus, be it known to you that we have made a league—all the Jesuits in the world, whose succession and multitude must overreach all the practice of England—cheerfully to carry the cross you shall lay upon us, and never to despair your recovery, while we have a man left to enjoy your Tyburn, or to be racked with your torments, or consumed with your prisons. The expense is reckoned, the enterprise is begun; it is of God; it cannot be withstood. So the faith was planted: So it must be restored."

What love for Christ! What love for the Church Christ founded! What love for neighbor! But why speak of this? For the sake of nostalgia? Are we merely gawking at the exhibits during a visit to the hagiographical zoo? No, I speak of Edmond Campion and his martyred Jesuit companions in order to prepare us for a challenge. And the challenge is this: Now it is our turn!

Consider this: one third of the members of the House of Representatives and of the Senate are self-identified Catholics. Nearly all of them are alumni of Catholic schools; and nearly all of them have almost perfect approval ratings from the National Abortion Rights Action League. Nearly all of them are prepared to vote for "health care reform" that will include federal funding for abortion. Their actions are a scandal. What shall we do about that?

Well, we could wring our hands, beat our breast, and shake our heads, tut-tutting our disapproval. We could pray the prayer of the Pharisee and give thanks to God that we are not like other men. Or we could follow the example of Campion and his companions, and tell these powerful people the truth, always with charity, and always without apology. Edmond Campion and his companions did not seek common ground, tolerance, diversity, and counterfeits of dialogue. They sought to win apostates to the truth of the Catholic faith for the sake of their souls—can we, dare we, do any less?

Let's get specific: Advent has begun. It is time to prepare for Christmas and the amazing grace of the birth of our Savior. Towards that end, I ask you to go online today, and identify a congressman and a senator who favor "abortion rights." Write to them, and tell them the truth. There is no need to write a book; the relevant sections of the catechism will suffice. Assure them that you will pray and sacrifice throughout Advent for their conversion. Assure them that you will pray that this year, the celebration of the birth of the Christ-child will not be immediately followed by Herod ordering the slaughter of the innocents.

If you are unsure about whether you have the time, energy, or obligation to undertake such an effort, consider these words from the great preacher Charles Spurgeon, who wrote: "If sinners be dammed, at least let them leap to Hell over our bodies. If they will perish, let them perish with our arms about their knees. Let no one GO there UNWARNED and UNPRAYED for."

And let's resolve that today we will commit to memory these words of Saint Edmond Campion of the Society of Jesus: "The expense is reckoned, the enterprise is begun; it is of God; it cannot be withstood. So the faith was planted: So it must be restored."

May God's Holy Name be praised now and forever.

Are You Exhausted?

Solemnity of the Immaculate Conception, Lectionary 190
Ave Maria, FL, 2011

Genesis 3:9-15, 20
Psalm 98
Ephesians 1:3-6, 11-12
Luke 1:26-38

A man volunteered to be a chaperone on a field trip for his son's kindergarten class for a field trip. Riding on the bus, one little girl kept running around and bothering the other children. Every time she acted up, her teacher said, "Sally, please don't do that. That's inappropriate." After watching this scene repeat itself four or five times, one little boy jumped up and shouted with exasperation at his teacher, "Don't just tell her it's *potpourri*—tell her it's wrong!"

I believe that story is a parable for our time. Nowadays, we have lost our sense of sin and our need for salvation. The world we live in tells us that there's nothing wrong with us that a little therapy and some shopping can't cure.

But the first step to sanity and sanctity is the admission that, in the words of a t-shirt I once saw, "Something wrong must have gone somewhere." Have we lost our ability to sense that something is not quite right?

G.K. Chesterton once entered an essay contest requiring a response to this question, "What is wrong with the world?" His response was, "Dear Sirs: What is wrong with the world? I am. Sincerely yours, G.K. Chesterton." He got it right. What's wrong with the world is me. And what's wrong with me is that I am a son of Adam and Eve and so was born alienated from God, lacking sanctifying grace. The whole enterprise of salvation was set in motion to remedy that malady, to bring my soul to life through grace and to prepare me for my destiny, which is eternal union with God.

And that fact should turn our attention to this feast day. All of God's plans for our salvation hinged upon the "Yes" of Mary to the message of the archangel Gabriel. For the plan to work, she had to be able to give a fully free and perfect "Yes," a yes without a single sin to restrain her or divide her heart.

To supply the "Yes" needed by Divine Providence, Mary needed to be "full of grace." And so by a special act of Divine Power, the merits of Christ's redemption were applied to Mary by anticipation. She was preserved from the defect of Original Sin, which is the lack of sanctifying grace. From the first instant of her existence, she was in the state of grace.

The dogma of the Immaculate Conception was defined by Pius IX in 1854. That was a time, some historians say, when the Church was "exhausted," and politicians and academics were welcoming "a new age with no place for Christianity." Sound familiar? The declaration of the dogma of the Immaculate Conception breathed new life into the Church and it challenged the world, as it reminded both the Church and the world, yet again, of the reality of sin and the wonders of our salvation.

And what about us? What about right now? We need to celebrate this feast because we too, like the people of 1854, live in a distressed Church and a cynical society. We too need to be reminded of the great truths, the tragedy of Original Sin and the drama of salvation.

But that's not all, and that's not enough. The doctrine of the Immaculate Conception should also alert us to the loveliness of Mary. There is a beauty that comes only from love, and so her beauty is the truest loveliness. In a hardhearted world, it is refreshing to see a person of purely innocent love. Thanks be to God, we can do more than merely think about Mary or view her from a distance, as if she were an object of art to be admired but not touched. We can in fact embrace her and know her as mother and friend, a partner in prayer and discipleship. The gift of the Immaculate Conception is Mary as a companion to our hearts' desire for God. We are never alone. We are never without love.

Let's resolve now to spend some time today with Mary Immaculate, to be reassured of our salvation, to be reminded of the beauty of love. Then we can say with Saint Paul, "...we who first hoped in Christ have been destined and appointed to live for the praise of his glory."

May God's Holy Name be praised now and forever.

How Are Martyrs Made?

Memorial of the European Martyrs of the Society of Jesus
Ave Maria, FL, 2012

2 Timothy 2:8-13
Psalm 123:1-2
Matthew 16:21-27

When I was a novice, newly entered into the Society of Jesus, I did some research. I found that if you were a saint or blessed of the Society of Jesus, it was 97% likely that you were also a martyr. So it is not surprising that today, when we call to mind the Jesuits martyred in Europe, that the list of Jesuits who gave their lives in Europe for Christ the King and the Church He founded extends to sixty-seven.

But what of it? Why might we here and now pay a bit more attention to this memorial of martyrs rather than to any other? I think that there may be two reasons that this memorial of the Jesuit martyrs of Europe might deserve special attention by us today. First, these men were all martyred by their fellow Christians. Second, they were all put to death by their fellow citizens.

In other words, there was a time when people thought that they could please God and please the state by killing faithful Catholics. The truths of the faith and the lives of the faithful was so repugnant to some that they believed that divine law and civil law conspired together to demand the death of these good Jesuits.

Would it be alarmist to ask if such times may be coming our way again? Perhaps. But let Catholics in America consider this: Where, in all of the gatherings of Christians, where, in all the seats of power, where, in all of the courts of law, where, in all of the halls of academe, where, in all of the precincts of popular opinion, where, in all these places, are faithful Catholics unconditionally welcome? Where, in all these places, are the symbols, sacraments, and Scriptures entrusted to us not held up to ridicule and scorn?

In how many places in this country, even among those calling themselves Catholic, is fidelity to Christ and the Church He founded considered a disqualification for employment, promotion, or praise? Is it possible that smirking scorn, muttered mocking, and crass contempt can turn into violence praised by Christians and mandated by the state? My martyred Jesuit brothers say, "Yes, yes indeed—it certainly is possible."

Jesus said that whoever would be faithful to Him must take up His cross and follow Him. The cross is proof that there is something more urgent than human approval, more binding than the state, more powerful even than death—and that is love, love lived faithfully to the end. The love of God demands that we allow no one on the throne of our hearts except Christ our King. And the love of neighbor for whom Christ died demands that we do not allow the saving truths of Christ entrusted to the Church He founded to be hidden, obscured, slandered, or distorted. The human race cannot become what God intended it to be unless Christ is known and loved throughout the world. Therefore, we should not be silent. We must not be afraid. We dare not run away.

Today, Christ our crucified and risen King, and my

martyred Jesuit brothers, call us to take up our cross. They call us to heroic fidelity, to unshakeable hope, and above all, to a most stubborn and generous love. Today, we must prepare for our mission and pilgrimage from death to life, by being fed at this altar the Body, Blood, Soul, and Divinity of Christ. Together, let us become prayerful, bold, humble, repentant, wise, and daring, like my martyred Jesuit brothers, and go where Christ sends us, and do what He tells us, and love as He loves us. Then Christ will share with us His victory, and welcome us into the home of our Heavenly Father, where already a banquet is prepared for us. Then we shall join the whole company of Heaven and echo the words of Saint Paul we heard today: "If we have died with him; we shall also live with him; if we persevere we shall also reign with him."

May God's Holy Name be praised now and forever.

Are You Crazy?

Memorial of Saint Agnes, Lectionary 316
Ave Maria, FL, 2012

2 Samuel 1:1-4, 11-12, 19, 23-27
Psalm 80:2-3, 5-7
Mark 3:20-21

Years ago, I found myself in Salt Lake City, outside the Mormon temple. The Mormons are fearless and relentless evangelizers. In front of the temple I was approached by a young woman with a magazine called "Family First Magazine." She said cheerfully, "Here's a copy of 'Family First Magazine,' full of fun activities that you can share with the family you have now or the family you plan to have later." As a priest and religious, I thought it would be misleading if I accepted the magazine from her, so I revealed to her my true identity.

Now, for many reasons, celibacy is unintelligible for Mormons. The poor young lady was confused and upset, and the more I tried to explain to her my vocation, the more upset and confused she became. Finally, I asked her: "If I'm not crazy, what must be true about God?"

We talked some more, and eventually we came to

following conclusions. If I am not crazy, then God must be real, personal, and sufficient for the human heart. We agreed that if any of these conditions are missing, then religious celibacy is a waste of my life. Then I went on to say, "But I do believe that God is real, personal, and sufficient for the human heart. In fact, I believe it so strongly, and I'm so sure that you need to believe it too, that I lead my life in this apparently odd way, so that we might have conversations like this one, and that you too might be moved to decide who God really is."

I don't know what became of that young woman, but I do know that I was glad to have that conversation, because it crystallized for me the conviction that some aspects of my life do not make sense unless God truly is Who He has revealed Himself to be to the Church.

I recall that scene in Salt Lake City because of the last line from today's gospel passage. The relatives of Jesus tried to seize him, for they said, "He is out of His mind."

Jesus could very well say to His relatives and to all of us, "If I'm not crazy, what must be true about God?" The life and death of Jesus only make sense if the greatest good is obedient communion with the Heavenly Father Who made us. And the martyrdom of Saint Agnes only makes sense if Jesus has told the truth about God.

We each of us must ask ourselves: How much of our lives only makes sense if God is our Creator, Redeemer, and Destiny? How much of our lives only make sense if God is our greatest love? And how happy are our lives when God is not the first, the center, and the goal of our lives?

Let's agree that we shall spend some time today answering those questions as specifically as possible. Only then can we know who we are and Whose we are. Only then will we be able to honestly echo the psalm we heard this morning: "Let us see your face, LORD, and we shall be saved."

May God's Holy Name be praised now and forever.

Lambs and Wolves

Memorial of Saints Timothy and Titus, Lectionary 520
Jesuit Spiritual Center, Wernersville, PA, 2006

2 Timothy 1:1-8
Psalm 96:1-2a, 2b-3, 7-8a, 10
Luke 10:1-9

When was the last time you contemplated doing something really dangerous? I remember a summer day when I was about 13. Our dog, Nipper, a delightful little mutt, was "in heat," as they say. This fact presented us with a problem. When Nipper had to "answer Nature's call," how could we get her outside to answer that call without affording her an opportunity to answer Nature's *other* and at that time more insistent call?

You see, if I went into the back yard with Nipper, neighborhood dogs and dogs I had never seen before but which had apparently gotten the memo would be in the bushes, lying in wait for her. At night, you could see their savage eyes glowing in the moonlight. So, when Nipper, in her delicate condition, indicated that she needed to "go potty," we'd have to take certain precautions. First, I'd put Nipper on the leash. Then, I'd arm myself with a big stick.

Finally, my sister would stand on the back porch with rocks at the ready, and together we'd drive off those interlopers who wanted to ravish my poor little dog and have their way with her. Unfortunately, Nipper never really appreciated the steps we would take to defend her honor.

As I headed out the door with the dog, my mother called after me. "Since you're going out anyway, I want you to run an errand for me. Take this delivery from the butcher shop and bring it around the corner to Mrs. Smith." She handed me a bundle of wax paper surrounding a pile of dripping meat. I froze, as I considered my mother's invitation to tempt fate. Think of it: Here I am, with a dog in heat and a big pile of raw, bloody meat, going for a walk. I'm a dog's dream come true! What could be better, from a dog's perspective? I'd never make it back alive! It's a suicide mission! They'd have to have a closed casket at my funeral! My God-given, delicate, inner sense of danger warned me that this was a very bad idea.

I call this to mind as we read from today's gospel, "I send you out as lambs in the midst of wolves." I want to respond: "Lord, this is a very bad idea. Do you know what the mortality rate is of sheep among wolves? They'd never be able to get life insurance! You need to reconsider this plan of yours."

Now, some of you might try to reassure me, by pointing out that today's gospel is complemented by today's other reading, from Paul's letter to Timothy, which says, "For God did not give us a spirit of timidity but a spirit of power…" Oh, I see. So what am I supposed to say to the wolves? "Stand back wolves—I'm a *powerful* lamb." Ooh—that sounds credible!

So, how are we to reconcile being sent like lambs among wolves, with being given God's spirit of power? Well, one way is to not even try. We could just say, "Lambs, power—there goes that wacky God again! You know, Job tried to get a straight answer out of God and look at what happened to him. With God, it's best not to ask too many questions."

But let's not give up so quickly. Let's try again to embrace what the Word of God gives us today. Believers can be said to be powerful because they are on the winning side. Through the cross and resurrection, Christ has conquered our two greatest enemies, namely, sin and death, and we are all promised a share in His glory. We are powerful because God offers to us the fullness of His final victory.

"Final victory." Ah, there's the rub... If we take an eschatological approach, true as it may be, and cling to the promise of God's final-victory-in-the-end, it's mighty tempting to resign ourselves to helplessness and slaughter now, and I'm not ready to do that just yet. And besides, we'd be open to the accusation that we're just offering "pie-in-the-sky-when-you-die."

But we cannot be helpless, because "our help is in the name of the Lord, Who made Heaven and Earth." In order to be true to the Scriptures, to the witness of the saints, and, please God, to our own experience, we must insist that "God is a present help in a time of trouble." We have been given a spirit of power—therefore, faith, hope, and love, wisdom, inspired words, endurance, and all the gifts and fruits of the Spirit are available to any who call upon the name of the Lord.

Yes, it's true that God's Spirit isn't magic; bullets don't bounce off of religious people. Oscar Romero proved that. But we *do* have offered to us the spiritual power to find the will of God and the grace to accomplish God's will. And what could be better than that?

May God's Holy Name be praised, now and forever.

Is Jesus a Gift or a Burden?

Feast of the Presentation of the Lord, Lectionary 524
Ave Maria, FL, 2013

Malachi 3:1-4
Psalm 24:7, 8, 9, 10
Hebrews 2:14-18
Luke 2:22-40

Do you want to hear a story? I should tell you that sometimes people ask me, "Father, are all the stories you tell true?" Yes. Yes, my stories are true. But I wish the story I will tell you today were not true.

I will tell you today about a man who called his father, and shared with him the news that his wife was pregnant with their first child. Hearing the news that he was to be a grandfather, he told his son, "Congratulations, moron! I hope you like working like a dog for the rest of your life, because that's what you're stuck with now!"

Oh, sweet Jesus! What we human beings do to each other! What must have happened in that man's life that caused the news of the gift of a child to stir up such anger and indignation? What did he lack and what did he fail at that led him to that outburst at that moment? We will never know, of course, and can only commend all the people in that story to the mercy of God.

I tell you this story today because our feast, the Presentation of the Lord, and the passage from the Gospel of Luke we heard this morning, show us how a child can be received as a gift from God, even though that gift is a strange and unlikely gift.

Luke depicts Joseph and Mary going to the temple to fulfill the demands of Mosaic law, as they offer sacrifice and prayer to give thanks for the gift of their son, their firstborn. They were acting as good parents and faithful Jews. But the Christ Child was no ordinary gift; in fact, it would be easy to think of their child as not a gift at all but rather as a terrible and terrifying burden.

Why do I say that? Let's listen again to what Simeon says: "Behold, this child is destined for the fall and rise of many...and to be a sign that will be contradicted—and you yourself a sword will pierce—so that the thoughts of many hearts may be revealed." What kind of gift is that? Would you want that kind of gift?

With his words, Simeon summarizes what will become the work of Jesus. He said that Jesus will bring about the fall of many. Why? Let's think this through: Jesus is the embodiment of the goodness of God. Yet many will reject Him precisely because He is good. They wish to name for themselves what is good and what is evil. There can be no greater fall than rejecting the Christ of God simply for His goodness.

Simeon said that Jesus will be the cause of many to rise. What does that mean? Jesus, in His life, death, and resurrection, offers to raise us up out of the tomb of death in which sin buries us. He offers to raise us up out of shame and lift us into glory. No one else can give us what Jesus offers to us.

And Jesus, Who is the Christ of God, will be a sign that is contradicted. What does Simeon mean by that? I will state this as bluntly as I can: Either all that the Church proclaims about the cross and resurrection of Jesus Christ is true, or life is a bad joke that should not have happened. We must say yes to the Church's proclamation with all of our lives, even at the cost of our lives, or we will have no life within us. We must have what only Christ can give us, and we can have it only if we choose to follow Him and imitate Him, faithful until the end. The fallen world, unredeemed flesh, and the devil will rage against such clarity and commitment.

Jesus tells us that we can become one with God but we cannot be God. Sinful pride cannot receive such a humbling and liberating gift. So, Christ and His faithful will be opposed until the end of time.

Simeon tells Mary that her heart will be pierced with a sword so that the thoughts of many will be revealed. What does that mean for Mary and for us?

The sword of sorrow pierced her heart most deeply when she held the broken corpse of her betrayed Son. At that moment hearts were revealed—those who truly loved Him stayed with Him. Those who merely thought they loved Him ran from Him in His greatest hour of need. And those who thought they knew enough about Him had Him killed.

That drama of love, abandonment, and murder is repeated in every generation throughout the life of the Church on Earth. In each age, Christ and His Church are loved by some, abandoned by many, and menaced by even more. That truth presents us with a hard question: When the sword of doubt, derision, and death comes in our time, what will pour out from our pierced hearts?

So—now what? What shall we do? Shall we panic? Shall we give up? Shall we simply cover our eyes and ears and mouths and hope that no one notices?

Not at all! God forbid! Consider these wise words from the late Classics scholar John Senior. He wrote: "For those who border on despair, especially now, it is essential to remember that the Church never looked so much like Christ as when She was broken and betrayed from within." So says John Senior. What can those words teach us?

I believe they teach us that when we look at the headlines, when we look at the world around us, and when we look in the mirror, we may see at least glimpses of a battered and broken Christ. At that moment—*at that moment*—that is when we should take heart. We should recall the words from the Letter to the Hebrews that we heard this morning. We are reminded in that letter that the death of Jesus will "destroy the one who has the power of death, that is, the Devil, and free those who through fear of death had been subject to slavery all their life." We must cling to the truth that the suffering and crucified Christ is also the risen and victorious Christ. That is the foundation of our hope.

We who have been baptized into Christ have been baptized into His death, and we shall rise with Him and we shall reign with Him—as He promised. *As He promised!* So, let us rejoice, for there is no lie in the Christ of God.

Now, let's take a deep breath. Perhaps then we can see that we should say to God, "That's quite a gift You gave us! This Christ Child, Who will bring the falling and rising of many, Who will be a sign of contradiction—that is a most unusual gift."

How shall we receive rightly that most amazing gift from God, the gift that we celebrate today on the feast of the Presentation of the Lord? Well, let's start by saying, "Thank you." Let's prove our gratitude for the gift above all by uniting ourselves with Christ in the Holy Sacrifice of the Mass. And let's proclaim our gratitude by striving every day to make Christ known and loved.

If we do that, if we live and pray through gratitude, union, and proclaiming, then we can echo the words of the psalm we sang today and say, "Who is this king of glory? It is the Lord!"

May God's Holy Name be praised now and forever.

Excuses

Solemnity of the Ascension of the Lord, Lectionary 58
Ave Maria, FL, 2011

Acts 1:1-11
Psalm 47:2-3, 6-7, 8-9
Ephesians 1:17-23
Matthew 28:16-20

You know how some people say, "There are no stupid questions," and then you wonder whether or not that statement is true? Well, one of my intentions this morning is to show that there are stupid questions. And more importantly, my intention is to show that some questions *appear* to be stupid, but are actually dangerous questions, because if we don't answer them properly, disaster will result.

Why do I say that there must be stupid questions? Well, there are stupid people, aren't there? And, if there are stupid people but there are no stupid questions, then it must be true that stupid people become smart when they ask questions, and then they revert to stupidity when you answer their questions, and that's how they remain stupid. Well, I've been teaching long enough to know that the experienced teachers here would agree with me that there really are stupid questions. For example, I tell my students that the question, "Is this going to be on the test?" is *always* a stupid question.

I have been a shepherd of souls long enough to know that there are also questions that appear stupid, but are actually important questions, because they are dangerous. These questions are dangerous because the wrong answers to them are both easy to find and quite plausible. If we answer these questions incorrectly, then we will miss out on what God asks of us and we will miss out on what God offers us. These questions are also dangerous because answering them properly requires both audacity and humility, which is a difficult combination to get right. Too much audacity, and we end up with presumption and arrogance. Too much humility, and we end up with passivity and despair.

So, here is my apparently stupid, yet subtly dangerous question: "Are you tired of making excuses for God?"

Now, when you first hear that question from me, you might wish to rush and correct me by saying, "Father! God doesn't need to have excuses made for Him! He's perfect! And He's also very touchy about having His perfection constantly acknowledged, so please, be careful with this crazy talk about 'making excuses for God'! If He hears you talking that way, He could get really upset, and you know how He gets when He's cranky. Let's not forget about what happened to Sodom, ok? 'Nuff said?"

If you admonished me like that, I would thank you, of course, and then I would repeat the question, "Are you tired of making excuses for God?" The reason I repeat that question is that I fear that we all do make excuses for God because, at least some of the time, we find God and His ways a little embarrassing. Let me give you an example of what I mean.

Imagine that you are having a conversation with a

friend—let's call him "Hitchens." Imagine that your old pal Hitchens says, "Hey, what is so great about God? What is so great about being a Christian? Why are Christians supposed to be joyful?"

You might say in reply, "Well, we are joyful because we celebrate the Hebrew word 'Emmanuel,' which means 'God-is-with-us.' And we Christians are joyful because, as we pray in the Angelus, 'the Word was made Flesh and dwelt among us.' That means that the Son of God became the Son of Mary, and became a human being like us."

And Hitchens might say, "The Son of God became a human being? How exciting! What does He look like? Can you introduce me to Him? I'd sure like to shake His hand!"

And this is where the apologies for God begin. Hitchens' request to meet Jesus and shake His hand may cause you to look at the ground, shuffle your feet, maybe rub the back of your neck. Finally you say to Hitchens, "Well, um, it's not quite like that. He's not here anymore. Well, He is here, but in a special way that you can't see. And it's supposed to be better that way. I remember reading that in a catechism or something like that. Jesus went back to Heaven, and that's so great that we celebrate it with a solemnity, and that solemnity is so important, that we're told that it is a Holy Day of Obligation, except when we're told that it isn't a Holy Day of Obligation."

Hitchens doesn't seem to be very convinced by your explanation of why it's great that he can't meet Jesus and shake His hand. Hitchens says to you, "Now, let me get this straight. The best thing about Christianity is that the Son of God became a human being so that He can live a truly human life that people could see and hear and touch, and it is also great that now you can't see or hear or touch Him, because He went back to Heaven, where presumably He governs the world from a distance, not unlike an absentee landlord, or a despotic government that demands taxes but doesn't care for the people. Is that what you mean to say?"

How would you respond? Would you say to yourself, "I wish it weren't so hard to stick up for God!" So, you take a deep breath, and you try again. You might say, "Look, Hitchens, it's not like that. It is better that Jesus goes to the Father. He says so—in the Gospel of John, I think—anyways, He said that if He goes away we will be sad but we will be sad only for a little while because if He goes away, then the Holy Spirit will come and console us. So, you see, Jesus going back to Heaven is actually a net gain."

Once again, Hitchens becomes excited and says, "Oh! The Holy Spirit is the consolation prize for the departure of Jesus. What is the Holy Spirit like? Can I meet Him? Can I shake His hand?"

And you reply, "No, Hitchens, you can't shake the Holy Spirit's hand. It doesn't work like that. But that's ok. The Holy Spirit is really awesome. The Holy Spirit helps believers perform all sorts of really cool miracles. Just look in the Acts of the Apostles—it's just full of miracles."

Now, Hitchens becomes very excited. "The Holy Spirit helps believers perform miracles? That sounds fascinating! Do you perform miracles?"

Once again, it's time to shuffle your feet as you make more excuses for God. And so you say to Hitchens, "Well, um, that miracle thing doesn't happen so much anymore, for reasons that were never really made clear. But that's ok, because the Holy Spirit gives really great gifts like wisdom, counsel, understanding, and knowledge. You can get by without miracles, but you sure don't want to live without wisdom, counsel, understanding, and knowledge! No sir! So, yeah, even though you can't shake the Holy Spirit's hand, He's still really important for a believer to have in his life."

But your answer just prompts more questions. Hitchens says, "Wisdom, counsel, understanding, and knowledge. They sound very similar. How are they different?"

How would you answer Hitchens? You might say,

"Well, they are different. I think there is an article in the Catholic Encyclopedia about all that. I looked it up once online, but I didn't read all of it, because the article is really long. But the important thing to remember is that the gifts of the Holy Spirit are really great and that you get those gifts in the sacraments, especially Baptism and Confirmation."

Now Hitchens smiles at you and says, "If everyone gets the gifts of the Holy Spirit, does that mean that every Christian you know, including everyone at Ave Maria, is wise?"

Do you see what I mean? Do you get it? Faced with persistent and awkward questions, we find ourselves in the difficult and painful position of having to make excuses for God. We think that it is necessary to make excuses for God because He doesn't seem to live up to His reputation and His promotional literature. I admit that the process of making excuses for God is painful and frustrating, and I also insist that it is quite unnecessary. The temptation to make excuses for God comes when we haven't moved beyond the surface of the truths of the faith.

Here is the position most Catholics find themselves in: We are told to celebrate the Ascension of Christ to the Father, yet we find it strange to do so because it appears to be a net loss. How can the Ascension mean anything other than, "Jesus is gone"? Then, we try to console ourselves for the apparent loss of Jesus by saying it is necessary so that the Holy Spirit will come, but we are really not sure what that means either.

So we find ourselves in the false position of "celebrating," under the threat of mortal sin, the disappearance of Jesus at the Ascension, and then we are expected to "celebrate" next Sunday the Feast of Pentecost, the coming of the Holy Spirit, the effects of which, I daresay, are not always readily obvious. If that is how we understand the faith, then it is no wonder that we lack joy and hope.

May I make an analogy? Most of us here of heard of "post-partum depression"; indeed, many here may have lived it. Well, I believe that every year we all experience "post-Pentecost depression." In other words, Pentecost, the climax of the Easter Season and the celebration of the giving of the Holy Spirit to the Church, comes along, and then it goes, and then Monday morning comes, and it is back to business as usual, with apparently nothing having changed. In other words, it seems that the "consolation" of the Holy Spirit falls flat.

Such an experience is not unique to this congregation. I was once in a parish in another state on Pentecost Sunday. At the Preface of the Eucharist Prayer I cried out, **"THE LORD BE WITH YOU!"** The response of the congregation was a sluggish, "And also with you…" **"LIFT UP YOUR HEARTS!** "We lift them up to the Lord." **"LET US GIVE THANKS TO THE LORD OUR GOD!"** "It is right to give Him thanks and praise." The celebration of the flaming descent of the Holy Spirit sounds like the "Night of the Living Dead," doesn't it?

Are you satisfied by that kind of "worship"? Of course not! Me neither! And neither is God!

We have to understand the wonder and joy of the Ascension so that we can welcome the genuine consolation of the Holy Spirit that Christ intends for us. So, let's try again to understand the Ascension, and do so in a way that precludes pathetic and mumbled "excuses" for God.

The wonder of the Ascension of the Lord to the Father is rooted in this: The Ascension proves that human flesh may stand before the glory of God. The completion of Christ's mission, the perfection of the Incarnation, demand that Christ ascend, so that He may open the gates of Heaven, and so allow a true man, body and soul, to stand before God without shame.

And the joy of the Ascension is that Christ calls us to do the same. He calls us to leave behind the limits of this life in order to be raised up with Him, beyond the grasp of earth and death, and enter entirely into the glorious presence of God.

Now it becomes clear: The Ascension doesn't mark the loss of Jesus; rather, it marks a gain of perfect hope. Because Christ returned to our Heavenly Father, we know that human life, body and soul, has an identity, a dignity, and a destiny beyond anything that the pagans could have imagined. And we are not left orphans, as we prepare in this life for our own fulfillment in the next life, a life made possible by the Passion, Death, Resurrection, and Ascension of the Lord.

Christ is still at work in the world, teaching, healing, saving, through the members of His Body, the Church. And to enable us to be His effective instruments and His credible witnesses, we are given the Holy Spirit. That means that next week, on Pentecost Sunday, we must celebrate, because all that we need to be faithful to Christ, all that we need to walk together to the home of our Heavenly Father, has been given to us.

This good news is not merely my opinion or my pious wish. God has revealed these truths to us in the writings of Saint Paul. Let's listen again to his letter to the Ephesians. Saint Paul writes: "May the God of our Lord Jesus Christ, the Father of glory, give you a Spirit of wisdom and revelation, resulting in knowledge of him."

In other words, the Holy Spirit opens the eyes of our minds, so that we may see Who it is Who is calling us to Himself.

Saint Paul also writes: "May the eyes of your hearts be enlightened, that you may know what is the hope that belongs to his call, what are the riches of glory in his inheritance among the holy ones, and what is the surpassing greatness of his power for us who believe."

In other words, by opening the eyes of our hearts, the Holy Spirit gives us the unshakeable confidence that we are the heirs of the kingdom of our Heavenly Father.

Brothers and sisters, be sure of this: By the power of the Holy Spirit, our Heavenly Father raised Jesus from the dead. By the power of that same Holy Spirit, our Heavenly Father call us, body and soul, with Christ, into His glory. Therefore, we *must* be a people of hope and joy and gratitude.

So, now what? How shall we live and pray until next Sunday, the Feast of Pentecost? How shall we live and pray so that the gift of the Holy Spirit may be renewed in us, inwardly, manifestly, and lastingly?

I will ask you to pray today and every day this week for three graces, for three special blessings. First, pray to receive light, that the eyes of your mind and heart may be opened. Second, pray to become light, so that others may see the path to Heaven. Third, pray to receive might, so that you may have the strength to persevere until the end.

If we do that, then we can know that someday, we will join the whole Company of Heaven, with Our Lady and all the angels and saints, and cry out, "God mounts His throne amid shouts of joy...Sing praise to God, sing praise; sing praise to our King, sing praise."

May God's Holy Name be praised now and forever.

What Difference Does It Make?

Solemnity of the Most Holy Trinity, Lectionary 166
Ave Maria, FL, 2013

Proverbs 8:22-31
Psalm 8:4-5, 6-7, 8-9
Romans 5:1-5
John 16:12-15

Today, I am going to begin a homily in a way I have never begun a homily before, in a way that I never imagined that I would ever begin a homily. Today, I will begin a homily by quoting Hillary Clinton. I will quote a line that I hope history will never forget, namely, her question: "What difference does it make?" I want to apply her question to this day on the Church's calendar, which is the Solemnity of the Holy Trinity. What difference does it make that God has revealed to us that He is Father, Son, and Holy Spirit, three persons in one nature? What has it do with me and with you? How are our living and dying and meaning touched by the truth that God is Father, that God is Son, that God is Holy Spirit? The short answer to that question is: "Everything." It makes all the difference to each of us and all of us and all of creation that God is Trinity. Let's reflect together on these very lofty, yet very practical mysteries.

To be a father is to take the initiative in creating life. Our fatherly God made you and me in His image and likeness. We are familiar with that statement—at least, it is familiar to our *ears*. I wonder if it is equally familiar to our mind and heart. So I will say it again: Our fatherly God made you and me in His image and likeness. What does it mean for us to be made, and to be made by and like our fatherly God? The Father is the origin of all creation. And creation changed the moment you were conceived. Why? Because God cherishes you in a way in which no one else has ever been cherished. Let's be clear: that is not an overly sentimental statement. It is a great truth. Blessed John Paul II said: "God created you as a *particular* image and likeness of Who He is." You are an unrepeatable and unique reflection of the abundant life and love of our fatherly God. That means you can bring God a reflection of His glory that no one else can. In the symphony of praise and thanksgiving that creation is meant to offer to God, no one can sing the note that only you can sing. Creation falls short of what God intended it to be if you do not make your unique "yes" in response to God's creative initiative. By God's work you have the potential to be a unique saint, holy in the way that only you can be holy. What a tragedy if you do not become aflame with that unique sanctity that only you can offer to God! Saint Alphonsus Liguori said that one of the greatest pains of Purgatory will be to see what we could have been if only we had embraced the gifts we had been given. Please, God—may we live our lives so as to avoid that pain!

Pope Benedict XVI told us that, "We are not the result of chance. Each of us is the result of a thought of God. Each of us is willed." He said that at the first Mass he offered as pope. And he is teaching that God loved you before you were conceived. He loved you so much that He did not want a world without you, so He created you. Now we can see what an act of vandalism, theft, and ingratitude is just one abortion. God made you in love; He made you for love; and that means that each of us and all of us are woven into a divinely-intended culture of life. I will say that again: each of us and all of us are woven into a divinely-intended culture of life. We can see how wide and grand a statement that is by asking ourselves this question, the question spoken of so eloquently by Saint Anselm, namely, "Why did God become man?" Our almost kneejerk response to that question is: "God became man in order to die for our sins." And that is true—but that is not the whole story. We can find the rest of the story if we ask the question "Why did God become man?" and then place it between the great feasts of the Annunciation and the Ascension.

At the Annunciation, Divinity descended into humanity. At the Ascension, humanity ascended into Divinity. Why are those two motions, the descending and the ascending, so important? Well, consider this amazing statement from Saint Irenaeus: "You are meant to become as divine by grace as Christ is by nature." The Divine Son, the Second Person of the Holy Trinity, became man to die for our sins—yes; He became man to save our souls—yes; but He also became man to dignify and divinize human flesh, to make human flesh unimaginably sacred and beautiful. So, we see again, the vandalism, theft, ingratitude, and even *sacrilege* of abortion, yes; but now we can say the same of the evils of pornography, promiscuity, contraception, and murder—all grotesque violations of the sanctity of the human body.

Consider this: God's love for you is so passionate and persistent that He would rather die for you than live without you. He would rather go through Hell for you than go to Heaven without you. He did not want an eternity without you, so He chose to save you at a terrible cost to Himself. He died for you so that you might live with Him. And He wishes you to live with Him, to be in His presence, both in soul and in body, in other words, as fully human.

But the story does not end there, because love calls out for a response. And so we turn to consider the role of God the Holy Spirit. We would not be able to love Jesus in return if He had not sent us the Holy Spirit. Saint John Eudes said that, "The Holy Spirit was sent to us so that we could live as continuations of the mysteries of Jesus Christ in the world." When I found those words of Saint John Eudes, I was delighted and consoled. He helped me to see that even though I, as a sinner, have made a mess out of my life, God the Holy Spirit can still make something beautiful and good, something truly Christ-like out of my life. And He can do the same for you.

Today, the Solemnity of the Holy Trinity is a gift, a life-affirming and life-changing gift, because it reminds us that we are created in love, redeemed in blood, and summoned to glory. Nothing and no one can change or erase those three truths. We who have received the revelation of the Triune God must bring that great light to a world still tangled in darkness. What we say, how we love, and how we worship can spread that healing and liberating light to our world. How shall we begin?

I will ask you to pray today and every day this week for three graces, for three special blessings. First, pray to be convinced—convinced that each of us is made uniquely in the image and likeness of our Triune God; second, pray to be compassionate—loving our neighbor for the love of our Triune God; third, pray to be courageous—courageous because, as Saint Paul said, "Hope does not disappoint." If we do that, if we live and pray as convinced, compassionate, and courageous, then we can lead the world to cry out with Saint Paul: "The love of God has been poured out into our hearts through the Holy Spirit that has been given to us."

May God's Holy Name be praised now and forever.

How Do You Know When You Are in Love?

Memorial of the Immaculate Heart
Ave Maria, FL, 2009

1 Kings 19:19-21
Psalm 96:10, 11-12, 13
Luke 2:41-51

How do you know when you are in love? How do you know when it is "the real thing"? I believe that Victorian poet Elizabeth Barrett Browning knew she was in love when she wrote these words after a brief encounter with her future husband, Robert Browning: "Thy touch upon the palm...leaves thy heart in mine with pulses that beat double. What I do and what I dream must include thee, as the wine must taste of its own grapes. And when I sue God for myself, He hears that name of thine, and sees within my eyes the tears of two."

Think of it! She went into ecstasy and rhapsodized because he touched her palm! And that simple touch changed her life. What a simplicity, generosity, and humility of heart she must have had.

Now we turn to Our Lady. Does she not also have a simple, generous, and humble heart? Oh yes, and so much more. Hers is an Immaculate Heart, a heart never stained by sin, never shrunk by selfishness, never bitten by bitterness. What kind of love and joy is such a heart capable of?

We can infer from the poem that Elizabeth Barrett Browning had a profound love for her future husband. But surely that love and intimacy paled in comparison with the love and intimacy Mary enjoyed with Jesus, the Word made Flesh from and in her body. What a joyful union—the innocent Immaculate Heart of Mary and the infinite Sacred Heart of Jesus!

Elizabeth Barrett Browning wrote enduring poetry in response to a touch upon her palm; surely Mary's own great poem, the Magnificat, is never ending, as she has marveled at her perfect union with perfect love.

But, love is not all wine and roses. To love is to offer your heart, and to offer your heart is to bind your life to the life of another, so that the victories and agonies of the beloved become your own.

Unlike us, Mary could never know the anguish of losing Jesus through sin. But in today's gospel we see that Mary felt the horror of being separated from Jesus, and that horror was just a foretaste of the agony of Calvary.

Because Mary's Immaculate Heart has known the dearest joy, the deepest union, the darkest pain, we should read again the words of Luke: "His mother pondered all these things in her heart."

Luke is telling us that Mary can be the great teacher of our own hearts. Her heart, her Immaculate Heart, her heart united with the Sacred Heart of Jesus—that heart of Mary, which has known the brightest and bitterest of human living and loving—her heart can teach us how to receive love, how to give love, how to savor love.

We, who rush through life as we race towards death; we, who run over each other as we run from God; we, who ache for love as we settle for lust; we, who long to be known as we hide from ourselves; we, who yearn to receive affection as we recoil from attention—we need to be taught what only Mary's Immaculate Heart can teach us. She, who pondered all these things in her heart, has so much to teach us.

She can teach us how to say yes; she can teach us how to trust; she can teach us how to be faithful; she can teach us how to suffer; she can teach us how to embrace innocence innocently; she can teach us how to love both tenderly and fiercely. She can teach us how to unite our hearts to the Sacred Heart of Jesus.

We poor sinners, starving for a love we fear we will never find, today let us join the whole Church in crying out, "O Mary conceived without sin, pray for us who have recourse to thee!"

May God's Holy Name be praised now and forever.

How Much Does Love Cost?

Memorial of Our Lady of Sorrows, Lectionary 639
Ave Maria, FL, 2010

1 Corinthians 12:31–13:13
Psalm 33:2-3, 4-5, 12, 22
John 19:25-27

How many weddings have you attended that included this reading from Saint Paul? I know of a wedding where this reading from First Corinthians was presented as a kind of psalm. A young lady, armed with a guitar, a lot of good will, and not much skill, sat in the sanctuary and sang, "The greatest of these is love, love, love, love, love, love; yes, the greatest of these is love, love, love, love, love…." until finally the bride's grandmother pushed herself up out of her wheelchair and shouted, "Okay, we get it! The greatest of these is love! Let's move on!"

That wedding disaster is a symptom of a larger problem: the word 'love' is used too casually, and even Saint Paul's great hymn to love is reduced to a mere platitude, something one expects to find on a greeting card, a bumper sticker, or a refrigerator magnet.

Like that deplorable Madonna wearing Rosary beads

around her neck or gangsta rappers wearing the cross as mere jewelry, our sacred words and symbols are now used by the world as decorations and trivialities or worse.

Today we honor the Blessed Mother as "Our Lady of Sorrows," and she shows us that love, real love, is always free, but never cheap. Real love is freely given, as Mary did when she said her "fiat," her "yes" to the Archangel Gabriel and agreed to become the mother of the Incarnate Word.

And real love, freely given, is always costly. It is costly because it demands that we put the center of our lives outside of ourselves. Real love is costly because it demands that we rebel against our fallenness, a fallenness that exalts a self-centered life. Love moves our hearts from "Me first!" to "You first!" Real love is costly because it moves us to be faithful until the very end. We know that because Mary stayed at the foot of the Cross until the last drop of the Blood of Jesus had been shed.

Today, the Feast of Our Lady of Sorrows, is in fact a day of hope: It is a day of hope because we see that real love is never truly alone. The disciple whom Jesus loved embraced Our Lady as his mother, and she embraced him as her son. As we grieve over the sorrows of our past, as we cry out from our present suffering, as we face the uncertainty of a future that will surely include pain, we may have hope. We may have hope because our own Blessed Mother, the Mother of Jesus, Mary who is Our Lady of Sorrows, Mary who was faithful to the end and is now Queen of Heaven and Earth, offers to be our companion, who will comfort us and walk with us from the tears of this life all the way to the happiness of Heaven, to our Father's house, where a banquet is prepared for us. And when we arrive there, we can join the company of heaven in singing the words of the psalm we have heard proclaimed today: "Blessed the people the Lord has chosen to be His own."

May God's Holy Name be praised now and forever.

Treasures and Riches

Memorial of Saint Ignatius of Antioch, Lectionary 660
Ave Maria, FL, 2011

Romans 4:20-25
Psalm 34:2-9
Luke 12:13-21

Do you want to hear a story? During the Second World War, the British Army fought terrible battles against the Nazis in North Africa. During a lull in one battle, a British general stood up out of his foxhole to have a look around. His soldiers cautioned him, warning him of the dangers of snipers. He replied, "Don't be ridiculous! They couldn't hit an elephant at this dist…" And those were his last words, speaking of his invulnerability.

Ordinarily, people in war zones do not need to be reminded of their mortality. But here in the US, with smoke detectors and bottled water and fire departments and antibiotics to keep us safe and healthy, we may need to turn to this parable from time to time to remind us that none of us, not even the rich, can make a claim upon the future with certainty. Steve Jobs, the brilliant founder of Apple Computers and a multi-billionaire, would agree with this parable, if he could, but he died of cancer this month at the relatively young age of 56. Neither his rare genius nor his abundant wealth could keep him alive longer than that.

So, we would not be wrong if we took the parable from today's gospel reading as a reminder of the fragility and uncertainty of life, and of the constant necessity of being prepared to meet God face-to-face in the life to come.

But it is not enough to do that. We must also be prepared, or at least willing, to meet God in unexpected persons, times, and places, and there to have Him bless us and make demands on us in ways that we could never have dreamed. The only way to live life well is to have more confidence in God's wisdom than our own, admitting that His timing and His agenda do not always seem wise to us.

But even admitting that is not enough. The parable offers more to us and requires more of us. This parable tells of the fool "who stores up treasure for himself but is not rich in what matters to God." I say that these days, we are in danger—we are in mortal danger and we are in immortal danger—if we do not see that this parable applies not only to individuals, but also to nations and even to civilizations, indeed to all of human desire and effort.

Many of us here are students of history. We know that the list of long-gone people, places, and things once thought to be indispensable or everlasting is extensive. Greece, the cradle of Western civilization, is now a basket case. Rome, the Eternal City, has fallen more than once to barbarians, and it looks like the barbarians took another crack at it again this weekend. Constantinople is no more. The thousand-year Reich lasted just twelve years. And the sun has certainly set on the British Empire. In this life, the only thing sure to last until the end of time is the Church—not regimes, not political parties, not banks, not armies, not tyrants, not ideologies, not nations, not corporations, not civilizations. They are from dust, and unto dust they shall return. All of them.

The Christian life is a long lesson in letting go, and letting fall what God will allow to fall, and receiving, with wonder and with hope, what God chooses to give us. And in this life we are especially to hold close and dear those vulnerable and weak and needy persons who have been entrusted to us by God. As we clasp to our heart those whom God has given us, and as the world begins more and more to wobble beneath our feet, let's resolve that together, as friends and scholars and neighbors and disciples, that we, each of us and all of us, will strive to become wise. Let us become wise in the sight of God, with a wisdom that will guide our hearts and minds and hands and voices, and govern how we spend our time, resources, and efforts. Wise with the wisdom of God, we can become "rich in what matters to God," faithful to the end in this life, and joyful without end in the next.

May God's Holy Name be praised now and forever.

SCHOLARS AND KNOWLEDGE

Memorial of Saint Ignatius of Antioch, Lectionary 470
Ave Maria, FL, 2013

Romans 3:21-30
Psalm 130:1b-2, 3-4, 5-6ab
Luke 11:47-54

Jesus said: "Woe to you, scholars of the law! You have taken away the key of knowledge. You yourselves did not enter and you stopped those trying to enter." What could these words mean for us today? I read them and I think of a prominent Catholic university in California that was in turmoil last week when the Board of Trustees considered *discontinuing* coverage for abortions in their employee health insurance program.

Faculty denounced the Board for even considering such a change, for doing so was a sin against that most distinctive quality of Catholicism, namely, "inclusiveness." To which I would reply: "Woe to you, scholars of the law! You have taken away the key of knowledge. You yourselves did not enter and you stopped those trying to enter." You do not have to be a genius or a saint to know that whatever includes everything and excludes nothing actually means nothing.

For example, being diabetic excludes being not-diabetic: otherwise, being diabetic means having diabetes and not-having-diabetes, which is nonsense. Likewise, being Catholic has always excluded tolerating the murder of children in the womb—always. If being Catholic also means including tolerating the murder of children in the womb, then being Catholic both tolerates and does not tolerate such murder, which means being Catholic means nothing, and I do not want any part of it. But all of that is a distraction, because it does not take the gift of grace in response to sacred revelation to know that murdering children in the womb is wrong—it only takes common sense. So again, I say: "Woe to you, scholars of the law! You have taken away the key of knowledge. You yourselves did not enter and you stopped those trying to enter."

Now, the people advocating such nonsense, these people who educate Catholic youngsters at great expense to their parents, they are not barbarians; they are not knuckle-dragging mouth-breathers. These are highly educated, highly cultured individuals, likely as highly educated and cultured as those who devised plans to herd Jews onto cattle cars and ship them to death camps. If you invited them to dinner, they would not burn down your house; they would likely bring a good bottle of wine and behave as charming dinner companions. However, if you did not include the murder of unborn children in the definition of Catholicism, they would likely accuse you of being an unfaithful Catholic. And again, I say: "Woe to you, scholars of the law! You have taken away the key of knowledge. You yourselves did not enter and you stopped those trying to enter."

How is this possible? How could highly educated, cultured Catholics who have worked for years in a purportedly Catholic environment become such enthusiastic supporters of tolerance of the murder of children in the womb? To understand how this is possible, let's turn to

Saint Paul. He wrote: "For there is no distinction; all have sinned and are deprived of the glory of God."

Oh dear—that means if educated, cultured Catholics at that other school can rationalize monstrous behavior, then so can I, and so can you. The capacity for evil, the capacity for rationalized evil, is not something foreign and extraneous; it is within every human heart, including yours and mine. And Saint Paul makes clear that our only hope is to run to the foot of the Cross and be washed clean in the shed Blood of Jesus. Our only hope is to run to our Risen and Returning Lord, and ask Him to share with us His victory over sin and death. And thanks be to God, we can do that right here at this very altar.

Then we need to go out into a world in need of evangelization, and especially among Catholics who need a re-evangelization, and declare the words that we heard from the psalmist today: "With the Lord there is mercy, and fullness of redemption."

May God's Holy Name be praised now and forever.

WHAT HOLDS YOU BACK?

Memorial of Isaac Jogues, John De Brebeuf, and
Companions, North American Martyrs
Jesuit Spiritual Center, Wernersville, PA, 2005

2 Corinthians 4:7-15
Psalm 126:1bc-2ab, 2cd-3, 4-5, 6
Matthew 28:16-20

What moves you to silence? When do words fail you? On this feast of the North American Martyrs I find myself on the verge of awed silence.

John the Baptist said that one was coming after him whose sandals he was unworthy to untie. This day I can say that there were some who went before me whose sandals I am unworthy to untie. I tremble at the thought of having to speak of them.

The North American Martyrs endured the hardships common to missionaries. They left behind everything that was familiar to go to a distant and alien land, language, and culture. Moreover, often and for long periods they were deprived of the benefits of religious community and the sacraments.

They endured physical hardships of backbreaking work,

lack of sleep and food, exposure to the elements, infestation by mosquitoes, and the hazards of primitive travel in the wilderness. Worst of all, they suffered almost unimaginable tortures: brutal beatings with clubs and sticks; burning with branding irons; flesh sliced off to the bone; fingers chewed off; thumbs hacked off with sharpened stones. And each died a gruesome, violent death.

None of these horrors took the martyrs by surprise. All of them knew that these trials were their likely fate. Yet all of them volunteered for the mission to North America and to the Native Americans. An uncomprehending world and a scarcely comprehending Church can ask, "Why?"

These men heard the call of the Eternal King. They took Christ the King at His word that "whoever wishes to join me must be willing to labor with me, that by following me in suffering, he may follow me in glory." They believed the Master when He said that the price of discipleship is a cross. They believed Saint Ignatius Loyola when he said, "Those who wish to give proof of their love, and to distinguish themselves in whatever concerns the service of the Eternal King and the Lord of all, will not only offer themselves entirely for the work, but will act against their sensuality and carnal and worldly love, and make offerings of greater value and more importance..."

These men volunteered for a life of heroic suffering because they believed what they were taught by the Gospel and the Spiritual Exercises. But there's a danger here. There's a danger in focusing on their exceptional heroism, their unstinting self-denial, their absolute sacrifice.

We run the risk of making the martyrs superhuman. And that's a tempting risk because if they're superhuman and we are mere mortals, then we are excused from imitating them.

But listen to this letter from Saint Isaac Jogues, written to a fellow Jesuit. Jogues is about to depart for a mission to the Mohawk Indians, a mission that he knows will almost certainly lead to his violent death. The letter is a prayer that we all could pray:

"Alas, my dear Father, when shall I begin to love and serve Him whose love for us had no beginning? When shall I begin to give myself entirely to Him who has given Himself unreservedly to me? Although I am very miserable, and have so misused the graces Our Lord has given me in this country, I do not despair, as He takes care to render me better by giving me new occasions to die to self, and to unite myself inseparably to Him."

In other words, there's hope for all of us, to live as heroes, if not martyrs then at least as witnesses, as Christ calls us to take up the cross and follow Him.

May I suggest a grace that we may pray for today, in the company of the North American Martyrs? It is an answer to this question: "What holds me back from heroic sanctity?"

May God's Holy Name be praised now and forever.

CAN YOU BE A SAINT?

Solemnity of All Saints, Lectionary 667
Ave Maria, FL, 2008

Revelations 7:2-4, 9-14
Psalm 24
1 John 3:1-3
Matthew 5:1-12a

Imagine this: You are attending the college graduation of your best friend. You are happy for your friend, proud of your friend's accomplishments. You are caught up in the excitement of the ceremony, the music, the academic regalia, and the celebrations which are sure to follow. You say to yourself, "Next year, it will be my turn."

Now imagine the person next to you, apparently reading your thoughts, turning to you and saying, "Admire it all you like—this is not for you. You will never graduate. You won't make it. You don't have what it takes. All this joy is for someone else. Spare yourself a lot of grief, set your sights lower, and admit your limitations. You will never graduate."

What then? You'd be crushed. You'd be indignant. Maybe you'd yell, "OH YEAH?!? Well, I'll show you! I'm not going to just graduate—I'm going to graduate *summa cum laude* and I'm going to be the valedictorian, and then you can....congratulate me."

Ok, that's about graduation. What has this to do with the Feast of All Saints? As we consider all the great heroes of the Church, the beloved of God, the stunning display of those with haloes, imagine the person next you turning to you and saying, "Admire it all you like—this is not for you. You will never be a saint. You won't make it. You don't have what it takes. All this joy is for someone else. Spare yourself a lot of grief, set your sights lower, and admit your limitations. You will never be a saint."

What then? Would you argue? Would you yell, "OH YEAH?!? Well, I'll show you. I'm not just going to be a saint—I'm going to be a Doctor of the Church and a martyr and my feast day will be a solemnity and a holy day of obligation! And then you'll pray for my intercession and I'll tell you to go to...Our Lady..."

Not very likely, right? Isn't it more likely that we'd say, "Yeah, you're right—I'll never be a saint. I'll be lucky if I can get the last seat on the last bus leaving for purgatory." And really, who can blame us for thinking that way? Who can hope to match the zeal of Francis Xavier, the eloquence of Edmund Campion, the discernment of Ignatius Loyola? Who can hope to match the profundity of Edith Stein, the simplicity of Therese, the purity of Maria Goretti? Isn't it more realistic, more honest, and more humble to leave holiness to the professionals, and we'll just muddle on with our messy little lives?

Well, we could try to do it that way, but I don't think that we should. If ever lukewarmness were a path to spiritual suicide, now is such a time. Pope Pius XI, observing the rise of fascism and communism, said, "Let us give thanks that we live in times such as these—for now it is permitted to no one to be mediocre." In these our times we have to confront our lack of magnanimity, our lack of heart and spiritual desire, our lack of striving for greatness of soul. We have to confront our spiritual sloth and cry out, "But the Church needs more saints! And God deserves them!"

I once saw a child point to a stained glassed window and say, "Saints are the people with the light shining through." That's what the Church and the world need! That's what God deserves! We must become the people with the light shining through. The light of grace needs to shine through our human nature. But God can't perfect in us what we don't offer to Him. Only if we offer God our body, heart, mind, and will can we be fully sanctified and so become the witnesses and heralds that the Church and the world so desperately need. Can we believe that?

Maybe, but it's hard to believe that the Church and the world need people like us, if only we would be sanctified. It's hard to believe that God could be glorified by the likes of us, even if we were sanctified. And it's here that Saint Ignatius Loyola warns us against the tactics of Satan. Ignatius says it is typical of the devil to work against "joy and spiritual consolation, bringing apparent reasons, subtleties, and persistent fallacies."

What are some of the apparent reasons, subtleties, and persistent fallacies that the enemy uses to cheat us out of our vocation to sainthood? I think the enemy, in order to keep us mediocre, might trick us into saying something like this:

"Well, like, we can't really be holy because it's too hard. God hasn't blessed us with the necessary character or strength. We have been burdened with lives that are too busy for the leisurely enjoyment of the things of God. We have families and businesses to attend to." That's one tactic of the enemy.

Once the enemy has our attention, he will have us say: "And our communities could never support us in a quest to become holy. Our fellow religious are too worldly and too uncharitable. Our parishes are divided, our liturgies uninspiring, our pastors are poor preachers. We've never been able to find a really good spiritual director or confessor, and we don't have the time to read Scripture and inspiring books."

Now that we've started believing the enemy's lies, we'll explain to all who will listen that, "the world's gone mad you see, and taken us along with it. The saints lived in a simpler time when holiness was still possible. We live in the age of global warming and AIDS and the war on terror. The circumstances just aren't right for holiness."

Now that the enemy has us convinced of the righteousness of our lukewarmness, we the mediocre would explain, calmly but firmly, that, "everything within us and everything around us is simply not conducive to holiness and, really, it's not our fault. It's all very well to admire the great saints, but they are such special cases that they are merely curiosities—entertaining to think about but otherwise irrelevant. God will simply have to get used to the fact that people nowadays just aren't capable of great holiness. That time has passed. He's going to have to accept us just as we are, just as we have accepted ourselves, as lukewarm, as mediocre."

That's how we the mediocre, under the direction of our mortal enemy, make our excuses. But here comes the communion of saints, our intercessors, who will blow down the carefully engineered maze of excuses which we have constructed for ourselves. The saints, who intercede for us, leave us no place to hide from God or from ourselves. The whole company of heaven, led by Our Lady, leaves us no excuse for not aspiring to great holiness. That's why this glorious, joyful, hope-filled Feast of All Saints should disturb us who are committed to mediocrity. They will tell us that if we are not holy, we have no one to blame but ourselves; in other words, God offers the grace, the saints offer the example and the intercession, and we lack the desire.

So, now what? Shall we just bow our heads, beat our breast, and try to think of something else? We dare not do that. More than ever, the Church and the world need saints. The Church and the world need saints who, as Jesus said, are as "shrewd as serpents and innocent as doves." We need to be smart, wise, holy, discerning, and bold. In this town, at this university, in this parish, we have everything we need to become the next generation of heroes, mystics, martyrs, scholars, warriors, and poets that the Church and the world need. Before you leave this church, promise yourself that you will beg God for a relentless, passionate, burning desire for sainthood.

Now, more than ever, we need to run towards sainthood. Why do I say that? Well, you might have heard that *"change"* may be coming to America. If that change comes, then we will fail unless we become worthy of these words of Jesus: "Blessed are you when they insult you and persecute you and utter every kind of evil against you falsely because of me. Rejoice and be glad, for your reward will be great in heaven." What have we done so far, what shall we do today and tomorrow and the next day and the next to be ready to receive such a blessing?

The best thing we can do to prepare for sainthood, always, is to come to our Lord in the Eucharist. Here at this altar, Jesus, the beloved of saints and angels, Jesus, Son of God and Son of Mary, Jesus the Lamb of God, comes to us, offers His Body and Blood to us, to win our hearts and feed our souls. We simply cannot be saints without the Eucharist.

If we divide our time between the chapel, the library, and the battlefield of the world, we can fight the good fight, we can receive the amazing grace that is offered us, and then lives will be saved, souls will be saved, and best of all, God will be glorified.

Please God, please God, let it be true of everyone here, let it be true of all our loved ones, that one day we will pass the final test. Let it be true of us and our whole Church, that one day the angels will point to us and ask, "Who are these wearing white robes, and where did they come from?" And, please, sweet Jesus, let the answer be, "These are the ones who have survived the time of great distress; they have washed their robes and made them white in the Blood of the Lamb."

May God's Holy Name be praised now and forever.

"I Miss You"

The Commemoration of All Souls, Lectionary 668
Ave Maria, FL, 2010

Wisdom 3:1-9
Psalm 23:1-3a, 3b-4, 5, 6
Romans 5:5-11
John 6:37-40

What are the greatest pains and joys of human life? Among the greatest pains must surely be missing a loved one. And among the greatest joys must be a reunion with that loved one so painfully missed.

Sometimes, when we have been separated from a loved one for a very long time, we don't realize how much we have missed him until we see him again. And then the joy of the reunion is tinged with sorrow. Why? Because the pain of the separation has finally stopped. We experience a kind of shock at the ending of the pain, as we do when a bad tooth is removed and the pain of the tooth is removed with it. We didn't know how much it hurt until it stopped hurting. And then there is a sorrow, a kind of proper pity for ourselves, when we see, upon the ceasing of the pain, how much pain we had been living with for so long. We are shocked by the tolerance we have for our own pain, but we don't realize it until the ache finally stops, as it does when we are reunited with a loved one. All of the ache of missing the beloved seems to come up and out all at once when we are reunited with the beloved. And like the ending of the toothache we had somehow learned to live with, so too the pain of separation ends when we are united with our beloved, a pain that we were not quite fully aware of until the joy of the reunion both brought forth and ended the pain.

So a reunion after a long separation can be bittersweet, as we embrace the long distant loved one we had missed so dearly, and we see all at once with pity and compassion our own pain at missing the one we love.

What does it mean to miss someone? Is it an absence merely acknowledged? No. Most of the world is absent from this oratory today, but I can't say that I miss them, at least not the great majority of them.

What does it mean to miss someone? The French have a wonderful way of expressing the active ache of missing someone, something that can't quite be communicated through the English phrase, "I miss you." The French say, "*Tu me manques,*" that is, "You are missing to me." That is so much better, isn't it? It says that you are present to me as being absent. It says that I feel you being absent from me.

On this day, All Souls Day, when we recall our beloved dead, many are missing to me. I actively feel their absence. Missing to me now are my parents who went to God just four months apart from each other, after fifty-three years of marriage; missing to me is my great aunt Catherine who even when I was a young man called me "Robbie dear"; missing to me is my mentor, Dr. Paul Weiss, who was writing books until he died at 101; missing to me is my best friend from college, Mark Maciag, whose violent death I witnessed just two weeks before we would have graduated together; and missing to me are more Jesuits than I can count, many who died full of years and some of whom died oh so young.

You too have your own list, your own long list of beloved dead who are missing to you. And in this Ave Maria community we can't help but think of Sister Theresa, and Theresa Lester, and Alex Klucik. We can say to all of our beloved dead, *"Tu me manques*—you are missing to me."

But because we are Christians, we have hope of a happy reunion with those who have gone before us. We have a firm hope of a happy reunion in heaven, and, as Saint Paul tells us today, hope "does not disappoint, because the love of God has been poured out into our hearts through the Holy Spirit that has been given to us."

There may well be tears of grief today, as we Christians grieve for ourselves and the pain we endure as our loved ones are missing to us. But today let's promise to console each other, and promise each other that we will help each other home to our Father's house, where a banquet is prepared for us and our loved ones are waiting for us.

And as we console one another, as we keep faith with our beloved dead by praying daily for their eternal rest, perhaps these words of Saint Ignatius Loyola will help. Shortly before his death, Saint Ignatius wrote:

> "If we had our fatherland
>   and our true peace in our
>   sojourn here in this world,
> it would be a great loss to us
>   when persons or things that
>   gave us so much happiness
>   are taken away.
> But as we are pilgrims on
>   this earth,
> with our lasting city in the
>   kingdom of heaven,

we should not consider it a great
 loss when those whom we
 love depart a
 little before us,
for we shall follow them before
 long to the place where
 Christ our Lord and
Redeemer has prepared for us a
 most happy dwelling in his
 bliss."

May God's Holy Name be praised now and forever.

Courage

Memorial of Blessed Rupert Mayer, SJ
Ave Maria, FL, 2009

Romans 12:5-16
Psalm 131:1-3
Luke 14:15-24

"Hate what is evil, hold on to what is good."

G.K. Chesterton said, "I do not believe in a fate that falls on men however they act; but I do believe in a fate that falls on them unless they act."

Chesterton knew that silence, like lethargy, is a form of consent. He knew that looking the other way, holding one's tongue, seeking to compromise with evil, are themselves a form of evil. And Father Rupert Mayer of the Society of Jesus knew it too.

He proved his physical courage again and again as a chaplain during the First World War. Given an opportunity to serve in secure areas, he refused and insisted on being put at the front, where the soldiers needed him most. He was renowned for his lack of hesitation to risk death to come to the aid of a wounded soldier. When people told him that he would soon be killed, he replied, "My life is in God's hands." The army recognized his courage, and conferred on him its highest honor, the Iron Cross.

A few years after the war, he was renowned as the "Pastor of Munich" and the "Apostle of Bavaria." And then he showed his moral courage. As early as 1923, he was sounding the alarm about the Nazi party. He said that one could not be both a faithful Catholic and a Nazi. I haven't done the research to verify my suspicion, but I suspect that he was denounced as being a "single-issue voter," one who did not respect the freedom of conscience or the separation of Church and State. I haven't done the research to verify my suspicion, but I suspect that he was derided for failing to find "common ground," and I imagine that he was accused of being close-minded, judgmental, and intolerant.

But he was undeterred. By the time Hitler came to power, Rupert Mayer was speaking in public as many as 70 times per month warning people against Nazism, insisting that a faithful Catholic could not be a member of that party. Mayer was horrified and indignant when the Nazis held parades in Munich and forced people to attend. As the Nazis marched through his parish, he emerged from the church, in his vestments, carrying the Blessed Sacrament in a monstrance. He marched right into the middle of the Nazi parade. The Catholics were so moved by the presence of Christ giving one man such courage, that they knelt in the streets and blocked the parade.

Hitler was furious and wanted Rupert Mayer killed. But Hitler was warned that Mayer was so revered and loved that if the Jesuit were murdered, the entire province of Bavaria would revolt. So, rather than trying to kill him, they tried to silence Father Mayer. The Nazis set up a special court, found him to be a traitor, and accused of him what we today would call "hate speech," in this case, hate speech against the Third Reich. He was forbidden to preach for six months.

Father Mayer was in anguish. How could he stop

preaching? His superiors feared for his life, and ordered him to comply with the sentence. Rupert Mayer was an obedient Jesuit. But it was not enough for the Nazis to silence him; they wanted to humiliate him, and, by implication, all priests. After Mayer was silenced, the mayor of Munich proclaimed, "The priests are all the same. Threaten them enough with arrest, rattle the keys of the concentration camp; they subside without further ado and shut up."

As a Jesuit, Rupert Mayer had sworn to renounce all honors, but also as a Jesuit, he would not surrender honor. He could not let such a defamatory remark go unchallenged. He sought and was granted permission from his superiors to preach once again. He told his congregation, "Despite the speaking ban imposed on me, I shall preach further, even if the state authorities deem my pulpit speeches to be punishable acts and a misuse of the pulpit."

As his superiors feared, Father Mayer was arrested and sent to a concentration camp. His health failed and he was near death. Not wanting to make a martyr of him, the Nazis locked him away in a monastery in the Alps, where he was able to recover his health.

In 1945, Rupert Mayer was liberated by American soldiers. He begged the soldiers to take him immediately back to his parish in Munich. They said that would have a celebration that night, and take him to Munich first thing in the morning. Mayer told them that he would just start walking to Munich. One soldier said, "Father, it's a very long way to Munich, we are in the mountains, and you have only one leg. Wait until morning." Rupert Mayer loved the people God gave to him.

Just a few months after returning home, Father Mayer was offering Mass. He turned to the people and said, "The Lord! The Lord! The Lord!" Then he collapsed and died. I think that is a good way for a Jesuit to die.

Why am I preaching about Rupert Mayer today? Am I just being nostalgic for the days of heroes long dead? Am I indulging in Jesuit partisanship by extolling the virtues of a brother Jesuit? Today I preach about Rupert Mayer because I believe that before long we will need priests with the raw moral courage of Rupert Mayer. I believe that right now we need priests who like Rupert Mayer will not be silent in the face of monstrous evil. I believe that today we need priests like Rupert Mayer who wish to give their very last breath speaking the Lord's name.

Today, on the feast of Blessed Rupert Mayer of the Society of Jesus, in this Year of the Priest, I ask us to pray for the priests we have; I ask us to pray for the priests we need; and I ask us to pray for the bishops of this country, that they may lead us well through times of darkness.

I will leave you with the words of a prayer written by Rupert Mayer:

> *Lord, let happen whatever you will;*
> *and as you will, so will I walk;*
> *help me only to know your will!*
> *Lord, whenever you will, then is the time;*
> *today and always*
> *Lord, whatever you will, I wish to accept,*
> *and whatever you will for me is gain;*
> *enough that I belong to you.*
> *Lord, because you will it, it is right;*
> *and because you will it, I have courage.*
> *My heart rests safely in your hands!*

May God's Holy Name be praised now and forever.

Who Needs a King?

Solemnity of Christ the King, Lectionary 162
Mass of Thanksgiving after Profession of Final Vows in the Society of Jesus, Ave Maria, FL, 2010

> 2 Samuel 5:1-3
> Psalm 122:1-5
> Colossians 1:12-20
> Luke 23:35-43

Do you want to hear a story? There was a man who fell down a long flight of stairs. He landed with a thunderous crash. Then he picked himself up, dusted himself off, and looked over his shoulder and said, "I wonder what all that noise was about?"

Those of you who were here yesterday evening may well ask the same question: "What was all that noise about?" What happened here yesterday? I hesitate to dwell on yesterday's Mass and what was done there, for fear of taking our attention away from Christ. What happened yesterday and what we are giving thanks for today is not some form of "McTeigue-Fest" or "McTeiguePalooza" or "McTeigue Appreciation Day." What happened yesterday and what we celebrate today is the certainty that Christ the King is still at work in the world, and that our King is able to do good things, even when using unlikely and flawed instruments such as you or me, even within a community that many would say is unnecessary or undesirable or impossible, whether that community be Ave Maria or the Society of Jesus.

Twenty-five years ago, I was cooking dinner with a friend and I said, "You know, in the long run, I don't expect to be happy. I don't believe that there is a place in the world for someone like me. What I value, what I believe, what I aspire to, what I think is important—I just can't imagine anyone or anything wanting what I have to offer or welcoming what I want to live. I can't imagine any place where I can put all my passion. I feel like I'm all dressed up and no place to go. That's why I say that in the long run, I don't expect to be happy."

Well, God had something to say to that despairing 24-year old man, and four years later, I entered the Society of Jesus, with the intention of serving God as a Jesuit priest, if God and the Church and the Society would have me. Two years later, I was moved to promise my life to God with the Society of Jesus. And the Society of Jesus said, in effect, "We'll see…"

Yesterday, I once again made an unconditional offer of my life to God in the Society of Jesus. And yesterday, the Society of Jesus made an unconditional "yes" to me.

To all of that, you might reply with two of the most important philosophical questions, questions I try to burn into the memory of my students, namely, "So what?" and "Who cares?" More specifically, what has all this do with today's Solemnity of Christ the King? And what has all this to do with our community of Ave Maria?

And since we've started asking pointed questions, we might well ask, "Why should there be a Solemnity of Christ the King at all?" Isn't the idea of a king passé? Isn't the celebration of kingship embarrassingly retrograde and sexist? Surely, no one would celebrate kingship as "progressive"! And don't democracies like ours have no use for a king?

I answer that now, more than ever, we need a king. A true king is a wise warrior who offers his people protection and vision; said another way, a true king gives his people boundaries that may not be crossed and horizons that must be reached. Without protection, the vulnerable suffer, and without horizons, the people wither. Even if a leader offers "change we can believe in," even if he offers change that we must believe in because we cannot avoid the change imposed upon us, even then—no, especially then—we need a true king.

Saint Ignatius Loyola can teach us what a true king is. In his Spiritual Exercises, he asks us to imagine a good, earthly king, who rallies his subjects to join him in a great cause. And how should one respond to the call of a good, earthly king? Ignatius describes the proper response to the call of a good, earthly king using these words. Ignatius writes: "I will consider what the answer of good subjects ought to be to such a generous and noble king, and consequently, if anyone would refuse the request of such a king how he would deserve to be despised by everyone, and considered an unworthy knight."

While on retreat as a young man, I read those words and shuddered. As someone who grew up on stories of heroes and kings and legends and adventures, tales of good guys with swords fighting dragons and demons, and dreaming one day of doing the same, what could be worse than being considered "an unworthy knight"? But then Ignatius raises the stakes. He says if a quick and generous response is owed to an earthly king, how shall we respond when we hear the call of Christ the Eternal King?

According to Ignatius, Christ the King calls each and all of us with the following words: "It is My will to conquer the whole world and all My enemies, and thus to enter into the glory of My Father. Whoever wishes to come with Me must labor with Me, so that following Me in suffering, he may also follow Me in glory."

When I heard this call of Christ the King, I knew in that moment that I had been waiting my whole life to hear that call, and that I had ached with a tormented restlessness until I knew that my heart was longing for Christ who, beyond my expectations, was calling me to His service.

When I was a college junior, just 20 years old, I went to the theater to see the movie "Excalibur," a rather imaginative retelling of the story of King Arthur and his famous sword. At one point in the movie, the young King Arthur jumps up on a horse—a *white* horse, naturally—waves his sword in the air, and calls out, "Any man who would be a knight and follow a king, follow me!"

And I found myself running down the aisle of the movie theater towards the screen yelling, "Take me! I wanna go with you! Take me! I wanna be a knight and follow a king! Take me! I want to be a knight and follow a king!" And yesterday, Christ the King, through the instrument of the Society of Jesus, said, "Yes, I will take you."

I believe firmly that Christ our King, our wise warrior, still offers His people protection and vision, boundaries and horizons. Christ our King still calls us to join Him in winning back the Kingdom for our heavenly Father. Christ the King today, as always, calls us to glory.

If you listen carefully to what the Church proclaims, if you listen carefully to the deepest stirrings of your own heart, you will find that Christ the King is calling you.

Each of us has a call; each of us, in his own way, is called, as Saint Ignatius said, to distinguish himself in the service of Christ the King. Whether in the daily routine of domestic life, or the high drama of fighting fires or fighting wars, we are called to follow Christ the King to glory, to the home of our Heavenly Father, where a banquet is prepared for us. And here, at this altar, as we receive the Body, Blood,

Soul, and Divinity of Christ, under the appearances of bread and wine, we are given a foretaste of what awaits us in the Kingdom that is coming.

Some folks here have known me for a very long time. They knew me at the outset of my religious life, when I was just a baby Jesuit. If you ask them, or maybe even if you don't, they will freely tell you that there was a time when I had more of a spring in my step and no gray in my hair. There really was a time when I was a young man. As I think about turning 50 next year, as I looking forward to starting my third decade as a Jesuit in service to Christ the King, I wonder who will come with me and who will come after me, and who will eventually replace me.

So, to adapt my favorite line from the movie "Excalibur," I say to the young men here: "Any man who would be a knight and follow Christ the King—follow me!" Follow me into the Society of Jesus, join me and take a place in that "Long Black Line" of Jesuit heroes that extends across the centuries back to our founder, Saint Ignatius Loyola. Join the ranks of Jesuits reaching back from Ignatius in Rome to Francis Xavier in Asia—Francis Xavier who baptized hundreds of thousands and who died face down in the sand pointing to the shores of China that he could see but could not reach.

Join the ranks of Jesuits from Francis Xavier to Isaac Jogues in North America. Isaac Jogues escaped with his life after his first mission in the New World, and chose to return and to face certain death, in order to ensure that the gospel would be firmly planted here.

Join the ranks of Jesuits from Isaac Jogues to Miguel Pro in Mexico. Miguel Pro shocked and shamed the Church's persecutors by shouting out "Vivo Cristo Rey!" ("Long life Christ the King!") at the moment he was being shot by a firing squad as a traitor to the state.

Join the ranks of Jesuits from Miguel Pro to Rupert Mayer in Germany. Rupert Mayer enraged Hitler with his fearless and relentless resistance to the Nazi madness.

Join the ranks of Jesuits from Rupert Mayer to the American, Walter Ciszek in Russia, who remained faithful to his vocation through years in Soviet prisons and Siberian exile.

Those names are familiar to many. There are other Jesuit giants likely not known to you, whom I was privileged to meet in my Jesuit life. I recall now great Jesuits whose example thrilled me and humbled me.

Today I remember Michael Kavanaugh, who served lepers in India, and offered Mass for them in graveyards, the only place where people would not try to kill them. I remember Jack Carboy, who, dying of cancer and giving thanks to God for his disease, gave spiritual direction to a prostitute dying of AIDS and who wished to give thanks for her disease. I remember Clarence Martin, who was starved and almost executed in Japanese death camps in the Philippines, who never lost the joy of the Lord, and spent his last years, old and blind, recalling and savoring the graces God had given him.

I know that all those men, my Jesuit brothers, are with us now, interceding for us, in the hopes that we might hear and answer the call of Christ the King.

Henry David Thoreau said, "The mass of men lead lives of quiet desperation." Not so for good Jesuits, who, on fire with love for Christ the King, always have something important to do, and always have a good reason to live and a good reason to die. Good Jesuits, striving always to distinguish themselves in the service of Christ the King, always have more to give, and always have a most urgent purpose.

Young men, if you want to find out how good your best can be, if you want to know truly how amazing is grace and how vile is sin, come clear-eyed, open-hearted, eager-minded, and with ready hands to the high heroism Saint Ignatius intended for his companions in the Society of Jesus.

So, now what? What shall we do? Now that we know that this festival of Christ the King is not merely nostalgia for medieval times, now that we know that speaking of Christ the King is not merely the use of a quaint metaphor, now that we know that in fact Christ the King rules and calls and leads, even in as remote a place as the swamps of southwest Florida, even in a servant as improbable and unprofitable as this loved sinner—now that we have seen all that, what shall we do?

First, let us give thanks, for Christ the King calls us all to heroic holiness. Next, let us discern, so that we might hear the true call of Christ the King. Finally, let us obey, quickly and gladly, the call of Christ the King. If we do that, if we live with gratitude, discernment, and obedience, then we can have great hope when we join that most famous loved sinner and cry out, "Jesus, remember me when you come into your kingdom!"

May God's Holy Name be praised now and forever!

MEDLEY

First Homily: Jesuit Companions

Feast of All Saints and Blesseds of the Society of Jesus
1990

(There is an old custom in the Society of Jesus. At the Jesuit novitiate, novices may preach at the community Mass on Jesuit feast days. Having been a Jesuit only three months, I was called upon to preach about all of our saints and blesseds. Below is the homily—my first time in the pulpit.)

> Deuteronomy 30:11-14
> Psalm 115
> John 12:23-36

When Martin Heidegger lectured, he was preceded into the hall by graduate students bearing stacks of books in triumphant procession, as though Heidegger had understood, vanquished, and transcended all the thinkers who had gone before him. To the surprise of at least a few, I hope, I do not intend to compare myself to Heidegger; and to the relief of all, I'm sure, I do not intend to lecture.

I've brought with me Tylenda's book *Jesuit Saints and Martyrs* as a visual aid. Tylenda lists 38 saints, 134 blessed, 36 venerables, and 115 servants of God of the Society of Jesus.

It is beyond my ability to even add up those numbers—even less am I able to do justice to the lives of these holy men and what God accomplished in them. I must note that most of these men died as martyrs, and most of the martyrs died in the company of their local community. That fact raises a question for us: How shall we live together now, so that if we needed to tomorrow, we could die together well? I must confess that at this moment I don't have an answer to that question.

Nevertheless, these men and this feast call us to holiness, and invite us to join "the long black line" of those who have shown us how completely a man can be consumed by the love of God.

Therefore, in the spirit of teaching a lesson which one has not yet learned, I have set for myself the less formidable task of explaining the hows and whys of becoming a saint in the Society of Jesus. In scholastic philosophy, this would be known as *ignotum per ignotius*: explaining what you don't understand by means of what you understand even less.

The key issue is that of choice. Each of these men, in the Spiritual Exercises and again and again throughout their lives, was asked to make a choice of life, a choice for or against the invitation of God to heroic sanctity. It is my belief that each of us is faced with the same opportunity for decision. This is seen in the lines immediately following our first reading from Deuteronomy:

> "See, I have set before you this day life and good, death and evil. If you obey the commandments of the Lord your God which I command you this day, by loving the Lord your God, by walking in his ways...then you shall live and the Lord will bless you. But if your heart turns away, and you will not hear, I declare to you this day, that you shall perish...I call heaven and

earth to witness before you this day, that I have set before you life and death, blessing and curse. Choose life, loving the Lord, obeying his voice, and cleaving to him." (Deuteronomy 30:15-20)

We are each free to choose between life and death. But we have to choose.

In my limited understanding of Ignatius' rules for discernment, I understand him to say that if our first discernment is good, then all our future actions and choices must be in harmony with that first discernment. We, like our brothers before us, have discerned a vocation to the Society of Jesus. What can follow from that discernment? There are really only two possibilities, life and death, but there may be different forms of these possibilities.

For example, I can discern a vocation to the Society, and walk away from it. I can decide that it is too much to bear: life in community, loneliness and a loss of independence, pilgrimage, vows, vow conferences, picking potatoes, scrod casserole on Friday nights, and all the other things they didn't tell us about in the vocation literature. And so I can decide to turn my heart away from God's call, to leave, and to go do something else. It might be something good or something bad, but I'll always know that I walked away, and will always be simply waiting for my bodily death to catch up with my spiritual death.

Or, I can choose to stay in the Society, but on my own terms. I can try to arrange a kind of armed truce with God, so that there are certain things that we won't talk about, certain places where we won't go. Under the terms of this truce, I won't allow God to ask anything great of me, and I won't allow myself to ask anything great of God.

And it's quite well possible that this form of spiritual mediocrity, this form of death, will be livable. After all, it's not likely that I'll be hanged, drawn, and quartered like

Edmund Campion, shot like Miguel Pro, dismembered like Isaac Jogues, or crucified, boiled, and burned like our martyrs in Japan.

And maybe I'll never have to accept an assignment I don't want. Maybe I'll never resent the command of a superior. Maybe I'll never have to live with a less-than-ideal community. Maybe I'll never be sent where I don't want to go.

And it's possible that I'll never be asked to console a grieving parent over the loss of a child. It's possible that I'll never be asked to help someone, even myself, to face illness and death. And isn't it possible that I'll never have to face danger while giving a voice to the voiceless victims of injustice?

Maybe. Possibly. But not likely.

But what is certain is the choice for life, for a holy life, for eternal life. It is the kind of choice that our saints and blesseds made, and by which all their decisions and actions were formed and guided. What does such a choice for life look like? We will find the answer in the Gospel.

Jesus says, "If anyone serves me, he must follow me; and where I am, there shall my servant be also." And where does Jesus go? Where does he require his servants to follow? "Unless a grain of wheat falls into the earth and dies, it remains alone; but if it dies, it bears much fruit."

Oh yes, now I remember. Jesus goes to the poor and lost, He goes to Jerusalem, He goes to the cross, and He goes to the resurrection. Our predecessors in holiness followed Jesus along the same path, and invite us, and I dare say even insist, that we do the same. In fact, they <u>must</u> insist that we follow, for the only way for a Jesuit to choose life, the only way for a Jesuit to be holy, is to be a true companion of Jesus, to live the kind of life He lived and to die the kind of death He died.

How does such a pilgrimage begin? How is such a life sustained? I suggest that you look to the Eucharist. Place your body in the bread, place your heart and soul in the wine. With Jesus let yourself be offered to the Father for the life of the world. This is the only way that a Jesuit becomes a saint.

Today our saints and blesseds, the Scriptures, and God Himself speak with one voice to us here, and to all the members of this our least Society: "I have set before you life and death, blessing and curse—choose life."

Called, Equipped, and Missioned

Mass of the Holy Spirit
Baccalaureate Mass, Ave Maria University
Ave Maria, FL, 2013

Acts 2:1-11
Psalm 104:1, 24, 29-30, 31, 34
Romans 8:8-17
John 20:19-23

Do you want to hear a story? When I was a little boy, my parents constantly reminded me of the importance of good manners, especially when someone had been kind to me. With a dangerous combination of enthusiasm and ignorance, I would try to show good manners by expressing loud gratitude whenever anyone gave me a gift. I would hold the gift in my hands and say, "Oh! Just what I always wanted!" The problem was that I had not yet unwrapped the gift, so I had no idea what I was expressing gratitude for, or if I even wanted what had just been given to me.

Those times of enforced enthusiasm in the name of good manners come to mind as we celebrate this afternoon this Mass of the Holy Spirit. Are we celebrating a gift that we do not really understand, and maybe do not know how to use or why should we even want it? Are we being asked to be as thoughtlessly "grateful" as I was as a child?

Let me explain. The Church speaks of the fruits of the Holy Spirit, that is, benefits of having the Holy Spirit at work in our lives. These include charity, joy, peace, patience, kindness, goodness, generosity, gentleness, faithfulness, modesty, self-control, and chastity. Well, that sounds nice, doesn't it? But can we really speak of those gifts and say, "Oh! Just what I always wanted!"? How many people are going to announce on Facebook: "Good news! God has loaded me up with modesty and self-control today! Just in time for the weekend!"

Wouldn't it be better if God gave us what we really wanted? Doesn't God know that what we really need is good health and flat abs and a winning lottery ticket and a job and better hair and a better grade point average and clearer skin and siblings who are not annoying and parents who understand us?

If God wants to give out gifts, we might ask, why not these? Why not give us gifts that we can understand and use and touch and feel? During this Mass of the Holy Spirit, might we not ask, "What's the Holy Spirit ever done for me anyway?"

But God knows us better than we know ourselves, and He knows what we really need. And if the Holy Spirit does not seem very useful or desirable, maybe that's because we don't know what to ask for. And we don't know what to ask for because we don't know what we need. And we don't know what we need because we don't know what are made for.

God made us for eternity and He made us for glory. He made us to spend this life, incomplete and imperfect as it is, to be a preparation for the fullness of life, united to Him forever.

What do we need, now, in this life, to get us ready for the perfect life that God made us for? Well, let's just look at two fruits of the Holy Spirit offered to us. Let's consider joy and peace.

Well, who doesn't want joy? Joy, Saint Thomas Aquinas tells us, is the delight that we have when we are united with our beloved. When we finally believe, when we know in our bones that God has made us for Himself and that nothing can take us out of His hands, then we will know a joy that nothing in this life can extinguish.

This is the amazing claim of the faithful Christian, namely, that the joy that God gives us cannot be taken away from us. Even when our world turns upside down—when the doctor says "cancer," when our spouse says "divorce," when our teenager says "pregnant," when our boss says "fired"—even then we can hold onto our God-given joy because we know that God's goodness and God's love for us cannot be defeated by anything in this world. We can rejoice, even in the face of pain, because we know that no loss, no disappointment, can touch what God has in store for us.

And with the gift of joy comes the gift of peace. When we trust God's goodness and His Fatherly love for us, then all the things that would otherwise threaten to give us ulcers and migraines do not seem so powerful anymore. There is a deep peace, a peace that remains even in the fiercest storm, when I can say, "Nothing can defeat God's love for me."

Joy and peace—does anyone have enough of that yet? If we lack joy and peace, then we have to wonder whether or not we have asked for them, really asked for them, from the Father Who loves us and Who has the best for us.

And what does all this have to do with our graduating students? Why do they need be here at this Mass of the Holy Spirit? Well, to all graduating students here I have a very simple answer to that question: "Just go away." Please. Get out of here! Run for the exits! Go into the highways and byways. Go from here, go from the heart of the Church, guided by the splendor of the truth. Go and set the world on fire! Take with you all that you have achieved here. Take all that you have learned. Take all the gifts that you have cultivated here. Take all of who you are, take the blessing of God that has been placed upon you here and offer it all to the world as only you can.

We are living in a world that will grow cold and die without the light, breath, and fire of the Holy Spirit. God wants to use you, wants to make use of what you have become here at Ave Maria University, to carry His life-giving Spirit into His creation that has been damaged by sin.

That is why we celebrate the Mass of the Holy Spirit today—to convince you that you are called, equipped, and missioned for a great and urgent task that is in the world and is for the greater glory of God. And you can fulfill your task—you can—if you ask for the anointing of the Holy Spirit to mark you, to make you wise and holy and generous. Before you leave this Oratory, ask for the spiritual gifts you need to be faithful and victorious.

If you do that, then I believe that you will hear the Lord's own words echo within your hearts, and you will know joy and peace, as you hear Christ say to you: "Receive the Holy Spirit."

May God's Holy Name be praised now and forever.

WHY WOULD ANYONE DO SOMETHING LIKE THAT?

Wedding Homily, 2013

Jeremiah 31:31-32a, 33-34a
Psalm 103:1-2, 8, 13, 17-18a
1 John 4:7-12
John 15:9-12

When was the last time you thought about doing something really dangerous? Did you do it? Or did you just think about it? If you thought about it, did you shudder, or did you just put that thought out of your mind? If you thought about doing something really dangerous, did you ask yourself, "Why would anyone do something like that?"

Let me give you some examples. When I see someone about to jump off a cliff into a body of water, I ask myself, "Why would anyone do something like that?" When I see someone strap on a parachute and jump out of a perfectly good airplane, I ask myself, "Why would anyone do something like that?" When I see someone strap strips of plastic to his feet and slide down the side of a mountain—in other words, skiing—I ask myself, "Why would anyone do something like that?"

And when we, we fallen, finite, flawed human beings, attempt to love each other, then I suspect we ask ourselves, at least some of the time, "Why would anyone do something like that?" After all, we have been warned. We have all been warned by unsettling cautionary tales of what was called love proving to be something else. If we are truly alert, we have been warned by even more unsettling cautionary tales of love proving to be true. And we have been warned eloquently, by no less an authority than C.S. Lewis. Lewis warned us that love—real love—is a most dangerous undertaking. Listen to his warning about love. Lewis wrote:

"To love at all is to be vulnerable. Love anything and your heart will be wrung and possibly broken. If you want to make sure of keeping it intact you must give it to no one, not even an animal. Wrap it carefully round with hobbies and little luxuries; avoid all entanglements. Lock it up safe in the casket or coffin of your selfishness. But in that casket, safe, dark, motionless, airless, it will change. It will not be broken; it will become unbreakable, impenetrable, irredeemable. To love is to be vulnerable."

So, I ask again: "Why would anyone do something like that?" I do not know why just *anyone* would attempt to love, but I do know why a *Christian* would love—first, because Christ said so; second, because Christ did so.

Jesus reveals that the call to love is in the nature of a commandment; it is not merely a suggestion or an option. Jesus said: "This is my commandment: love one another as I love you." The commandment we have received from our Lord is not merely obligation to embrace an abstract, disembodied love, for Jesus said, "…love one another as I love you." This is not the kind of love we find in pop culture; it is not trite or merely sentimental; it is a love that reaches beyond the heat of human passion and desire. The love that our Lord speaks of, the love He revealed and lives is a love that is practical, soulful, and total. Practical: It is a love that is shown more in deeds than in words. Soulful: It is a love that lasts beyond the death of the body. Total: It is a love that gives everything.

But, once again, our awkward question returns: "Why would anyone do something like that?" Our Lord tells us why. Jesus said in the Gospel of John: "I have told you this so that my joy might be in you and your joy might be complete." Oh….well…joy is a good reason to do something, even something as difficult as true love. Joy, Saint Thomas Aquinas tells us, is the delight that comes from seeing the good of the beloved fulfilled, and from being in the presence of the beloved. The joy our Lord offers us is the perfect fulfillment, the perfect rest, the full delight that is His in His union with the Godhead. In striving, with grace, to love as Jesus loves, in imitating Him and becoming like Him, we can share, as much as any human is able, in the joy of God Himself.

That is why it is not foolish to love. That is why the only sane course of action is to be a Christian who loves. That is why a Christian would willingly set his heart and mind, body and soul, upon the good of another, and promise with God's grace to offer an unending embrace, in good times and in bad, in sickness and in health, for richer or for poorer, faithful, faithful, *faithful* until death. Whoever would lose his life in loving as Christ loves, will find it. Whoever takes up his cross to love as Christ loves, will receive from the hand of Christ Himself a glorious crown.

What our Lord has revealed about love, we so very much need it to be true—*all of it*—or life would be too great a burden to bear. So, with thanksgiving we celebrate today because John and Elizabeth have heard Christ's call to love as He loves, and they have chosen to say, "Yes." They have chosen to love each other with all of who they are, to love with all the grace that God can give them, not only for God's glory, not only for their benefit, but for our benefit. With God's grace, they will prove that the world is wrong about the foolishness of love; they will prove that the world is wrong about the wisdom of selfishness; they will prove that our Lord has not given us impossible commandments. They will prove that the world is wrong and that God is right, when, day by day, in the sublime and mundane events of sacramental marriage, they choose to love as Christ loves.

John, Elizabeth, you both know that grace is not magic but is the life of God poured out on nature, which He made in love. And it is at that meeting point of nature and grace that the rest of us here will have a job to do. We, your family and your friends, we who love you, want and need for you to succeed in your sacramental marriage, so, today, we, like you, make promises. We promise that you need not live your marriage alone. We will serve you, assist you, and cheer you on, through all of the light and dark of the coming years. When you ask for help, we will help you. When you wish to share your joys, we will rejoice with you. And when you need to cry, there will always be another shoulder to cry on.

Now let's move from speaking of the love of Christ to doing what the love of Christ demands. Let's gather up every bit of our lives and unite it to the sacrifice of Christ to our Heavenly Father. And as we offer ourselves with Christ, let's throw our hearts wide open to fully receive Jesus, Son of God and son of Mary, Who is the Christ of God. Let's have His pattern of love inscribed again in our souls and in our flesh. And let's pray that John, Elizabeth, and all of us will love as Christ loves—freely, fully, faithfully, and fruitfully.

May God's Holy Name be praised now and forever.

ABOUT THE AUTHOR

Father Robert McTeigue, SJ, is a member of the Maryland Province of the Society of Jesus. A professor of philosophy and theology, he has taught and lectured in North and Central America, Europe, and Asia and is known for his classes in both rhetoric and medical ethics. He has long experience in spiritual direction, retreat ministry and religious formation and now works in seminary education.

Made in the USA
San Bernardino, CA
24 August 2018